'I have known Michael Green for more than 40 years and nothing that he has ever written, said or done has been boring. This book of stories from his experience is fascinating and fun to read.'
VISCOUNT BRENTFORD

'My friendship with Michael Green spans 45 years and his contribution to my spiritual development has been most significant. He is a gifted teacher, erudite scholar and passionate evangelist who continues to inspire. For him, as for me, the Christian life is an adventure and this compelling book is the story of his exciting journey of faith.'
MOST REVD. GEORGE CAREY, Archbishop of Canterbury

'Michael Green is quite extraordinary. A scholar of New Testament and Greek, with first class degrees, doctorates and professorships littered about, his greatest delight is to see someone come to a living faith in God through Jesus Christ, in the power of the Holy Spirit. He personifies the combination of enthusiasm and intellectual rigour. I know no one like him, and I thank God for him.'
MARTIN CAVENDER, Springboard

'One of the great Christian warriors of this age, my friend Michael Green has a lifetime rich in Christian wisdom to share with the world.'
CHARLES W. COLSON, Prison Fellowship Ministries, Washington, DC

'Michael has outstanding gifts both as an evangelist and teacher which have enriched the world church.'
BISHOP JACK DAIN, Australia

'Gifted evangelist, prolific writer, able theologian, and Apostle Paul for our own age.'   EDWARD ENGLAND, Publisher

'A fascinating and frank account of a lifetime's work for the Lord, brimful of insights and suggestions, which deserves to be on every pastor's bookshelf.'

ALISTER MCGRATH, Professor of Historical Theology, Oxford University, Principal, Wycliffe Hall

'From 1963 when I, as a nineteen year old student at the University of Cape Town, first met Michael Green, he has retained a deep concern for South Africa and, so typically of him, also, over nearly forty years, for me as an individual. By challenging me to see and emulate the quality of love that Jesus had for people; by stretching my mind to recognise and boldly affirm that in society, family and politics, this is God's world; by encouraging me to study further, Michael laid a foundation, set an example and opened a process of living for Christ which has been a joyful battle ever since.'

GRAHAM MCINTOSH, MP, South Africa

'Breezy brother, sharp scholar and eager evangelist Michael Green has an enviable gift for making you think, squirm, laugh and get real all at the same time, and his review of his full and fruitful life runs true to form. This is vintage Green.'

J. I. PACKER, Professor, Regent College

'Few people have had such a variety of gifts, and such a range of experiences, as Michael Green. So he is able to evaluate first-hand many different ministries, movements and contro-versies. His views are always forthright, often humorous, sometimes mischievous (as he admits), but never lacking in thoughtfulness or generosity.' DR. JOHN STOTT

'I have known Michael since my days at Oxford, when he filled St Aldate's as a popular, ever-accessible preacher and counsel-lor. And like so many others, I have been encouraged and stimulated by his outstanding scholarship – his commentary on 2 Peter will remain a classic. Rare are those who, like

Michael, combine profound learning with evangelistic zeal and vision.' REVD. PROFESSOR CARSTEN THIEDE,
Paderborn, Germany

'As a young student of theology I first came across some of Michael Green's books. After reading them I knew I had to meet this man. In 1981 I was able to do a short-term internship at St. Aldate's, Oxford, with Michael Green. What I experienced there has profoundly influenced my life and ministry. The combination of evangelistic passion, academic scholarship, openness to the work of the Holy Spirit as well as deep-rootedness in the historic church and a truly world-wide perspective has always been an inspiration and guiding light. Michael's input and example has borne much fruit for the church in Germany.'

DR. ROLAND WERNER, Marburg, Germany

'Michael has finally put into writing his 50 years of exciting ministry in the Lord. He is a gifted writer; a passionate scholar for Christ; and a humble servant of God who deeply appreciates others serving the same Lord. His new book will be a real source book filled with encouraging, challenging and inspiring personal experience in the Lord.'

MOST REVD. DATUK YONG PING CHUNG, Primate,
Province of Southeast Asia

MICHAEL GREEN
ADVENTURE
of FAITH

REFLECTIONS ON FIFTY YEARS
of CHRISTIAN SERVICE

GRAND RAPIDS, MICHIGAN 49530 USA

ZONDERVAN™

Adventure of Faith
Copyright © 2001 Michael Green

Requests for information should be addressed to:
Zondervan, *Grand Rapids, Michigan 49530*

First published in Great Britain and the USA in 2001 by Zondervan

Scripture quotations are mainly taken from the
HOLY BIBLE, NEW INTERNATIONAL VERSION.
Copyright © 1973, 1978, 1984 by International Bible Society

Michael Green asserts the moral right to be identified as the author of this work

ISBN 0 00 710542 8

Printed and bound in Great Britain

02 03 04 05 / ❖ CPD / 5 4 3 2 1

For Rosemary,
my wife of more than 40 years,
and best friend,
who is my inspiring partner in this
adventure of faith.

Contents

PART 4 – FAITH AND THE GOSPEL

PART 5 – FAITH AND THE FUTURE

A Word from the Author

I have been approached by more than one publisher to write my autobiography. I declined. They asked if I would agree to someone else writing a biography. Again I declined. This was for two reasons. In the first place, I did not regard my life as being sufficiently significant to write up: to do so would have seemed pretentious. In the second place, I have an indifferent memory and have not kept a detailed record of events. Then, one night at a small dinner party, my colleague the Rev. Dr Graham Tomlin said, 'Why don't you write some reflections on things that you've seen as significant?'

So I did. Blame Graham for the idea!

I have been particularly privileged to have been allowed 50 years, no less, in Christian ministry. I began to exercise Christian leadership as president of the Christian Union at Oxford University. This continued during National Service, and then I moved on to ordination via Ridley Hall, Cambridge. During those 50 years I have seen a great deal of change in the culture of our society, in Christian approaches to that society and in the world Church. I have had the privilege of being involved in many of the significant events within the Church which our students now read of as modern history! In the course of my ministry I have had the joy of preaching and teaching in a great many countries across the world. I have had the good fortune to be the principal of a theological college, a professor overseas, an evangelist in all five continents, an author, a theological teacher in several countries and the rector of a dynamic church. This breadth of experience – which has been both humbling and inspiring – and my unusual journey as a combination of academic and practitioner, have bred various convictions in me. In this book I would like to share them with others. I have found it all an exciting adventure of faith.

I want to thank Hodder Headline for allowing me to use, in Chapter 1, slightly modified material which I originally wrote for them in *The Best Decision I Ever Made* (1999). I am also most grateful to SPCK for allowing me to summarize parts of my book *Asian Tigers for Christ* (2001) in Chapter 15.

It has been a delight to work with HarperCollins, and I want to pay tribute to their Publishing Director, James Catford, for his assiduous encouragement to write the book, and to his Senior Commissioning Editor, Amy Boucher Pye, for her detailed, warm and invaluable help and advice. Her friendship, interest and skill have made a tremendous difference to the finished manuscript. I would also like to thank Bryony Bénier for her careful work and gracious spirit in editing the text.

I am very grateful to Dr Michael Ramsden and the Rev. Professor Alister McGrath for helpful critique of a couple of chapters, and I want to thank my wife Rosemary and my four children, Tim, Sarah, Jenny and Jonathan, for their constant love and patience with my sometimes over-busy life. Most of all, I want to express my gratitude to God as I look back over 70 years of life and the privilege of working for the best of all employers, Jesus Christ. Without him, it would have been a very different story.

Michael Green
Wycliffe Hall, Oxford University

PART 1

FAITH AND NURTURE

CHAPTER 1

Conversion

I was born in 1930, in the Depression. Perhaps that is why I had no brothers or sisters: finances did not allow it. Or maybe it was due to my father's reaction to having been one of 12 children. My parents were poor in money but rich in love, generosity and self-sacrifice. My mother was an Australian who had given up her native land and come to Britain to marry a Welshman she had met only once on a visit, but who pursued her with his letters. My father was a country clergyman looking after two tiny rural parishes in Oxfordshire, Shenington and Alkerton, the only incumbency he ever held. He served those parishes faithfully for more than 30 years. They were wonderful parents to me. I loved them deeply.

We lived in one of those massive old country rectories which immediately set a barrier between the parish priest and most of his parishioners. It was 'the big house', and to live in it inevitably isolated the vicar and his family from the villagers. So there was quite a solitary aspect to my youth. I went to the village school just across the road, but most of my spare time was spent behind the large gates which closed off the rectory drive. I made my own entertainment in our three acres of garden. Situated as we were, seven miles from the nearest town, I began to develop a deep love for nature and the countryside, a love which has never left me. Birds, fish, wild animals, butterflies – I was fascinated by them all.

Schooldays

When I was seven years old, a big change occurred. My uncle ran a preparatory school in Devon, and he offered to take me as a pupil for the princely sum of five pounds a term. This seemed too good an opportunity to miss, because my parents could never have afforded the full fees. Looking back, I am most grateful for my uncle's generosity, but at the time I felt I was being wrenched hundreds of miles away from my home into an environment which I did not understand and where I was left very much to sink or swim.

I loved the holidays. When that battered old black suitcase was loaded with me onto the train for home, I was elated. I knew a royal welcome awaited me. As my father's ancient Austin Seven, which had met me at the station, puttered into our drive, my mother would run out with almost unbearable joy to hug me and bring me into the house, where a great treat was to have pork sausages for my first evening meal. One thing was clear to me about boarding school: it did lead me to appreciate my home all the more.

While I was at home I regularly went to church on Sundays. It seemed the least I could do to help my father, who (as was very obvious to me at an early age) was battling against the decline of organized religion that marked the whole of the twentieth century in the West. He was struggling to keep the church an effective force in the village. Naturally I backed him up, and so did my mother. It would have been unthinkable to do anything else in those days, and in any case I wanted to help. That is why I gave as much assistance in the house as I could. I regularly hand-mowed the interminable lawns in the garden. Others might think it was a privilege to live in a big house, but even my young eyes could see that, with no finances to keep it up and no help to speak of in house or garden, my parents needed any small contribution I could make. I even sang in the rudimentary choir which the church boasted, though I croaked like a raven.

At school it was very different. We had formal prayers every day, and formed a long crocodile to a particularly dreary church on Sundays, where my headmaster uncle was a sidesman. I was lazy but bright, and in addition to my five canings I remember getting the odd prize for school work, including Scripture. I was a lawbreaker by instinct, and was generally involved in the illegal activities that went on – smoking, beating other boys up, climbing out at night and so forth. A disturbingly violent streak was starting to become evident and my language grew increasingly foul – a habit I could not stop even at home, where it was a distinct embarrassment.

Enough of those early days. In my penultimate year at the preparatory school, I realized with a shock that unless I started working, the future of my education was very much in doubt. So I applied myself, lazy though I was by temperament and experience, and in due course got a scholarship to Clifton College, Bristol, which the school authorities generously increased because we were not able to afford even the reduced fees. Thus in the autumn of 1944 I began what I suppose proved to be the most decisive five years of my life.

I had not really enjoyed my preparatory school, but I loved Clifton. When I first went there, the school was still in the evacuation quarters it had taken over during the war. Bristol was a dangerous target area for German bombs, and in any case the Army had soon requisitioned the school buildings. My first two terms were spent in what had been, in peacetime, a terrace of hotels by the seashore in Bude, Cornwall. It was wonderful: freedom, wild midnight excursions, rock-climbing and abseiling, opportunities for entomology, shooting, cricket, fencing and all my other distractions. On top of all that came the privilege of a good education which offered a wide variety of specializations.

I have fond memories of that first term, when six of us junior boys were herded into what had been a single hotel bedroom but now comprised six bunk beds, roughly lashed together, which left practically no floor space. That was where we lived. We quickly formed a close bonding and before long were making gunpowder, which we delighted to explode in all the most inappropriate situations. Little monsters that we were, we constructed blowpipes which shot darts at people, dipped in formic acid which we distilled ourselves. Our human targets would scratch the offending spot where the dart had touched their skin, and the inflammation grew.

Such was the scene when a boy in my House invited me to come to a private – almost secret – meeting. It took place in the cricket pavilion on a Sunday afternoon, after the school had returned to Bristol. It was to do with Christianity, and it amazed me, because it immediately showed me that Christianity was very different from what I had hitherto assumed it to be. Some 40 boys were listening attentively to the Professor of Surgery at Bristol University, who also, I discovered, edited the *British Medical Journal*. He was talking about Jesus Christ and, to my astonishment, he spoke with a quiet conviction that Jesus was alive!

Now, I knew a good deal about this Jesus. He had formed a background warmth to my growing up. I had read the Gospels and had even won a prize on them. Nobody, however, had ever suggested to me that Jesus was still alive and could make a real difference to the lives of twentieth-century people. Yet here was a highly intelligent scientist who not only believed it and lived in the light of it, but thought it so important that he was willing to give up his valuable spare time to instruct a bunch of schoolboys on the topic.

It set me thinking. If this professor and the group into which I had unwittingly tumbled were correct, then they had made the most important discovery of all time. If they were wrong, I need not trouble myself further with Christianity. It would prove to be merely a matter of following the ideals and teaching of a revered but dead teacher, and that need not make any serious impact on my life. I resolved to find out whether or not they were right.

I decided to do two things. I would regularly attend the meetings of these enthusiastic friends of Jesus, and see what I made of their teaching. I would also watch the members during the week, and see if this profession that Jesus was alive made any difference to the way they behaved. I could see this was an intensely important issue. Was Jesus really alive, risen and relevant? Or was he just one more great teacher who had come to a sticky end? This question, and its implications, was the most important issue one could possibly consider. It was quite literally the key to the meaning of human existence. I was determined not to be taken for a ride. I needed to examine it carefully for myself.

Conversion

I watched the members of this meeting for some eight or nine months, and regularly attended their weekly gatherings. These were led by Richard Gorrie, the head boy of the school, who was a brilliant academic and a distinguished athlete. One summer Sunday he gave a talk on God's guidance. By that time it was clear to me that I could no longer resist the claim that Jesus was alive. The difference he made to the boys who professed to believe it was too blatant. I had turned from investigator to seeker. I was now convinced that this Christian story was true. I realized it was all to do with Jesus. To me, however, he was still the stained-glass-window Jesus, the Stranger of Galilee encased in the dusty books of the New Testament. Yet I was fed up with religion: I was hungry for reality.

I went up to Richard Gorrie at the end of his talk and asked him how God guides us. It was not a very flattering question, come to think of it, since he had just delivered an excellent 20-minute dissertation on the subject. He looked at me with a wisdom beyond his (nearly) 18 years, and invited me to come to the upstairs storey of the cricket pavilion. There he led me to a living faith.

I cannot recall all that happened that Sunday afternoon, but the main outlines are burnt into my memory. I remember the cricket bats and pads, the spikes in the boots and the divots of turf on the heavily scored floor. I remember Richard gently pointing out to me how I had affronted God by my way of life. I did not argue. Only the term before, he had been obliged to give me a richly deserved punishment for illegal entry into his House at the school. I knew my life was a mess. I did not need to have it rubbed in.

Then he showed me something obvious enough, but I had never seen it before. He showed me that Jesus Christ had done all that was necessary to bring me back to God. On the cross he had taken responsibility for all the dark side of my life. I already believed in my vague way that Christ had died for the sins of the world. After all, it came across in almost every service. Yet it had never meant anything much. That afternoon I saw that he had died for *me* personally, bearing responsibility for *my* failures and deliberate bad things. It was the evil in me, among others, which had held him to that cruel cross. He had done it willingly, in his great love.

I seem to recall that Richard gave me a graphic illustration of the difference Calvary had made. He used the prophecy in Isaiah 53 and illustrated the phrase 'all we like sheep have gone astray' by placing a black object between his left hand and the light. That represented the responsibility for my misdeeds resting upon me, cutting me off from the light and warmth of God's holy love. 'We have turned every one to his own way.' I could not quarrel with that. I knew it was true. 'And the Lord has laid on him the iniquity of us all,' continued my friend, transferring the dark load to his other hand, which he used to represent Christ dying on the cross. Of course this released the left hand, which represented me. No longer need there be a 'cloud of unknowing' to separate me from God. I saw for the first time in my life that Christ had carried my burden of evil; he had taken personal responsibility for all that was wrong in me. The whole lot was poured on his loving, sinless head, so that I could go free. The love of such a God broke me down.

That was not all. My second shock that afternoon was occasioned by my friend's gentle question about whether I believed that Jesus Christ had risen from the grave. I had long been able to say the Creed without it affecting me in any way. My searchings over the previous months had convinced me that Jesus was indeed alive, and I had no difficulty in telling Richard so. He then faced me with a crunch question. 'What are you going to do about him, then?' I began dimly to see that I was faced with a massive choice. I could either disengage from this Christ who had loved me and given himself for me, or else I could yield my whole life, future and career to him. There was no middle way. I was on the horns of a dilemma. I had to choose.

That led to my third discovery. I must have told Richard that I had no idea how to react to the enormity of what God had done for me. He took me to a verse in the Bible which has led millions to a personal commitment. It was Revelation 3:20, where the risen and ascended Christ says these wonderful words to a lukewarm church – lukewarm because they had kept him excluded from their church and personal lives: 'Here I am! I stand at the door and knock. If anyone hears my voice and opens the door, I will come in and eat with him, and he with me.'

Although there was much I did not understand, the heart of the matter was now sufficiently plain. The Jesus who had dealt with the barrier which seemed to make God so far away, the Jesus who had smashed the power of the Last Enemy by the great victory of Easter Day – this Jesus, Son of the living God, was alive. He was willing and able to enter my life by means of his Holy Spirit. Of course, Christ himself had returned to heaven at the Ascension, but I do not recall that this posed any problem to me. He was apparently willing, even enthusiastic, to place his unseen Spirit in my life and start living in me. What an exciting, if daunting, prospect! It was undreamed-of generosity for God to act like that.

It would be very demanding, however. It would require the cleaning up of the mess in my life. I could not do that: I had tried. I vaguely realized that Christ could do it, but I had to be willing for the revolution to start inside me. My sins were comfortable. Like ivy on a tree, they had been intertwined with my life for many years. It would be hard to break free from them. It would also mean that Jesus, not I, was henceforth to be number one in my life, behaviour, decisions, ambitions and relationships. Was I prepared for such a costly takeover? What is more, I would not be able to keep quiet about this overwhelming discovery. I would have to be willing to 'let my light shine' as the Gospels put it. Once I knew a bit more, I would need to be Christ's vocal ambassador as well. How much I understood of all this that Sunday afternoon I do not recall, but I know I counted the cost of discipleship as best I could.

Richard helped me to see what needed to be done by showing me a postcard of Holman Hunt's famous painting, *The Light of the World*. It was inspired by Revelation 3:20 and shows Jesus Christ, clad in dazzling white with a blood-red cloak, standing outside the door of a dark and desolate cottage. In his hand he holds a lantern – is he not the Light of the World? Clearly he looks for access, and then the light will illuminate all the house and shine out of the windows. Equally clearly, however, he will not enter until he is invited by the tenant. The door is choked with ivy: it has never been opened. Yet patiently Christ stands knocking, with the nail marks in his hands. He is waiting to be invited in. He is offering to come in and stay for ever.

The imagery of the painting was lucid and compelling. That afternoon I gladly and deliberately accepted Christ's offer. I did so with tears of gratitude (yes, tears from a reserved male in his mid-teens; tears that hit the dust on the floor, and bounced). I blurted out my response to him in a prayer, and I am grateful that I was encouraged to begin my active discipleship with an audible prayer. Many churchpeople spend 50 years and more in church and seem unable to pray out loud. It has no particular merit, of course, apart from concentrating your thoughts and enabling others to share in your petitions – but that in itself is not unimportant.

When I had recovered from what, for me, was a very emotional act of will, my friend started to give me some immediate aftercare. He told me how to meet the initial doubts that were sure to come from the Father of Lies. To begin with I would have no experience to depend on, but I had the promise of the Christ who could not lie: 'If anyone opens the door, I will come in.' Well, that 'anyone' covered me. I had 'opened the door' of my will, so he *had* come in – because he had pledged to do so. I could rely on his promise. He could not break his word. This was a great help to me later that very day. I relied on his promise even before I found it beginning to become true in experience. I suppose I was learning one of the basic lessons of faith: believe the promises of God and rest your weight on them.

Richard then tried to get me introduced to a rudimentary devotional life. He suggested that I should get up when the first bell went in my House, at 7.10 a.m. There was a second rising bell at 7.25 and all boys had to be on parade for 'call-over' at 7.30 (on pain of a caning for three absences). Those of us with some bravado made a point of not stirring until the second bell went. In fact, I never even used to hear the first bell. When I told this to Richard, he was somewhat nonplussed but responded very wisely, 'Ask the Lord to wake you up at the first bell, and then get up and spend a bit of time with your Bible and in prayer before the day gets underway.'

I was prepared to give it a try. To my amazement, I found that I did wake up the next morning at 7.10, and continued to do so every morning during the rest of my time at school. Those 15 minutes or so before call-over, in the privacy of a loo, proved invaluable for getting me into the habit of devotional Bible reading and prayer. I remember I started reading Romans. I had never been able to make head or tail of the Epistles before my conversion, but now they began to speak to my new experience of life with Christ.

Before I left that afternoon, Richard encouraged me to talk to the Lord as I went along the road back to my House. I did not need to shut my eyes or kneel down. I had encountered 'the Friend who sticks closer than a brother' and it would become the most natural thing in the world to speak to him and listen to him, at any time and on any topic. In this way I began to learn how to 'abide' in Christ and live my life with growing awareness of his companionship.

Change

There were two particular ways in which Richard Gorrie was of further help to me. In the first place he invited me to a Christian house party for boys in the holidays, at a place called Iwerne Minster in Dorset. I had heard of this, and had already turned down an invitation because I very much enjoyed my holidays at home. Now, however, I saw that it would be a great way to develop my Christian life and I accepted enthusiastically. That house party became an important part of my adolescent and young adult life. I learnt a relevant and attractive pattern of Christian discipleship among boys my own age, specifically related to life in a boarding school. When I became an undergraduate and began to help in the leadership of this house party, I found I was given a marvellous training. Indeed, in three areas I have never met anything superior: how to give an attractive talk, how to lead an inductive Bible study and how to engage in basic pastoral work. All this lay in the future, but I know that the friendships, worship, fun and teaching of this holiday house party and the term-time school meetings were an enormous help to me in the formative period of my active Christian discipleship.

The other great help Richard afforded me was to make himself available about once a fortnight to answer the questions and objections I had about the Christian life. I used to make a note of them as they cropped up and save them up to talk over with him. He would answer the questions to my satisfaction and then choose a short passage of the New Testament to read with me, showing me how to draw thoughts from it for my own life. This personal one-to-one care is sadly missing in many parts of the Christian world today, and it is immensely valuable. I might well have foundered without it.

You may wonder what differences began to emerge. They were fairly visible, because I had been quite a high-profile troublemaker! One was my language. I found that the habits of swearing and obscenity which had held me in such a tight grip disappeared almost overnight. I learned to pray with the psalmist, 'Set a guard over my mouth, O Lord; keep watch over the door of my lips,' and to my amazement, within a few weeks every trace of obscenity had gone. The other thing was my violent temper. I was a passable boxer and I used violence on people outside the ring too, when my Welsh temper flared up. Once I had entrusted my life to Christ and asked him to work on this problem, I found I no longer wanted to hit anybody.

I do not think that these two failings were particularly important in themselves, but they mattered to me and I had been quite unable to get rid of them. The power of the risen Christ made short work of both. It was an enormous encouragement to me, as you can well imagine. I think God often gives graphic and immediate answers to prayer in the early days of our Christian lives to help us get started in trusting him. Later on it seems to be much slower and more gradual.

The remaining years at school saw solid growth in my Christian development. I began to try to please Christ in every aspect of my life, probably becoming for a while unnecessarily narrow in what I allowed myself – but maybe that was a good failing. I found I was becoming very keen to share the joy of Christian faith with others who seemed as blind to it as I had once been. Naturally, I was not yet competent to explain to them the way to faith, and that would have been politically unacceptable within the closely bound network of an English public school. I was, however, able to invite them to the same house party which had so helped me, and had the joy of seeing several boys become firmly committed Christians as a result. I guess that is where the seeds of evangelism were sown in my heart. They have persisted and indeed grown ever since.

I also discovered the joy of close Christian fellowship with my peers. A number of us who were school prefects were also committed Christians, and we used to meet regularly to pray for each other and for the school. No doubt we were somewhat precocious, but all the same it gave me a taste of close Christian fellowship. This has seemed to me to be one of the most lovely aspects of Christianity as I have, in subsequent decades, moved widely around the world. The trinitarian God, who not only invented fellowship but *is* fellowship, has so arranged things that it is in fellowship that we find our greatest fulfilment, and supremely in fellowship with those who have Christ in common.

Oxford

I had two somewhat painful experiences during my school and undergraduate days which taught me an important lesson. In my last year at school I was very surprisingly picked as the opening bowler in the school cricket eleven. This was a high honour in those days, and we all greatly looked forward to the culmination of the season, a three-day match against Tonbridge School at Lords. Well, I was dropped before the Lords match. It hurt. Yet it taught me not to make an idol of sport, as I was tending to do. Then, after five terms at Oxford, we classicists had an examination which constituted the first half of our degree. It consisted of 13 papers, and you needed six alphas in order to get a first-class degree. I worked hard, and hoped I might make it. In the event I got five alphas and six b++ marks. I later learned that they had discussed my case at length, and in the outcome I was given a second. That taught me not to make an idol of academic success, as I was tending to do.

If those were examples of God teaching me through comparative failure, one particular incident from my student days stands out as God guiding me very clearly towards the life work for which he had designed me and in which I would be most fulfilled. At the start of my penultimate year at Oxford I would have expected to try either for the Foreign Office or maybe academia, after graduation. I often prayed that God would guide me between the two. One day I heard a sermon saying that we should not give God a choice of options, but should rather ask what he wanted us to do. So I began to pray like that, and gradually the conviction began to take shape that I should offer myself for the Christian ministry.

That was most certainly not part of my plan! I loved being a Christian, but had no desire whatever to be a professional cleric. One night the local curate dropped in for a coffee and I remember asking him, 'Teddy, why should I be a wretched parson? I'm just not going to do it!'

Rather than arguing, he sat down, clutched his coffee mug and roared with laughter. 'Of course you are, Green!' he said. 'It's perfectly obvious.'

It was just the treatment I needed. That night I knelt by my bed and prayed with great sincerity. I told God I was willing to be ordained if I must, but that I did not want to make a mistake which would mess up my life and the lives of thousands with whom I would come in contact. I asked him to give me a sign. I do not advocate this procedure, by the way, but I did ask for a sign that night.

The next morning, the president of the University Christian Union called in, most unexpectedly, and asked if I would be willing to become president the following year. This was a great surprise to me, because I had been conspicuous in not toeing the party line on several occasions. I went to see my tutor and asked him if I was likely to get a first in the final part of my degree. He told me that I would get a second standing on my head, but would not get a first. Had he told me that I was a likely candidate for a first, I would have turned down the presidency of the Christian Union. As it was, I felt free to take it on. What a good decision that proved to be. It meant gaining experience of leadership among several hundred of my fellow students at a particularly important time, when Michael Ramsey (then Bishop of Durham) was about to come and lead a mission to the university. It also meant that I met my future wife on the Executive Committee! Then, at the end of it all, when I sat my finals, I turned out not merely to have got a first, but to have gained one of the best in the year. It taught me a powerful lesson about God's guidance. I began to realize that, when you start following the path of obedience to God, you are not the loser.

That year of leadership in the Christian scene at university was invaluable for me. It confirmed my call to ordination. It launched me on the path of public speaking, thoughtful leadership and extensive reading as a Christian. Followed, as it was, by the practical knockabout of two years in the Army on National Service, with the opportunities for evangelism that offered, it prepared the way for a research degree at Cambridge while I was training for ordination.

That calling is clearly what the good Lord designed me for. I have been extremely happy and fulfilled in it. If I had my time again, I would take precisely the same route. It has meant teaching in theological colleges and universities in England and abroad. It has meant travel in the cause of the gospel over much of the world. It has meant many missions in universities, towns, cities and villages in England and overseas. It has meant seeing many men and women turn to Christ and many enter ordained or missionary service alongside the majority who have allowed their faith to shine through so-called 'secular' careers. It has meant a good deal of writing, radio and television work as a Christian communicator. It has opened the way for the great privilege of spending 12 years as a pastor in a very lively church. And it has led to the joy of seeing four Christian children all launched on useful careers.

If, from one perspective, it all began in the mysterious election of God before I was born, from another it sprang from the decision made back in those mid-teen years to entrust my life to Jesus Christ. It was without question the best decision I ever made.

New life

It is that decision of the will to follow Christ which is so vital. Alas, many people seem to drift into church attendance or even the ordained ministry without it. For some this surrender of the will comes gradually, like the dawning of the day or the gentle unfolding of a flower. For others it comes with sudden, overwhelming force, as I suppose it did in my own case. All our lives are like a journey, and at some stage along that journey we all need consciously to join up with Christ. As we look back in later life we can see that, however gradual or shattering our conversion may have been, God was at work on us long before we were aware of it, let alone responded to him. In that sense there is probably no such thing as a sudden conversion, and William James's distinction between 'once-born' and 'twice-born' Christians is invalid.

Conversion is the name we give to the human side of Christian beginnings. It literally means 'turning to'. That needs to happen at some time or other in our lives, and of course the surrender it enshrines is constantly being renewed in a healthy Christian life. The most important part of Christian initiation, however, is the new birth about which the New Testament is so insistent. Regeneration, 'new birth', is the name theologians give it – and, if conversion is the human side of the process, regeneration is the divine side. Without that new life, imparted by God, signified by the once-for-all-ness of baptism, we simply have not begun. That is the problem one frequently meets in church life. There are people involved in church life who have never bowed the knee to Jesus Christ and asked him to give them the new birth, the presence of his Holy Spirit in their hearts and lives.

Suddenness has nothing to do with it. Take the image of birth itself, as at least four New Testament writers do in order to illuminate this concept. Birth is more or less sudden, but there has been a long process of pregnancy beforehand and there are, hopefully, many years of growth to come. Nevertheless, the actual birth is essential if there is to be any subsequent life. So it is in the spiritual realm. It does not matter if one cannot remember when this new birth took place. Some, like John the Baptist, are filled with the Holy Spirit from their mother's womb. Some date their regeneration to the fact that they were born in a believing family and have never needed a radical change: the direction of their lives was Christ-centred from their earliest days. For some, their regeneration happened at their baptism, whether as infants or as believers. For some, it comes with powerful force later in life. It is God's gracious gift of new life, and we cannot organize its timing. Still less can we insist that all those who are baptized are necessarily born again: you have only to glance at the lifestyle of millions of baptized unbelievers to see that this is not the case. Baptism is the sign and seal both of the divine initiative and of the human response, but it is not magic. It symbolizes the new life, but does not necessarily convey it.

The new life is God's gift, but always there must be human response. God will have no conscripts in his army. People will not be dragooned into heaven. His generous grace is always open to rebels like you and me, but we have to close with it and embrace it personally. It has been well said that God has many children but no grandchildren. St Paul has some remarkable words on the matter. He tells us that his conversion was a pattern for those who would subsequently believe (1 Timothy 1:16). Now surely that must be nonsense! Are we

18

all expected to fall to the ground and go blind? Of course not. The physical manifestations that accompanied his conversion were particular to him, but the principles that his conversion embodied apply to us all. That is the sense in which his conversion is a model.

It seems to me that there were four quite clear elements in Paul's response to the grace of God. First, his *conscience* was stirred: he had, after all, held the clothes for those who stoned Stephen to death. He realized he was in the wrong with God despite all his moral and religious diligence. Second, his *understanding* was illuminated. He came to see that in persecuting Christians he was persecuting the shadowy figure behind them, Christ himself, the crucified one who was alive again for evermore. 'Who are you, Lord?' he cried. 'I am Jesus whom you are persecuting,' was the reply. No doubt he did not appreciate very much on that Damascus road, but he did realize that Jesus was Lord of the universe and must be his Lord as well. Third, his *will* was surrendered, and he went into Damascus with his proud self-centredness broken and his career plan in ruins. Then, of course, his whole subsequent *life* was changed – his experience of the Holy Spirit, his relationships, his desire to reach others with the gospel and his willingness to suffer for the Christ he had once despised and persecuted.

Those four elements are vital in every conversion, whether it is sudden as in the case of St Paul, or gradual as in the case of St Peter. They may come in different orders, but in every true Christian there is always a recognition of unworthiness; there is always at least a recognition that the crucified one is risen, that Jesus is Lord; there is always a surrender to his claims; there is always a change in lifestyle. Without those elements, the human side of Christian beginnings is dangerously incomplete. Without them, we may have good reason to doubt that the divine aspect of regeneration has taken place. There has to be a new life. Yes, and there has to be a new lifestyle. That is where Christian discipleship begins, and the older I get, the surer I am that this message of new beginnings, new life, new birth, new relationship with God needs to be at the very centre of the proclamation of our churches. It is always crucial in growing churches. It is often muted or absent in churches that are simply into the maintenance business. Christianity begins with conversion.

Support

You may wonder what my parents made of these changes in their only child. I can only say they were most understanding. My father was a clergyman of the classic old High Church spirituality. He would have liked to have worn vestments in the two small country churches over which he presided, but he knew that these would not be appreciated by the congregation, so he never did. When I was invited to the house party at Iwerne Minster, he wrote to one of the bishops who was a sponsor and asked him if it was reliable. He got an affirmative answer, and when he saw how much I profited from the experience he was delighted, and was only too willing for me to go regularly. I felt that was very big of him. As time went on, he became increasingly interested in the Evangelical faith which had captured his son, and wanted to read the books I valued and in due course wrote. What drew us together theologically was, I think, the orthodox Christian faith that we both espoused. He had been trained at Lampeter, which combined a High Church spirituality with a firm biblical orthodoxy. We found a deep spiritual unity, and I cannot thank God enough for his love and example.

As for my mother, she should have had a dozen children – she was so affectionate. As it was, she had to make do with me. She was initially a little bemused by my personal commitment to Christ, though very encouraging. In due course, she was able to enter into it as well. She had always been a believing churchgoer, but that personal encounter with the risen Christ had, I think, eluded her. Her practical Christianity, goodness and sympathy with everyone in the village made an enormous impact on the villagers, and even more so on me. I thank God for those parents of mine, and the gracious way they handled my conversion. I am well aware that not all are so fortunate.

CHAPTER 2

Nurture

I was extremely fortunate in many ways. After I had made my initial commitment to Christ, I was given a great deal of help. Without it, I doubt whether I would have survived as a Christian. I might simply have become part of the extensive casualty list of those who profess a decision for Christ but never carry it through to discipleship.

One of the most significant elements in my development was the house party for boys from public schools held at Iwerne Minster three times a year, under the leadership of a remarkable Christian who shunned the limelight, the Rev. E.J.H. Nash. He was known to one and all as Bash, and 'the Bash Camps' played an immense part in the training of many who now hold senior positions in Church and State. For a short time Bash had been the chaplain at a public school, but in the more restrictive situation which prevailed in the 1930s he found he did not have the liberty to bring boys to a personal faith within the school set-up. Accordingly he left, and hit upon the strategy of setting up these 'camps' in the holidays for public schoolboys – house parties where they could be introduced to a living faith in Christ and the discipleship that has to follow. He had the remarkable knack of gathering around him an astonishingly able and committed band of men whose prime aim it was to serve the boys, to help them to begin and grow in the Christian life.

It would be easy to criticize this work. In those days it was secretive: yet it had to be, because it would have attracted much opposition among school headmasters, creating an impossible situation for 'campers' in those schools. It was sexist: yet it would be hard indeed to concentrate on spiritual issues with attractive members of the other sex sitting next to you. It was elitist: well, that is perfectly true, it was. Yet think what would have happened if you had tried to win Etonian teenagers for Christ at the same house party as underprivileged children from the East End. There would have been mutual suspicion, massive cultural divergence and, on the part of the Etonians, an unconscious arrogance which would have made them impervious to the gospel. The elitism was deliberate. It was a tunnel-visioned but very fruitful attempt to reach public schoolboys who had leadership potential. Once the work of nurturing was done and the boys left school and university, they carried the principles learnt at Iwerne into a wide range of careers which were not elitist at all. It is those principles which I found so invaluable, and which I would like to outline here.

Nurture at Iwerne

One vital factor was the talks, morning and evening in the library of Clayesmore School, where these 'camps' took place (and still do). Boys new to them were amazed how relevant these talks were to their lives and how different they were in tone and content from the formal school chapel services which they were forced to attend. The worship sessions were notable for their simplicity, the carefully chosen short songs or choruses sensitively introduced and applied, the variety of winsome 'officers' leading the sessions, and the talks themselves, which were outstanding in terms of clarity, pungency, illustration and insight.

The programme of talks was carefully planned for the week or fortnight concerned, so that there was a gradual progression, building up after three days or so to a talk on personal commitment and then moving on from there to assurance, growth and service in the Christian life. Clear, practical help was given on how to be sure you were a Christian, how to grow in intimacy with God, why and how to pray, how to read the Bible for yourself, how to gain from Holy Communion. One of the talks would involve a leader giving an example of his own daily quiet time, done out loud for the benefit of us all. Then there would be a talk on how to face and overcome temptation, how to let your life and lips witness as a Christian, and the critical importance of wholeheartedness. We would always end the camp on a note of laughter, hope and encouragement.

sounds like Alpha!

The talks were invariably drawn from the Bible, attractively and imaginatively presented, and they showed us teenagers that the Bible is a living book: it understands me, speaks to me and can feed me. The menu in the series of talks did not vary very much, but it was wholesome and reasonably comprehensive for the 14–18 age bracket it covered. The talks were given by different camp officers, and although the subjects were much the same, the treatment was very different each time.

The morning and evening talks were the staple diet of the camp, but that diet was enhanced in many ways, all of which contributed to my development. There was a period set aside before breakfast for personal Bible reading and prayer, and notes were provided to help with this. Then there was the warm Christian fellowship with fellow believers of my own age and above. It was wonderful to engage in active sporting pursuits and intellectual discussion with boys alongside whom I worshipped morning and evening. Friendships were born there which survive to this day: some of my closest friends are people I met at Iwerne, and I know that is true for countless others as well. Friendships were deepened last thing at night, when each dormitory of boys sat around with their leaders, reading a passage of Scripture, making their own comments on it and learning to see its application to their lives. We turned many of those insights into short prayers before tumbling into bed – and were often then regaled with a hilarious story by one of the officers as we went to sleep.

Pastoral care did not end there: far from it. There were two officers in each dormitory of boys, and between them they made a point of having at least two personal chats with each boy in their dormitory during the house party. It was, if you like, the evangelical counterpart of spiritual direction, though none of us had heard of the expression at that time. It enabled the leader to sense how much had gone in, what the difficulties were and where encouragement or instruction was needed, and it gave us boys a great sense of being cared for. Here were gifted adults who not only gave up their time for our benefit in coming to run these camps, gave excellent talks and engaged with us in varied activities, but also took pains to help us in our personal discipleship. That meant a lot. What is more, they wrote to us at school between the camps, and always had some word of spiritual encouragement to include in the letter.

Another feature of camp as one grew older were the daily voluntary Bible studies. These were topical studies on issues like leadership, sex, the authority of Scripture, Bible difficulties and so on, designed to help the older and more spiritually hungry camper to grow. In this way we were introduced to biblical teaching on a number of important topics, and we began to think biblically and see the Bible as a book for all seasons.

Even this was not enough. The really enthusiastic boys were introduced to so-called 'keen books', a selection of approved spiritual books – usually covered in brown paper lest they *wow* should attract unfavourable notice from a parent or schoolmaster! Looking back, it was perhaps a narrow selection, but very appropriate for our age. If nothing else, those books gave us a thirst for good Christian literature, particularly the biographies of men and women who had really invested their lives for God.

Nourished in these ways, we went back home and then to school, where we were encouraged to join a weekly (and somewhat subterranean) Christian group composed largely of Iwerne Minster campers. This was intended to keep the flame burning, and it largely succeeded. Speakers included schoolmasters, clergy, athletes, doctors and professors. We learned that dynamic Christianity was not confined to house parties in the holidays, but was a matter of daily living for people in a wide variety of careers. As we became more senior in the school, a few of us used to gather weekly in a classroom or study to pray for individuals in the group, for those we hoped to invite to camp, and for the meeting on the forthcoming Sunday. Indeed, as very senior boys, we were sometimes allowed to give the talk at the meeting, which was a marvellous introduction to the art of speaking. I vividly recall the first occasion I spoke. I was very nervous in any case, but imagine how I felt when someone passed by outside and stood staring through the window! I froze completely, and for a while could not continue. Most of us were not very good speakers, but the example of a senior boy getting up and talking to 40 fellow students about the difference Christ makes to life certainly had an effect, particularly on the younger boys to whom the head of House or School was an awesome figure.

Such were the influences from camp which played a major part in my development through my teens and leading up to university. As a result, when I went to Oxford I was intellectually equipped to help someone else to faith, which I did in my first term there. The training in discipleship had been thorough and effective. That was not all: once we reached undergraduate stage, many of us were invited back to help run the camps. The really skilful part was that we were initially invited back to sweep the floors, clean the lavatories, make packed lunches and wash the dishes – indeed, to do any practical type of servant ministry that was needed. That was an invaluable test of character. Those who learned to serve with cheerfulness and generosity in these menial chores were the ones who were subsequently invited to become 'officers'.

It was overwhelming to join the officers' room and become a junior colleague of those I had long admired as leaders of the enterprise. It was an awesome experience to give one of the morning or evening talks, knowing there were 20 people in the room who could have done it better, some of whom subsequently offered gentle critique and suggestions. The atmosphere in that officers' room was one of mutual interdependence and great loyalty to the institution of 'camp', to Bash and to the boys entrusted to our care. There was a strong – perhaps too strong – party line on what was 'done' and what was 'not done', but there was plenty of room for individuality. Different officers undertook responsibility for different sides of camp life – games, expeditions, entertainments, administration, food and so on. 'White papers', the fruit of much experience, were available for us to study on many aspects of the leadership which was expected of us: how to bring someone to faith, how to help him to assurance, how to introduce a personal chat without embarrassment, what not to say in letters sent to a boy at school. There was a strong white paper on the reliability of the Bible as the source for Christian belief and behaviour.

We younger ones worked alongside a senior dormitory officer, and watched him running the inductive Bible study at night, entertaining the boys and generally giving a lead. In this way we developed our own style of leadership. It was not so much taught as caught. Iwerne became a hugely important part of our lives – so much so that those of us who were undergraduates or schoolmasters would try to spend time each vacation doing a camp at Iwerne, while officers in other careers came as often as they could, frequently giving it priority over a holiday abroad. We wanted to see those boys and our colleagues again. We wanted to help in the work of spiritual development. In term-time there was (and still is) a weekly extended prayer meeting in some of the universities for the boys, who inevitably undergo a variety of pressures in their schools. Who knows how much has been effected by those regular prayer meetings?

All of this was magnificent nurture. I have no hesitation whatsoever in regarding it as the main ingredient in my own spiritual growth. I have gone into such detail about it because I believe that nurture of this quality is seriously neglected in much Christian work today. Evangelical Christians are quite good at bringing people to Christ – probably better, by and large, than Christians of other traditions. Yet they are not distinguished these days by careful nurture. Much of the work is shallow and slap-happy. It looks for decisions, but is weak on discipleship. It lays great emphasis on an overt commitment, but little on subsequent development. As I look around many Christian organizations today, I see very little of the quality of follow-up which I was privileged to experience over about eight years, at school and university. It was the making of me.

In particular, I learned three things at camp which I have never encountered so effectively anywhere else, and I have spent much of my life in theological colleges of one sort or another. None of those colleges taught me how to do personal evangelism and nurture as well as Iwerne did. None of them taught me how to lead an inductive Bible study without dominating it. None of them taught me so well how to give a talk that is attractive and biblical, with a clear structure, gripping illustrations and effective application.

Nurture of that sort is not easy to come by today, but it is sorely needed. It does not have to be at a holiday camp. It can be done in any context. Reflect for a moment on the principles that lay behind the nurture I received: the value of going away in a congenial group; the coherent, organized series of talks; the personal conversations with a 'soul friend', leading to spiritual growth; the inductive Bible studies where everyone was encouraged to contribute and to pray out loud; the experience of both expository and topical talks, the first taking a passage of Scripture and letting it speak to you, the second using a concordance to discover the biblical teaching on a particular topic. Reflect on the value of a short period of personal daily prayer and Bible reading with the assistance of some helpful notes. The influence of this habit throughout life is incalculable.

Think, too, of how helpful it can be to have a more experienced Christian revealing in a talk how he uses his devotional time. When did you ever hear such a talk replacing the sermon in your parish church? When, as a preacher, I have done just that, the expressions of gratitude have been profuse. People need that practical help on how to approach different aspects of the Christian walk. The delightful and relaxed mixture of natural and spiritual elements in relationship, the friendships, the encouraging letters – all of this was excellent nurture. So was the use of literature: Bible-reading aids, devotional books, biographies, books dealing with current moral and intellectual problems. Remember also the intentional prayer for others, the way younger leaders were brought on by being apprenticed to more experienced colleagues, and the sacrifice involved on the part of the officers.

All of these are principles I first learned at Iwerne, but they seem to me to be of universal application. They make for growth and spiritual development. We shall need more of that pastoral care of Christians in the years to come if we are to breed strong leaders and regain lost ground in this country and beyond.

Many years later, I was privileged to have the chance of working out some of these principles on a fairly large canvas when I became Rector of St Aldate's, a leading church in Oxford with a large congregation drawn from both town and gown. If, as I passionately believe, God's Church exists not for itself but for the benefit of those who are not yet members, then strenuous efforts must be made to reach them and to nurture them. The Church at large has a poor image, and this will certainly not be overcome if things continue the way they have been in the past half-century. A definite initiative is needed, and I would like to share some general principles which have helped me.

Nurture in the parish

First and foremost comes the ministry of prayer. Without that, nothing happens. Unless we are praying for the conversion and nurture of those with whom we are in contact, and doing so regularly, intentionally and corporately, we shall not see much fruit. Therefore a parish prayer meeting of some sort is an essential. I do not mind whether people pray in silence or out loud, whether they use liturgical or extemporary forms, whether they pray in small groups or at a central meeting, whether it involves prayer breakfasts, prayer walking, prayer partnerships or whole nights of prayer – but prayer there must be. The reason is simple and does not need to be dressed up in abstruse theological argument. The plain fact is that frail human beings cannot achieve the conversion or nurture of anyone else, nor will fallible human efforts ensure the growth and development of a church. We are entirely dependent on God. In prayer we tell him so, and we express our dependence on him 'without whom', as the old Prayer Book has it, 'we can do nothing'.

Moreover, a local church must be seen to care in a practical way about the needs of people in its area. So often church-going seems to be a private hobby for those who enjoy that sort of thing. If it is to cut any ice, the church must be seen to care, as Jesus cared. It must be involved in the struggles and problems of ordinary folk. Thus the local church may need to contend for the supply of playgroups, and help to meet that need from its own membership. It may need to take a visible stand by supporting racial minorities in the face of many types of discrimination – and make crystal clear that no discrimination of any sort is tolerated in the church. It may need to start up or help to staff some facilities for young people if there is little of the sort in the area. Unemployment is likely to remain a scourge in many parts of the Western world: the weakest go to the wall. Very well, the church must be seen to care about this in practical ways, perhaps by helping to put together a retraining scheme, even using some of the church property as a night school or workshop venue. I have known churches do both. Perhaps computer buffs in the congregation could be encouraged to give an evening a week to train unemployed teenagers in computer skills. Perhaps others could help staff a night shelter for the homeless or organize a soup run on the streets.

Care shows itself in myriad ways and the church, if it is to attract anyone to its Master, must embody that practical care for others in need which so characterized the life of Jesus. Incidentally, such projects can be a marvellous way of nurturing younger Christians. They can help in practical ways like these when as yet they may know very little about the faith. They will be drawn deeper as they engage in practical caring for others in the company of those who have been Christians for a much longer time.

The church must be a friendly place. The average pub is much more inviting and relaxing than the average church. People are so estranged from the church these days that many have never crossed the threshold. Consequently we have to make the most strenuous efforts to help people feel welcome. We need to pay attention to the physical impression that the building gives. We need to have attractive and frequently changing publicity prominently displayed outside, together with a tidy approach and maybe a bed of flowers. We need to have warm-hearted greeters on the door. We need to avoid burdening people with several books when they come in: today we do not live in a book culture, and people are embarrassed when they are unable to find the place in an unfamiliar book, let alone three of them! The use of PowerPoint display software or overhead projection is much more welcoming, and nowadays there are competent operators in many congregations who would be delighted to offer their talents for service in the church. A five-minute 'buzz' of mutual greeting at the outset of a service is far more attractive than the solemn procession of a choir in strange robes. The serving of coffee afterwards and the ready invitation for visitors to have a meal or spend a night make an enormous impact, because, to our shame, they are so unexpected. I know of churches where several members always plan extra food for a Sunday lunch so that they can invite newcomers to share it with them. Of course, if we can have meetings in the local pub or golf club, this removes at one stroke the dread many have of entering a church building. However it is shown, love and welcome must be the keynote of any church which hopes to win and nurture others.

Evangelistic preaching to the congregation is something which every church should incorporate into its programme. It not only brings newcomers into the family of God, but it is very encouraging for young Christians to hear afresh the good news of the gospel. If there is any turnover at all in a congregation, it is safe to assume that at least some of those present will not have a personal attachment to Jesus Christ, but will be visiting the church out of habit, family pressure, mild interest or honest enquiry. On three or four occasions in the year it would therefore be good to have a well-prepared, well-advertised evangelistic talk which is unashamedly designed to lead people to faith. The worship, the music and aids such as drama, dance or testimony can all be very valuable – so long as they, along with the sermon itself, are all subordinated to the one aim of drawing men, women and young people to Christ. At the end of the service an opportunity should be given for people to stay behind and make a decision. They are then going to need a lot of loving nurture. They will also need to be incorporated into a group for new believers.

The Christian life is one of obedience and discipleship. How is a church to conserve and build up the results of its outreach? Perhaps we should begin one stage further back. In the religious confusion and spiritual search which are common today, it is vital for people to have relaxed opportunities to discuss and argue about Christian claims before facing the challenge to respond. This is just as important as the need to have a good nurture group to follow commitment. At St Aldate's we found it useful to arrange small groups for people who were unsure about the Christian faith and were prepared to look into it together. We called them Agnostics' Groups, and they were run by one or two experienced Christian leaders with a group of eight or ten agnostics. Sometimes the group worked out its own agenda; sometimes it tackled basic issues, one each week. The purpose was to help members discover their way to Christ by uncovering and removing their difficulties and objections along the way.

I loved taking these groups. Like St Paul among the agnostics at Athens, I was happy to let the discussion roam where it would – often the agnostics would resolve some of each other's questions, or shoot down each other's objections – but I constantly drew them back to Jesus and the resurrection and insisted they examined the powerful evidence for these two cardinal points of the faith. Obviously the leadership of such a group calls for knowledge of the gospel, understanding of people, patience and empathy. It is important to expose enquirers to Scripture, which has its own power even when people profess not to believe it. A meal and unjudging friendship are important ingredients in forming trust and promoting openness. The loan of books on different aspects of Christian belief and behaviour can help; so can the companionship of other Christians and the testimony of those who have recently been agnostics themselves.

Such groups ought to be a common feature in our churches. In my experience, however, they are rare. Why? The minister is supposed to be trained in the content of the Christian faith and other world views. He or she ought to excel in such a group. Alas, that is not always the case. It may well be that other members of a congregation have greater gifts in this particular and exacting ministry. If so, let them loose. It does not matter who does it: it does matter that it happens, and on a widespread scale in a post-Christian country like Britain. I am fascinated that the Roman Catholics have well-publicized courses of instruction advertised in the papers. Why not the Anglicans? Why not the Methodists? The non-Christian is not going to come to church. The church must go to him or her. Christians must be prepared to engage in open discussion in home or pub. I have just been engaged in work of this nature in my own local pub. It is challenging, but very reward-ing. When we ran those Agnostics' Groups at St Aldate's, we found that more than half of those who began the course became Christians before the end.

Initial nurture

It makes no difference whether people come to faith through an Agnostics' Group, an evangelistic address or gradual osmosis. They all need intentional nurture afterwards. At St Aldate's we made Beginners' Groups a cornerstone of our work. The church had the peculiarity of being set in the con-tinually changing, open-minded context of intelligent and enquiring young people, but every church which expects to win and nurture new believers needs to find an appropriate way to look after them. In a word, every church needs a nursery! Attendance at church alone will not do the job of nurture. Church will probably be a strange world to new Christians at first. Being plunged into an already existing house group will not necessarily be helpful either. It will be too advanced for their situation and they might be intimidat-ed. New Christians are full of doubts and questions, and need careful, specialized attention. They need to be in a group for beginners.

Our Beginners' Groups lasted eight weeks. There is no magic in this number: it was simply the length of an Oxford term, and convenient for that reason. A group consisted of two or three leaders and a dozen or so new believers, or people who were on the edge of commitment. Each week we examined a basic area of Christianity – the person of Jesus, conversion, assurance, prayer, the Church, the sacraments, the Bible and how to feed on it, the Holy Spirit and his power, and Christian service. Different leaders would handle their group in different ways. There might be a shared supper. There would almost always be an introductory talk. A verse of Scripture might be memorized. There would usually be a small book table, appropriate for the topic of the week. There would certainly be a time for sharing joys and disappointments, answers to prayer, problems and doubts.

There would also always be a time of Bible reading in small groups. If the Beginners' Group was large, we would split it for this part of the evening. (If you keep the groups small, there is a tacit pressure for all to participate.) After a passage chosen by the leader had been read aloud, a period of silence allowed everyone to fasten on something that he or she found helpful. Then everyone contributed a thought, and the discussion was usually lively and relevantly applied. This was followed by a brief time for prayers – short, simple prayers and thanksgivings, usually based on a verse of the passage the group had just read, or arising from a personal need. This open prayer was a totally new experience for almost all of our 'beginners', but immensely valuable for their future growth and Christian fellowship. I am still astonished that people who had been going to church for 40 years could not bring themselves to pray aloud, while these youngsters, who had only been followers of Jesus for a week or two, were delighted to do so. Notes on the evening's topic were distributed as people left. By the end of the eight-week course, members had a mini-theology of the Christian life in their hands!

Notice what has happened by this stage. These beginners have learnt so much even after two or three such evenings together. They have discovered Christian fellowship in the small group – before ever having heard the word 'fellowship'. They have found that others have problems in belief, just as they do. They have found that the Bible is a book which speaks to their condition, and have begun to learn from it. They have gained insight, through the theme of the evening, into some central aspect of life as a Christian. Many of them have learnt to pray aloud in the company of others and discovered its strange power to link people in profound fellowship. They have discovered that their stumbling comments actually help other people. They begin to make Christian friends. They start the habit of learning verses of Scripture and reading Christian books. They are no longer embarrassed to talk about their spiritual discoveries and doubts. All of that constitutes serious advance.

A great deal goes on in the dynamics and interaction of these small groups. In addition, however, new believers need the sort of care that I got from Richard Gorrie. They need personal attention. They need the chance to talk through their own problems and to discover how Christ can impact their personal difficulties. We tried to facilitate this by ensuring that each member of a Beginners' Group had at least two unhurried personal sessions with one of the leaders. In the first, the leader would try to ensure that the member had a sure and solid foundation for his or her Christian life, fielding outstanding difficulties (which often consisted of moral issues like sleeping around or excessive drinking) and helping the person to develop a regular daily time of Bible reading and prayer, so that the foundations of a strong devotional life were in place. The second session usually involved a review of how the person had grown during those electrifying eight weeks, including a discussion of changing priorities, promising spheres of service and the next step in Christian nurture.

The next step was usually twofold. The first part of it was to find a sphere of ministry for the young Christian. It might be to go on the large house party we ran each spring vacation at Lee Abbey. It might be to take an active part in the college Christian group. It might be to join a Christians in Sport group. It might be to undertake training to go on the two-week mission we regularly organized each September in a different city. Those were appropriate areas of service for a student. In a normal church situation the areas would be rather different, but the principle remains: it is crucial for growth that young Christians engage in some activity for Christ that they would not otherwise have done.

The second part, undertaken at the same time, was to graduate from the Beginners' Group and join one of the basic cells that permeated the life of the church. We called these Fellowship Groups, but the name is immaterial. The young believers had tasted the joy of informal Christian fellowship in the Beginners' Group. It was important for them to have a suitable and more advanced group in which to develop this taste. Most of the students in our church threw themselves into the Christian Union in their college. Most of the towns-people (and some students) joined one of the many Fellowship Groups in the church. These groups were geographically arranged, which meant you were very likely to bump into another member of your group in the course of a normal week's activities. The groups could meet weekly or fortnightly, depending on the other structures within the church. Anything less frequent than a fortnightly meeting is too little to enable a group to grow together in openness and cohesion.

Such groups become the basic pastoral units in a church. The members do indeed learn to 'bear one another's burdens and so fulfil the law of Christ' (Galatians 6:2). Problems are shared, joys celebrated, the Scriptures studied and applied – and sometimes the group can take a night out for recreation or for an act of service. Members get to know, love and depend on one another. Close friendships often develop. Some groups will lay on the occasional extra breakfast meeting for particular prayer, or go away together for a weekend to relax or to conduct a mission. They become, in short, 'the church in the home' in their midweek meetings, and 'the church gathered' on Sundays. I was fascinated to find on a recent visit that this is precisely the principle adopted in a very fast-growing church in Sabah, Borneo, where they have more than 300 midweek 'cells' and great celebrations when all come together on a Sunday.

We need at least three levels of nurture: the individual mentor for personal growth, the small group for caring fellowship, and the larger church gathering for celebration and instruction. All three are important for healthy growth. It is not enough to stop there, however, if we are to facilitate growth into maturity. Training is a very important, and usually neglected, aspect of church life. At St Aldate's we attempted to answer this in a number of ways. From time to time we had training courses for various needs: basic counselling, marriage preparation, mission, leading youth and children's ministry, thinking Christianly. For the most part, these courses were of short duration – up to eight weeks or so. Increasingly, we found that a concentrated time away from the pressures of regular life, be it a day, a weekend or a week, was more effective for training purposes than an extended course involving one evening a week. Thus we gradually developed our Away Days, our Training Weekends and our Parish Holidays. They were an invaluable part of our nurturing work.

In addition, Christian students in a particular discipline – be it politics or medicine, engineering or theology – tended to get together and discuss how their faith impinged on their academic work. Outside a university environment, this could be organized just as effectively on a factory shop floor by Christian shop stewards, or in an army unit by Christian NCOs or officers. Such informed interaction can be a great learning tool, although there is no formal instruction involved.

At St Aldate's during term-time we put on a regular Sunday lunch for those who cared to stay on after the morning service. It was a marvellous opportunity to meet and greet new faces, and to quiz the preacher on his sermon. The sermon should never be one-way communication. It is very helpful (for both parties!) when the preacher interacts in free discussion with his congregation on the address he has just given. I fancy that, if this were more common, and clergy knew that they would face a bunch of cheery interlocutors afterwards, it would improve the quality of their sermons dramatically.

One of the ways in which we sought most intentionally to build up young Christians was through the mission training we offered them. Each year we took about a hundred members of the congregation, mostly students, away on a two-week mission. We went to some part of the country where we had been invited and where a year of preparation had taken place beforehand. Such a mission was very good for us. It enabled our members to share in the spreading of the gospel and see it take root in other lives. It was also good for the parishes to which we went. They got drawn together ecumenically by the venture, and they received converts after the mission was over. They may also have seen something to model in their own churches. Naturally, such a mission cried out for training before we went, and this we attempted to do by an eight-week course and a preparatory visit to the town or city. Yet those who took part learned most through experience, during the mission fortnight itself. We used debate, drama, dance, street parties, testimony, school teaching, open-air work and preaching. Invariably we saw God powerfully at work, and we always came back rejoicing.

In such varied ways, we saw new converts grow rapidly in the Christian faith. Some of them wanted to become speakers for Christ. We ran a course on preaching and gave them opportunities to practise. Some wanted to learn New Testament Greek and study the Gospels in the original. We had the resources to teach them. Some wanted to exercise leadership in home fellowships or college groups. We offered training for leadership courses. In due course, some of the Fellowship Group leaders became lay pastors, each monitoring the development and encouraging the leaders of three Fellowship Groups, or taking responsibility for some major area of church life. Such was the aim of every aspect of our nurture programme: to 'present everyone mature in Christ Jesus' (Colossians 1:28).

Nurture through Alpha...

Curiously enough, there is a link between the approach I have outlined above and the Alpha course which has spread so widely round the world. When Nicky Gumbel was doing his theological studies at Wycliffe Hall, Oxford, he became one of the leaders of our Beginners' Groups at St Aldate's. The Alpha course which he developed so brilliantly owes something to those courses for Christian beginners in Oxford, though of course it has eclipsed them – to my delight. It is amazing how Alpha has spread all over the globe and is now a major industry, with its manuals, videos, training courses and books. It is designed for conversion and nurture combined. It seeks both to bring people to a living experience of Christ and to ground them in Christian discipleship. It is the most effective tool for winning and nurturing that I have seen in my lifetime.

The Alpha course is designed quite literally for anybody. It normally lasts for 15 weeks and comprises teaching and discussion, based round a weekly meal. There is a superbly crafted and professionally videotaped talk each week on a basic Christian theme, following an initial talk designed to woo people into the course, called 'Christianity: boring, untrue and irrelevant?' The course handles the following topics: Who is Jesus? Why did Jesus die? Can I be sure of my faith? Why and how should I read the Bible? Why and how do I pray? Who is the Holy Spirit? What does God the Holy Spirit do? How can I be filled with the Holy Spirit? How can I resist evil? How does God guide us? Why and how should we tell others? Does God heal today? What about the Church? How can I make the most of the rest of my life?

The talks are all given and recorded by Nicky Gumbel, a barrister-turned-clergyman who works in partnership with Prebendary Sandy Millar at Holy Trinity Brompton, the largest Anglican church in England. This course is now being run by thousands of churches of every denomination in well over a hundred countries and a vast variety of languages throughout the world. In many ways it differs little from the much more amateur efforts at Christian induction practised by many churches for a long time. Look at it more carefully, however, and you will see some of the distinctives which I think make it superior to courses such as Emmaus, Christianity Explained, or anything else on the market.

For one thing, the presentation is brilliant and the Alpha material is magnificently packaged and distributed. There are various supporting materials for leaders and members of the groups, including a number of books by Nicky Gumbel, a newspaper, conferences and so forth. Nobody leading an Alpha course need feel on their own or unsupported. That is a real benefit, especially to people working in isolated or very restricted situations.

Another factor is the nature of the course itself. It is brilliant for church members, offering them an attractive and clear refresher on Christian essentials which will bring into focus disparate elements of teaching that they may or may not have partially grasped previously. Once they are persuaded of its value, they will branch out and invite their friends the next time round. Alpha's main thrust is towards outreach beyond the Christian community.

It proves to be very appealing indeed to people who are not Christians. They like the quality meal, normally offered free. They appreciate the lightness of touch and humour: why should Christianity be dull when Jesus was the most exciting person who ever walked this earth? They like the fact that they do not have to believe anything before they start. They like the free and unfettered discussion. They like the clarity and directness of the talks. They like the fact that it is not generally held in a church but in a home, hall, restaurant or theatre. They like the fact that it may well not be taken by a clergyman – thus obviating some of the ecclesiastical objections which many people harbour. They like the Christian fellowship which they experience without even realizing it. The course is open to anyone, believer or unbeliever, and no question is deemed inappropriate. Learning about Christianity is thus not didactic, one-way traffic from the expert to the others, but involves debate and lively discussion. Course members are not listening to someone else's bright ideas, but are going back to the basic document of the Christian faith, the Bible, and seeing what it has to say. Nobody is asked to believe it at first encounter, merely to listen to an attractive presentation of what it has to say. Before long, the innate power of the Scriptures have their own convincing and life-giving effect.

Another important emphasis is the length of the course. It tests the seriousness of those who come, and it stresses that discipleship is no sudden decision but a journey, like life itself. It is not dogmatic, either, despite its constant reference to the teaching of the Bible. Each talk is couched as a question, allowing people to come, discuss, argue and disagree. Alpha is promoted not so much as an explicitly Christian course as an answer to the fundamental question we have as human beings: is there a purpose to life and, if so, what is it? Although it may begin in a church as a refresher for the more fringe or ill-instructed church members, its main impact is deliberately aimed at those who never go to church and make no Christian profession. It has led hundreds of thousands of such people to Christ, and is currently the most effective form of outreach and initial nurture to be found anywhere on earth. All denominations have come to see its value. Without trying to be, it has become a modern ecumenical tool.

In due course Alpha will pass away, but the principles behind it will not. The opportunity for enquiry; the clear teaching; the openness to discussion; the importance of individual relationships and fellowship within the group; the element of gradual infiltration of the gospel through weekly exposure; the joy of leading someone else to Christ; the experience of the living God; the universality of the gospel for a wide variety of ages, types and nationalities – all of these things are essential both for the start of the Christian life and for the early days of discipleship.

...and beyond

Of course there is more to nurture than this. I could have said a lot more about prayer. After all, prayer is openness to the living God who acts. Without prayer we shall not grow, nor shall we achieve anything in his service. The basic forms of prayer – corporate and individual, silent and verbal, informal and liturgical, involving confession, intercession, thanksgiving, contemplation and adoration – have filled many a volume, and rightly so. Prayer is the lifeline of the Christian.

I could have said a lot more about Bible reading. It is one of the major means by which we appropriate God's grace. There is incalculable blessing available to those who humbly and regularly expose themselves to a part of God's Word day by day. It is first milk and then strong meat to feed us. It is a lamp to guide us. It is a sword to pierce our indifference or to wield in spiritual battle. It is honey to our lips. It shows us our inheritance in Christ. It builds us into maturity of Christian judgement and holiness of Christian living.

I could have said a lot more about service. It is in serving the Lord that we develop our Christian muscles. There are many types of service which Christians undertake, enough for all tastes and abilities. The important thing is to show our gratitude to the Lord 'not only with our lips but in our lives, by giving up ourselves to his service'. We can serve God through integrity in the workplace, through compassion for those in need, through cheerful acts of helpfulness and generosity, through fearless witness to Jesus, through the 'cup of cold water' given in his name, through conforming our lifestyle to that of Christ, through using our strength or our intellect, our marriage or our singleness, our career or our retirement explicitly for him. All Christians are called to serve the Lord, be it in the land of their birth or in ministry overseas. Without service there is no possibility of being nurtured into Christian maturity.

I could have said much about the Eucharist, or Holy Communion. This is the supreme means by which Jesus invites us to remember him. It drives us to our knees as we recognize the failures on our part which led the Lord of glory to the gibbet of Calvary. It elicits in our hearts profound gratitude for what he has done for us on the cross. It binds us together with other communicants as members of the Body of Christ on this earth, who are called to live in harmony with each other and in usefulness to our Lord. It is one of the great means whereby the Lord pours himself into our lives and nourishes us with the bread of heaven. It is strength for the journey. It is a supreme foretaste of the heavenly banquet, when the redeemed will be with the Lord and each other for ever. All that and more could have filled another volume, to add to the thousands already written on the subject.

I have chosen not to major on these other important areas of growth, for the simple reason that they are well known in the Christian community. Less well known are the principles I have recounted above – principles which proved so significant in my own nurture. If they were practised throughout the Church, there would be a great difference in the quality of Christian holiness and maturity. That should be our primary goal.

CHAPTER 3

Student Religion

Contrary to commonly held opinion, Christianity is very much alive in the universities, and a far higher number of students are to be found at worship than is the case with the rest of the population. Whether this is all part of the openness to exploration which marks most undergraduates, I do not know, but the fact remains: the student world is often a hotbed of religious attachment, opposition and controversy.

When I went up to Oxford in 1949, this was as true as it is today. Perhaps more so, because many were coming to the university after being demobbed from the Forces. These men had seen action. They did not share the frivolity of the generation between the wars. They had faced death, and had dealt it out. They were in search of something to live for, now that they had seen off the Nazi menace. Others, like myself, had arrived straight from school. There was formal religion in the college chapels, and that drew a quorum on Sundays, especially those who liked singing in a choir. There was the contingent of committed High Churchmen whose spiritual home was Pusey House. There were interested searchers, who were drawn to the attractive galaxy of preachers at St Aldate's. The serious Evangelicals were to be found in St Ebbe's under the leadership of Maurice Wood, who had recently won a DSO on the Normandy beaches and was destined to become Bishop of Norwich. And then there was the OICCU.

The Oxford Inter Collegiate Christian Union was the university's branch of the countrywide Inter Varsity Fellowship of Evangelical Unions (now UCCF). It existed to present the claims of Jesus Christ to members of the university, to unite in fellowship those who desired to witness for Christ and to deepen their spiritual life, and to promote involvement in God's work worldwide.

The OICCU and the SCM

You either loved the OICCU or hated it: few remained neutral. It consisted of Evangelical Christians, drawn from a variety of denominations. These Evangelicals were not willing merely to go to church or chapel and leave it at that. They had a real enthusiasm to bring Jesus Christ to the notice of their peers and invite them to start following him seriously. Inevitably, that proved divisive. Thus the OICCU was derided. It was called spoilsport, because many of its members would neither drink, smoke nor go to the theatre or cinema. It was called narrow, because it regarded other Christian organizations – particularly the Roman Catholics and the World Council of Churches – with suspicion and was very wary of co-operating with them at any level. It was called obscurantist, because it took the Bible very seriously and regarded its teaching as infallible. It was called crude, because it insisted that Christ died on the cross as the substitute for sinners. It was called all sorts of names, because its members pestered their friends to come to the evangelistic services which were held every Sunday night of full term. Saturday nights were reserved for solid teaching sessions among the Christian undergraduates.

Every college had its group of these enthusiastic Christians. My own college, Exeter, was no exception. They had a problem, however. It so happened that in 1949 no room in college was assigned to any of the Christian Union members.

Within a few hours of unpacking my belongings in a little room on No. 9 Staircase, I was asked if I would allow my room to be used for an invitation tea, called a 'squash', where some senior Christian from outside the university would come and talk about Christ and encourage people to join the Christian Union. I gladly agreed.

I did not actually join the Christian Union at that stage. I was not enthusiastic about signing bits of paper on which other people had written my beliefs. Yet I found my spiritual home with this group of people, and I stayed with them throughout the four years that I studied Literae Humaniores, or 'Greats' as it is known at Oxford: Latin, Greek, Philosophy and Ancient History. In my final year, as I mentioned earlier, I found myself president of the OICCU, and it proved to be an invaluable training in leadership.

That is to go too fast, however. I had not been at the university more than a few days when I discovered the Student Christian Movement. This was a group of several hundred students who sought to work out their Christian commitment in social and intellectual endeavours. They explored Christianity and the arts, Christianity and social justice, Christianity and prison reform, and so on. The OICCU folk pilloried the SCM as 'woolly', because they had no firm doctrinal basis and no strong views about personal salvation. Many of them would have been quite agnostic about that, but they were attracted by Jesus Christ and wanted to see how discipleship might work out in the postwar world which was dawning all round us.

Sadly, the SCM has now more or less died. It occupies no place in the university religious scene today. That is a pity, because it emphasized a very important aspect of Christianity to which Evangelical Christians were blind in those days: the social and political implications of the gospel. These were entirely neglected in the OICCU, and indeed among most Evangelicals until the Keele Congress in 1967, when the social imperatives of the gospel were roundly asserted. Indeed, they were not only asserted, but acted upon, and a plethora of Evangelical organizations emerged for relieving poverty, meeting needs in the Two-Thirds World, lobbying parliament and so forth. Concerns like these had, of course, figured largely in the Evangelical Christianity of the previous century, when a spiritual revival had triggered a host of caring agencies in factories, prisons, education, mission work and justice issues. Sadly, however, Evangelical outlook contracted to tunnel vision during the first half of the twentieth century. Great Evangelical reformers of the past like Wilberforce, Newton, Fry and Barnardo were honoured but not emulated in the days when I was a student. Serious Christianity was a matter of personal conversion and growth, followed by determined attempts to reach others with the gospel.

This attitude had prevailed for several decades. Back in 1910 there had been a great Missionary Congress, and the Christian student movement had been fired by the glorious vision of reaching the whole world with the gospel within a generation. After that date there was a parting of the ways. Those with the greater evangelistic zeal concentrated on evangelism to the exclusion of most other aspects of Christianity, and were influenced by the fundamentalist approach to the Bible common in Protestant circles after the 1920s. That was the stream to which the OICCU belonged.

The other stream was broader. It was unconcerned with personal conversion or theological niceties, though increasingly it favoured a liberal approach to the Scriptures and Christian teaching. It concentrated on the liberation of human beings, on the relief of poverty, on justice issues, on what became known as 'the social gospel'. Sadly, a growing polarization took place between these two aspects of Christianity which so obviously need each other. The Evangelicalism of those days often had a millennial flavour, expecting at any moment the return of Christ which would wind up human history. The important thing, they felt, was not to improve society, doomed in any case to pass away, but to save souls.

You do not find much of that attitude around today, thank goodness. Evangelicals are frequently in the forefront of social and political concern for a better world. It was very prevalent then, however, and led to a quite unnecessary polarization among those who could have complemented one another in the Christian cause. It was obvious that, if they were to survive, either the OICCU mentality had to embrace social action, or the SCM mindset had to make room for personal conversion and growth. The SCM did not make that adjustment and has died. The Christian Union did adjust to a considerable extent, and is by far the most significant Christian influence in every British university today.

Strengths and weaknesses

The strengths of Evangelical Christianity in the universities are enormous, and often under-rated. The commitment to Christ, the devotional life, the strong fellowship, the desire to grow and to bring all life under Christ's control, the willingness to submit major issues like career and marriage to God's will – all this was admirable in the students 50 years ago, and still is today. So is the evangelistic passion, which has led thousands into ordination and overseas missionary work.

Then, as now, this evangelistic zeal reached its climax in a triennial mission within the university. The Christian Union college groups invite an experienced guest from outside to come and help them evangelize within the college. The OICCU itself invites a gifted evangelist to come and proclaim the gospel for a week in the Sheldonian Theatre, and also puts on a multitude of lunchtime apologetic sessions, covering most of the main objections to Christianity. I have been involved in these triennial missions for many years, as a young student, as president of the Christian Union and as the main speaker. The aim has not changed – to give every student an opportunity of hearing a coherent explanation of the Christian faith at least once during his or her time at university. The sophistication of these missions has, of course, been refined over the years and is currently impressive.

Nowadays nobody in their right mind could say these missions are over-emotional or pressurizing. Nobody could say they are obscurantist. Nobody could say they have a fixation on instant conversion. Nobody could say (as they often have, quite justly, observed in the past) that due care has not been exercised in following up the week's outreach. In this regard, we hit upon what proved to be a very good idea for nurture during the 1997 mission at Oxford, which I had the privilege of leading. Instead of challenging people to respond to Christ there and then in the meeting, we invited them to 'sign up for the Mars Hill Tavern' – a phrase with good vibes! This was a series of dinners in attractive, non-churchy surroundings, with Greek food and wine. People sat at the same table every week, and each table had a couple of postgraduate Christian helpers attached to it. After the dinner, a competent talk was given on Christian basics and discussion followed at each table. Friendships emerged, and so in due course did decisions for Christ. We ended the mission with some 200 people signing up for the Tavern, but within about three weeks this number had risen to 460, as *non-Christians* told their non-Christian friends that this was something they should not miss! In the course of several months, a great many students professed Christian faith and were drawn into ongoing discipleship.

Yes, Evangelical Christianity at Oxford and in other universities had many strengths, and as one who has constantly been involved with students, I am delighted to have seen the Christian Unions remain steadfast and grow over five decades. Needless to say, there are real weaknesses too. In universities with large Christian Unions, like Oxford, Cambridge, Durham and Southampton, the CUs run themselves under student leadership and do not take too much notice of the regional helpers provided by the central UCCF. As a result, they produce real leaders but are prone to make the same mistakes year after year. In universities where the CU is smaller, they rely much more on senior guidance and therefore may produce less in the way of leadership while making fewer repeated mistakes.

There have been other discernible and common weaknesses. It used to be the case that you threw away the chances of a good degree if you were involved in the time-consuming work of the Executive Committee. That is certainly not true today. Many Executive members get first-class degrees. It used to be the case that Evangelical students tended to be obscurantist, and to keep their faith in a watertight compartment. This, too, is much less true today, and I discern among students a wide-spread desire to integrate their faith both with their academic discipline and with their personal life. It is also no longer the case that Evangelical students have an exclusively substitutionary view of Christ's atonement, although they find that is the most helpful aspect to emphasize to people who are aware of their guilt before God. Nor is it the case that they espouse a literalist approach to the Bible, although they incline in that direction because of their profound suspicion of a sceptical criticism of Scripture which robs it of its authority. Nonetheless, I think the OICCU, and its parent body the UCCF, are a little unwise to insist that all members sign assent to what the Americans call the 'inerrancy', and the British the 'infallibility' of the Scriptures.

John Stott, a man of unimpeachable orthodoxy, has given several reasons why he does not like the word 'inerrancy' in his book *Evangelical Truth*. It does not do justice to the richness of Scripture to reduce it to a string of propositions which can be labelled 'truth' or 'error'. The word is a double negative and sends out wrong signals: instead of encouraging Bible study in order to grow, it leads to defensiveness in relation to discrepancies. Moreover, it often misses the point: submission to Scripture, not subscription to statements about it, is what matters. In any case, it is impossible to prove that the Bible contains no errors. I can subscribe to the concept of infallibility if it is taken in its strict etymological sense that the Scriptures are incapable of leading you astray: they represent an utterly reliable road for the pilgrim to travel towards God. If, however, the word is taken to mean that there can be no possibility of error in any statement in the Bible, and if its proponents go to absurd lengths to harmonize what cannot be harmonized, then they are asking for trouble.

Indeed, trouble has come. Over the years an enormous number of people who have been converted and nourished within Christian Union circles at university have gone on to study theology, and have found that a narrowly infallibilist attitude to Scripture is almost impossible to maintain with integrity. As a result they have become liberals, and often very militant liberals. I think of several professors I know who were once enthusiastic CU members, but when they came to study theology they found they could not reconcile the UCCF doctrine of infallibility (in its strongest form) with what lay before them in the plain text of Scripture. As a result they became vociferous and sometimes very acid opponents of all that the CU stood for. This is a great pity. For one thing, it robs the CUs of some of the senior friends who could other-wise be of great help to them. For another, it breeds in student Christian circles a deep suspicion of the whole theological process: 'It will poison you. Keep clear.'

Of course, there are historical roots for this sort of myopia. The Christian Union at Oxford was swallowed up by unwise co-operation with more liberal bodies back in the 1920s, and has felt the need ever since to define its position with the utmost clarity. The infallibility of Scripture has never been part of the historic Christian faith, however. It does not figure in any of the great creeds of the Church. It was not asserted by the Reformers. Scripture does not claim infallibility for itself. Nonetheless, its foundational importance, its reliability, its supreme authority for belief and behaviour – this can and should be maintained by all Christians. Holy Scripture is inspired by God and normative for us. It might be helpful all round if we avoided the word 'infallibility', and substituted a phrase such as 'complete trustworthiness and divine authority'.

This is, of course, a very tender area for students anxious to maintain an orthodox position. They may feel I am being dangerously lax. If so, they should be encouraged by 'Evangelical Affirmations', a careful statement produced by some 650 Evangelical leaders in 1989: 'We affirm the complete truthfulness and the full and final authority of the Old and New Testament Scriptures as the Word of God written. The appropriate response to it is humble assent and obedience.' In their conclusion they wrote, 'Evangelicals hold the Bible to be God's Word and therefore completely true and trustworthy (and this is what we mean by the words infallible and inerrant).'

Constructive co-operation

If a narrowly infallibilist view of Scripture is one problem with which CUs need to wrestle, another is the matter of co-operation. Fingers have been badly burnt by co-operation in the past with other Christian bodies which have compromised the gospel by non-biblical teaching and lack of impact. As a result it has become policy to stand aside from any co-operative mission. I can understand that. Indeed, in the light of history I can agree with it – so far as organizational unity is concerned. Yet organizational unity need not have the last word.

When I was president of the Christian Union at Oxford we were presented with a particularly teasing problem. There was going to be a mission in the university organized by the college chaplains. Such missions often invited rather unsuitable people who did not win the minds or hearts of the students and generally proved ineffective. In 1952, however, they invited the distinguished Professor Michael Ramsey, who had just been made Bishop of Durham, to take such a mission in the Sheldonian Theatre. He was well known as a holy man, a forceful speaker and an orthodox theologian and believer. It clearly would not do to brand such a mission a liberal waste of time. It was best to see it as an opportunity, not as a problem.

I therefore encouraged the Christian Union members, while maintaining our organizational independence, to take their friends to the meetings and to the chaplains' sherry parties afterwards, and to use the teaching of Michael Ramsey to help their friends face up to Christian truth. We knew that the Bishop would be unlikely to challenge people for a decision then and there, so we maintained the normal OICCU evangelistic meeting on both Sundays during the mission, inviting speakers who had a known gift for precipitating decision. As a result, a good many people were led to recognition of Christian truth through Michael Ramsey's preaching during the week, and came to a personal commitment to Christ on one of the two Sundays. That seemed to me a good way of maintaining the distinctive biblical witness of the CU, at the same time as encouraging personal participation in any venture that would uplift Christ. Any perceived inadequacies in the missioner's presentation could be made good in personal conversation.

I confess that I found the intransigent attitudes of the OICCU leadership rather trying when I was appointed Rector of St Aldate's in 1975. They had already invited me to lead the OICCU mission in 1977, and I had agreed. That, however, was before I was appointed to St Aldate's and was still Principal of St John's College, Nottingham. In the minds of the OICCU Committee, St Aldate's was deemed 'unsound', although at the time far more OICCU students went there than to the 'approved' church of St Ebbe. Moreover, St Aldate's had for 20 years and more had a thoroughly orthodox and evangelistic Rector in Keith de Berry, who led hundreds of students to Christ. Nevertheless, some of its visiting preachers were not 'true blue' and memories of its more liberal past remained, so St Aldate's was regarded as non-kosher in OICCU circles. As soon as I became Rector, although I was presumably personally acceptable because they had invited me in the first place, the OICCU rescinded the invitation to lead the 1977 mission. This was very painful, and caused me a lot of careful reflection.

In the mid-1970s, the CU was getting increasingly out of touch with the student scene, because it continued to provide 'modern' apologetics and approaches to an increasingly 'postmodern' situation. I and my colleagues at St Aldate's therefore set out to reach a much wider cross section of the university. We began a worship and dance group which operated before services in the street outside the church. We arranged late-night debates in the church with Cabinet ministers, trade union leaders and controversial figures of the day. We invited all new students to come to a free lunch on one of three days at the beginning of their first term, and told them what St Aldate's and, more importantly, the gospel stood for, inviting them to church on the first Sunday of term. Hundreds came, and we included testimony, drama, humour and profound worship in those services at the start of each academic year. The large congregations of young people, the contemporary approach and the clear focus prepared people for an attractive but very direct evangelistic sermon.

This was followed by a challenge to come and join a Beginners' Group for people who had just come to faith or were approaching it. Sometimes as many as 80 people would sign up for these groups on that first Sunday of term, and many more as the year went on. It led to a large number of conversions, and, because the evangelistic challenge was integrated with the eight-week Beginners' Groups which provided good pastoral care, there was very little fallout. Before long, we were leading far more undergraduates to Christ than the OICCU was. I was determined, however, to do nothing to embarrass the OICCU. We were in partnership, not competition. At the church we sought to maintain our evangelism and nurture, since no church could responsibly renege on that. Yet we urged those we had helped to faith and put through

Beginners' Groups to take things further by getting fully involved in their college Christian Union. We did not set up an alternative structure, although it would have been easy to do so.

We had public baptisms, often down at the river, because that was something the OICCU could not do. We had weekly informal Eucharists, often with a hundred or more students attending, because the OICCU was not a sacramental body. In many such ways we sought to complement the Christian Union, and before long we were very much at ease with one another. In ways like this, co-operation without compromise can flourish between church and CU, and I am glad to see that there are now many examples of such partnership throughout the country. The opportunities for lively churches near universities are enormous. We had the privilege of the Oxford Pastorate being attached to our church. This was a tremendous asset. It meant that while I was Rector we were able to have at least one clergyman and several lay assistants whose task was to undertake pastoral and evangelistic work in the university: a truly marvellous job for those who have the skills. The Pastorate, founded in the nineteenth century by visionary people with a heart for students, paid the bills. I realize that this was a most privileged situation, but many churches in university cities could do a significant work in partnership with the Christian Unions if they saw it as a strategic part of their ministry.

Strategic it certainly is. Not only is the student scene the fastest growing and most fertile soil for Christianity these days, but many of these young men and women are destined to hold high positions of great influence in a whole variety of careers in the future. Their potential influence is incalculable. Perhaps the most significant mission work in the world today is through the International Fellowship of Evangelical Students, the worldwide body to which the OICCU is affiliated. In just over 50 years of life, it has become the single most effective instrument for the gospel in our world and has a membership of over a million. In Nigeria recently they had a missions conference among Christian Unions. Twenty-five thousand people attended, and resolved at the end to make the spreading of the gospel throughout Africa their lifelong aim. In war-torn Ethiopia, one university student in every 15 is a member of one of the Fellowship's Bible study groups, and much the same could be said for many other parts of the developing world. I am deeply grateful for this remarkable work for Christ that is going on all over the globe. There are Evangelical student Christian groups in all but a dozen or so countries of the world, and often they produce a substantial part of the future Christian leadership of their country.

In our own church in Oxford we had occasional meetings for those who were considering missionary work or ordination. Many came to these meetings, and many became clergy or missionaries. This was not because we gave these meetings a particularly high profile, but because they could see from the leadership team of our church and the stature of the overseas Christians we invited to speak, that a lifetime of ordained ministry or missionary work was one of the most fulfilling projects anyone could attempt, and one of the greatest callings anyone could follow. To win, equip and send students into a lifetime of service for Christ and their fellows is one of the most treasured privileges that has ever come my way.

CHAPTER 4

Family Life

When Rosemary and I got married in September 1957, we were almost immediately plunged into ministry at a large church. In December of that year, having finished my ordination training in Cambridge, I was taken on as curate at Holy Trinity, Eastbourne. We loved it. We had a marvellous, wise, caring vicar and his wife. We had a lot of freedom for initiative. And we were very much involved in it together. Although Rosemary had been a maths teacher at a girls' public school, this came to an end with our marriage and my curacy. She did not mind a bit. Occasionally she would do a couple of days' teaching at the local College of Education – and would earn more in those two days than her curate husband earned in a whole week! Both our hearts were in ministry, however. We loved the job and the people, the opportunities and the large youth fellowship for which we were responsible. We had great fun inviting students from the nearby College of Physical Education to come for an evening to our home, where they would jostle for space and there would be plenty to eat, party games and a talk about Jesus. A number of students found faith at these evenings and are effective Christian workers to this day. It was a wonderful three years.

Then the big change came. I was pressed repeatedly to accept a post as tutor at the London College of Divinity. Eventually, after exploring an Oxford chaplaincy and a university lectureship in Ghana, we said a cautious 'yes' to the theological college. It was a significant decision which was to have repercussions later on. For me, it was a challenge. It made use of both my intellectual and my pastoral gifts. Teaching for the London Honours BD and the College Diploma, spending quality time with the men and starting to write – all this was fulfilling. Yet the college was very old-fashioned by today's standards, and no modern theological students or staff would tolerate it. Staff and students were expected to have all meals in college. We had to be in for chapel by 7.15 in the morning and were not free to return home until after supper. This did not make for the quality of partnership which Rosemary and I had previously enjoyed. Furthermore, women were distinctly unwelcome in the college. They never entered the place except for the annual Christmas revue, which largely consisted of a take-off of the staff.

All of this was very discouraging for a young wife who had just produced our first baby. At least there was a lively parish church nearby, where we worshipped on Sundays, and Rosemary succeeded in finding some fellowship there. Increasingly the church family became her sphere, and the college mine.

Neither of us realized that this move into a theological college would consume a substantial part of our lives – 15 years in all. I had expected it would be a sort of second curacy, four or five years at the most. It did not turn out like that. Increasingly I was invited onto significant Church commissions, like the Doctrine Commission and the Anglican–Presbyterian Conversations in the UK and Scandinavia. I also began to undertake at least one major international speaking engagement a year, and to write serious books such as *The Meaning of Salvation* (1965) and *Evangelism in the Early Church* (1969).

Home and family

Life was becoming very busy. Between 1960, when we moved to the college, and 1966 our other three children were born. Rosemary had her hands full, and I was not around as much as either of us would have liked. The vacations provided some relief, but as I look back, I know the young family and Rosemary got squeezed by my job, and I much regret it. That is not to say that we did not have a lot of fun together. We did. Sunday afternoons were particularly good, as we got out and played wide games in the nearby woods, or engaged in rough-and-tumbles and hide-and-seek in the house.

Both Rosemary and I had athletic skills. She exercised hers by playing lacrosse for her club on winter Saturdays, while I looked after the children. She had gained a blue at Oxford in this sport and was still very good. I played cricket for a local club in the summer, while she looked after the children – they often came to watch. Cricket was a game I loved, and still do. I recall one remarkable day when, opening the bowling with a certain John Samways, at that time a university teacher, we bowled out the opposition for 14 runs. That was surprising enough, although the conditions were very much in favour of the bowlers, but what was really amazing was that he and I had a precisely equal bowling analysis. We each got five wickets for seven runs in six overs. For some reason, the *News of the World* latched onto this the next morning! John, by the way, found his way to a decided Christian faith soon afterwards, and has since become a most effective clergyman.

Christian families are often at a loss about family prayers, but we found that evenings together before bedtime were a joy when the children were young. We would tell them stories from the Bible and then illustrate them by primitive pictures drawn in an old exercise book. A simple expedient, perhaps, but one that maintained high interest and enthusiasm. On one occasion Michael Ramsey, by then Archbishop of Canterbury, was speaking to the students at the college, and I invited him to come over to our home. Rosemary was conducting family prayers with the children at the time, and the Archbishop happily joined in. At the end Jenny, aged three, looked solemnly at Michael Ramsey and announced, 'You not got much hair.' He replied with a great laugh and a waggle of those famous eyebrows, 'Neither has your Daddy!'

Holidays were much looked forward to by the whole family. We had a car and often went camping or borrowed a house from friends for the summer holidays. These were usually good times and some of the most memorable holidays were in Kenmare in Eire, where we went three or four times. A remarkable and generous Christian lady, Mrs Schofield, had a wooden cottage called 'Tigh' which we were allowed to colonize. There was a donkey to ride, endless space, hills to climb, rivers to fish, rowing boats and even a small sailboat for the sea. The children loved it, and so did we. Rosemary did some sailing and I got some trout-fishing in. I would often also get a rabbit for the pot as I drove back from the river, because the bumper of our little car was just the right height to knock a rabbit out without spoiling the meat.

On one occasion I got back in the dark with several trout after the evening rise and found a considerable commotion. Rosemary had taken the sailing boat out and it had capsized. Most people would have been glad to forget the boat and try to swim back to land. Not Rosemary. She managed to right the boat, but was unable to bail it out, so she pushed it in front of her as she swam slowly back to land. The old lady had seen all this from her sitting room window (she missed very little!) and ensured that a boatman and hot drinks and blankets were on hand by the time Rosemary landed.

Sometimes, I fear, I spoiled the first part of the holidays by being gloomy, because I found it so hard to relax and clear my mind of work. Fortunately, that bad trait of holiday blues improved, but I know that it took the sparkle out of the initial days of more than one family holiday.

In 1968, when we had been at the London College of Divinity for nearly eight years, we were surprised by the resignation of the Principal, Hugh Jordan. He had recently been instrumental in securing a house and field up in Nottingham, near the research area of the university, which looked as if it would be a much better place for training ordinands than the leafy surroundings of Northwood, where the college was currently located. Furthermore, London University was cutting down on the institutions which were allowed to teach for the internal London BD, and we were due to be removed from the list. So the need to move became urgent, despite the fact that we occupied the most modern buildings of any theological college.

To my astonishment, I was made Principal after Hugh's resignation, and had to undertake the new and heavy responsibilities of moving the college to its new site in Bramcote, Nottingham. By this time we had a fresh, young staff, with able colleagues such as Colin Buchanan, Julian Charley and Stephen Travis, but it was a formidable task and engaged all our energies. Once again, time for the family was limited. Rosemary, however, proved to have a very good eye for detail when it came to scrutinizing the architects' plans, and she saved the college many a mistake and a good deal of money.

Of course, the move meant major disruption for the family. Our eldest son, Tim, was of an age when he could have gone to Nottingham High School or to a Christian preparatory school. We found it a difficult decision, but eventually agreed on the latter and had no cause to regret it. Initially very shy and withdrawn, Tim found that school a great help. He really flourished there, and later at Dean Close where he got a full-fee scholarship and ended up as head boy. He went on to win a scholarship to Queen's College, Cambridge. Both girls, Sarah and Jenny, settled down very happily at Nottingham High School for Girls, while Jonathan, our youngest, went to the local primary school.

We had a splendid black rabbit as a pet. It was given the freedom of the sitting room, and had a penchant for chewing through the flex of the electric light. On one memorable occasion we had Metropolitan Anthony Bloom for a Quiet Day at the college, and naturally he stayed with us. At breakfast the next morning, this imposing figure with black hair and beard, black cassock and shoes, happily shared his porridge with the black rabbit who bounded cheerfully up onto his lap.

On another occasion we were privileged to have the saintly Bishop Trevor Huddleston to stay. He made a great impression on the students and, indeed, on our family. I went for an early morning walk with him, and he told me that the cost of a celibate life was, for him, not so much the lack of a wife as the lack of children, whom he adored. When he returned to Stepney, where he was Bishop at that time, he sent our children a wonderful parcel. Inside was a black ebony tortoise with a legend reading something like this: 'I asked my master where he had been, and he told me that he had been in Nottingham with a family with four children. I like children, so I asked him if I could go and live with them, and here I am.' It was typical of the generous and imaginative spirit of that great man. I invited him to St Aldate's years later, and once again he made a profound impression on the large crowd who came to hear him.

Any account of our family life in those days would be very incomplete without reference to dogs and horses. Sarah had long pleaded for a dog, and when she was 11 we got one, on the condition that she should exercise her and generally look after her. This she did most assiduously. The dog was Judy, a liver and white springer spaniel, and before long she won all our hearts. One of the most touching presents I have ever been given was quarter-ownership of Judy, which Sarah generously bestowed on me! Although bred for show, not for working, she had a superb nose and both boys and I occasionally used to go out with her shooting rabbits and – if we were lucky – the odd pheasant, on a friend's farm. We all enjoyed it, none more than Judy, and the pot benefited. She had some delightful characteristics. There was an old shed near our house at the college, adjoining the sports field. We used to keep hens there in deep litter, and often let them out on free range. At night, if any of them were still absent without leave, Judy would find them and either chase them back in or carry them tenderly in her mouth.

In due course Judy died, but her daughter Jester was a great delight to the family, although she missed her mother a lot. I acquired another springer, Tarka, as company for her. She was a working dog and was much more disciplined than either Judy or Jester in the field. She was wiry and fast, and was my special delight. When I was fishing one evening on the Wye, Tarka jumped into the water and caught a duck before it could take off. On another occasion, when we were staying in a little cottage used by David Watson on the Yorkshire moors, Jester twice flushed a small covey of grouse and on each occasion caught one of them in midair, retrieving it to me in copybook fashion. We were somewhat embarrassed when we fell in with a gamekeeper on the way down from the moor, but he did not see the birds and we did not feel bound to inform him!

The dogs became an important part of our lives, especially when we moved to St Aldate's in the heart of Oxford. They provided a very friendly welcome to the countless people who came to the rectory, and made it easy for them to relax. Tarka was particularly well disciplined, and I could walk across a busy Oxford street with her walking to heel in the midst of the traffic without a lead. Once she provided a superb illustration in a Sunday service of the sort of loving obedience Christians owe their Lord. She dropped at my hand signal, waited while I continued preaching and walked away down the aisle, then a click of the fingers brought her to my heel, and so forth. I doubt if anyone present forgot either the theme or the illustration of that address.

The dogs were shrewd, too. On one occasion we had taken them for an extended walk on Shotover Hill, an extensive wild area some miles from the centre of Oxford. They had turned deaf ears to our whistle and call, so preoccupied were they in trying to find rabbits. We searched long and hard, but returned home disconsolate without them and had a bad night. By the next morning, one of them was sitting smugly on the doorstep and the other was found up on Shotover Hill, sitting exactly where we had parked the car, waiting for us to collect her. But enough of the dogs. They were very dear to us and became a sort of trademark. It was exceedingly hard to give them away, even to excellent homes, when we moved to Canada.

Unwittingly, the dogs have brought me to mention the 12 years when our family lived in Oxford. St Aldate's rectory was a remarkable building, erected towards the end of the nineteenth century by public subscription in gratitude for the powerful and lengthy ministry of Canon Christopher. It was an enormous house and it suited us well enough, although my successor turned it into well-appointed offices and reception rooms, along with an invaluable Christopher Room which is in constant use. We managed to erect an inner door which separated the private part of the house from public rooms and office – even though that door was more often open than shut. At least it meant that, in a house where sometimes a hundred people would come in the course of a day, there was space for the children to have some privacy. They each had a room of their own, and that was a blessing in such a busy home.

[handwritten margin note: 100 visitors a day to the home! wow!]

The pressures were not so great on the boys, because they were away at school for much of the time, but the girls felt it. They both transferred to Oxford High School for Girls, somewhat similar to the school they had left in Nottingham, but more academic and with fewer 'fun' things like cooking and sport. We were fortunate to discover a friend who had grazing rights on Port Meadow, a 400-acre field adjoining the city. This enabled us to acquire a horse each for the girls, and it was one of the best investments we ever made. They cared for their horses every day after school and went in for various Pony Club events, revelling in the rosettes they won. This certainly kept them from other, less healthy pursuits during 'the slippery days of youth'.

At that period both girls were rather disenchanted with God. Why had he taken them away from their friends in Nottingham? In due course they returned to their committed allegiance to Christ, which persists today. The horses perhaps played a big part in this, because we never insisted that the girls should come with us to church, and they were often off on the horses on a Sunday. Returning from the service one day, we found that Jenny's horse had climbed up the steps to the house, had entered, and was surveying itself in the hall mirror! I think we were wise not to insist on churchgoing when their hearts were not in it. The greatest help spiritually came through a good youth group and one or two caring members of the congregation who took them under their wing and listened understandingly to their often justified complaints against their parents. I think it is important, especially for families in full-time Christian ministry, to have a safe refuge where the children can go and complain at their lot if need be, and find love and sympathy. I know how grateful we were for it. The children were too.

Marriage difficulties

The years in Oxford were intensely busy and I know that we – and particularly I – did not give enough quality time to the children. I would take one or other of them away with me on a solo jaunt from time to time, and that was special, but it was not often enough. One of the biggest problems a church minister faces is the tension between the family he or she loves and the job, which is also a love affair of sorts. Some resolve this by selling the parish ministry short. There are some lazy clergy around, and you can certainly be lazy if you are so disposed, because there is little accountability on your use of time. Probably more of us err on the other side, and give too much priority to the parish and not enough to the family.

This was a lesson that was forcibly and painfully brought home to us around the middle of our time in Oxford.

Rosemary and I came to see that we were drifting away from one another. I was totally engrossed in the work, and she had for years taken the brunt of caring for the family and a large number of guests. It is not easy to remain spiritually on top of the world when you are the mother of four children with only six years between them. Rosemary's inner spirituality had been dwindling, and I had failed to recognize and minister to this. When the charismatic movement affected me, it led to the recognition of gifts I previously knew nothing about, such as the gift of tongues and the ministry of deliverance. Rosemary remained untouched by all this. When I had meningitis in South Africa, however, this was something of a crisis and Rosemary was constrained to let down her barriers and allow both God and other people to minister to her.

That was when the Spirit revitalized her and gave her a fresh love for Jesus and a new openness to people. She was still very suspicious of charismatic gifts, but when she realized that the Lord was encouraging her to ask for some spiritual gift, she said something like, 'Lord, what is it to be? Please, not tongues or healing!' The two-word reply seemed crystal clear: 'Wise counsel.' That was the start of what developed into a very effective pastoral ministry, helping people with deep personal problems.

Later, when I was away on a mission and she was feeling dismal and dispirited one day, she ventured to ask God for the gift of tongues. Her prayer was answered. Tongues flowed copiously – and enhanced both her prayer life and her ministry. Not long afterwards, she went to a conference on counselling where the leader declared that she was a 'natural'. She then went on a rather less helpful counselling course run by the Westminster Foundation, but it was in actual practice that her gift developed and matured. She often deliberately made herself vulnerable when speaking in public, and this attracted needy people to her as a light attracts moths. She became a very shrewd and patient listener, and would then encourage the person with her to wait on God and sense his direction.

Often people would get some mental picture, usually of Christ, which became intensely significant to them. They went away profoundly helped. She would maintain contact with such people for ages, long after I had forgotten about them.

Nonetheless, while I rejoiced in this new and valuable spiritual gift that she had received, it did not make any difference to the rift that was growing between us. I continued in a ministry that was being very fruitful in evangelism, teaching and leadership. She gave herself for many hours to one needy person after another. As one friend put it, 'Rosemary and Michael are walking in broadly the same direction, but on different sides of a river.' That was true, and painful.

Even more painful was an unexpected accompaniment to the spiritual spring-clean Rosemary had received. The Spirit was digging into hidden recesses, and latent anger emerged. Hurts from the past began to come to the surface, particularly the death of her father in an avalanche when she was only six weeks old. At times it made her frustrated, at times violent, and both the children and I were affected by it. Sometimes the inner unrest coupled with the counselling skills led her to unwise actions. After an incident when the rest of the staff were away on a mission, it was felt right that Rosemary should withdraw from active work for a time and be ministered to by some of the team, particularly David Prior, who led St Aldate's in partnership with me.

Of course, I needed ministry as well as Rosemary. After all, it was my over-busyness and neglect which had been a substantial part of the trouble. We reached a very low point during that year, and Rosemary's thoughts sometimes turned towards divorce, sometimes even to suicide. She graphically described her affection towards me as being like one solitary little white flower crushed in on every side by brambles. The love was flickering and almost gone. We began working on it, however, and the leadership team in the church helped us. By the end of that year we were very much together again, and have been ever since. Nobody meeting us now would ever imagine that we had ever had any difficulties in our marriage.

We did have very serious difficulties, though, and I am writing this because I hope it may be of help to others. Most people have difficulties in their marriages, and hush them up until they erupt into divorce. It is naïve to imagine that Christian leaders are immune to such problems. David Watson, that most gifted evangelist and charismatic leader who died at the untimely age of 50 in 1984, seemed to be – and indeed was – the most outstanding, godly leader imaginable. He was a dear personal friend. Yet, as he revealed in his autobiography, he wrestled with serious problems in his marriage. He did not give up, however, and neither did we. I am so grateful for that now. We have a very good relationship, but it would all have been thrown away, and both our ministries would have been ruined, had we yielded to the impulse to break away from each other. Our marriage vows and our allegiance to God kept us together when nothing much else seemed to hold us. We worked at it, prayed about it, deliberately set about serving one another and allowed others to help us – and, because of these things, the marriage was restored and is the joy of our lives today.

Rosemary has now developed a remarkable gift in speaking, writing and giving wise counsel. Many come to her for advice because she is so approachable, so experienced and so willing to make herself vulnerable if it will help anyone else. As a speaker she goes direct to the heart, and people are profoundly helped. She has what is probably the unique distinction of being licensed by both Archbishops to preach anywhere in the UK. Her writing has also developed very significantly in recent years. In addition to her book *God's Catalyst*, which has helped many people to counsel others, she regularly writes notes for the Bible Reading Fellowship. These notes go out worldwide, and letters and messages of appreciation come to her from all over the world. Moreover, we normally undertake overseas speaking engagements together, and find that our styles of speaking are wonderfully complementary. We are so grateful to God for the way he has restored and gloriously used our marriage. Indeed, he has made our partnership in ministry something of an example to others, and many comment on it. We could never have imagined such a thing in the dark days when our love had burnt low and our paths were diverse.

Divorce is now such an easy option that people go for it much too easily. The romantic glow of first love is bound to wane and, unless there is deep commitment to each other, together with loyalty to God and to the marriage vows, the easiest thing to do is to cut the knot and start again. Nowadays nearly one in two marriages fail, while nearly as many people do not get married at all, and various alternative lifestyles are coming in. Yet God gave marriage as a special gift to humankind: an exclusive and permanent bond, transcending feelings and other attractions. A society which flouts God's ordinance of marriage as carelessly as ours does is headed for trouble. In history, whenever a civilization has become promiscuous in sexual matters and careless of marriage, that society has rotted from the inside and collapsed. It was so in the Roman Empire. I fear it may soon be so with our Western civilization.

The older I get, the more convinced I become of the rightness of the divine plan. 'One man, one woman, for keeps' is the ideal. I know it is very difficult, but it is the most fulfilling state, as even the sexologists Masters and Johnson have come to realize. I have just been revelling in John Stott's charming and superbly illustrated book *The Birds Our Teachers*, and he has this to say about the marriage of humans in contrast to the mating of birds. Even though some birds mate for life, 'human love is unique, because it is a reflection (pale perhaps, but authentic) of the eternal, selfless love of God himself, revealed on the cross, affirming the worth of its human objects, and leading to the "steadfast love" of his covenant pledge to his people ... The real mystery is not that birds can behave like humans, but that humans can behave like God.' Faithfulness in marriage provides many opportunities to do just that, despite the many failures.

Money and children

Financial problems, like divorce, tend to bedevil marriages. Rosemary and I started with very little behind us and a curate's salary of £400 a year. We know how fortunate we were compared with many, and I think we did a few things right. We invested what we had in the education of our children, and that has proved invaluable. We determined not to go into debt, but to live within our means. We have always had a joint account and trust each other in its use. We have also tried to save. Early on in our marriage, we looked at what capital we had and divided it into five. We wanted one part to go to each of our children and one part to God. We set up a little charitable trust with a fifth of our capital, and this has grown over the years. I have done a good deal of book-writing, and I have kept some of the proceeds, given some to the children, and the rest has gone to swell this little trust. It is a great joy to us. It means that when we see a need we can generally give something from the trust, in addition to using it in planned giving. There is no temptation to use it for ourselves, because it is not ours. I would recommend those who are able to do so to start a trust fund like that, or to join the Charities Aid Foundation. It is a source of joy and usefulness.

I hesitate to say anything about the bringing up of children. What parent can claim to have made a success of it? Yet it is the most important thing we ever do. Rosemary and I look back and see the many mistakes we made, but we also did some things well. I believe the children always knew that we loved them dearly. We trusted them and, for example, never gave them a time by which they must be in at night. Consequently they never betrayed our trust. In general we gave them a long rope as they grew up, and if we had our time over again we would do the same. We did a lot as a family, having meals together every day, for example. Many families today never eat a meal together. That cannot be good for family cohesion. Another small but important thing was that we made a point of apologizing to our children and begging their forgiveness when we had done something wrong. This seems very obvious, but I find that few parents do it. That is not only discourteous: it is unwise. Children are not fools. They know quite well when a grown-up has hurt or injured them. We cannot hide from our children. If they see us willing to apologize and admit our failings, that encourages them to do the same.

We think our children have turned out wonderfully well. Tim studied natural sciences at Cambridge, where he was president of the Christian Union. After a spell in industry, he became a long-term missionary in Pakistan. He has a marvellous wife, Rachel, and three strapping children who do not seem to suffer at all from being heirs to two cultures. In fact, it has enriched them. Sarah, our second child, went into veterinary medicine after Cambridge and has since married Marshall Riley, a distinguished Irish chest consultant. They live in Belfast with their three children. Jenny, our doctor daughter, is very athletic and won more than one blue at Cambridge. She has married Cal MacLennan, another doctor, who managed to combine being a member of the Olympic Rowing Squad with doing a DPhil. They have a little son, Robert. Our younger son Jonathan is a lawyer, and he has married Sally, another charming and gifted lawyer. As I write, they are revelling in the arrival of their first baby, William.

We are so blessed by this enlarged family. If we could have chosen partners for our children, we could not have done nearly as well as they have! All the adults are committed Christians, and we trust their increasing clutch of children will follow in their steps. The Psalms encourage us to look for blessing upon our children's children. We are beginning to experience that blessing as we draw near to (or in my case achieve) the age of threescore years and ten.

In this book I have deliberately set out to write my reflections on various matters, not to attempt an autobiography. I am aware, however, that this chapter in particular is distinctly autobiographical. The reason is simply this: I have read some autobiographies which tell you a lot about the activities of the person concerned, but little about their inner lives and relationships. I did not want to write in that way. It is only as you see a person in the context of their family that you begin to understand who they really are.

PART 2

FAITH AND WORK

CHAPTER 5

Parish Work

The last thing I ever intended to do was to be ordained. My father served as a country parson in the same tiny village for 33 years, in the wake of a predecessor who did no less than 57 years. For most of a century these two men led the little village flock. It was a (very ill-paid) ministry of word and sacrament, visiting, daily offices, meetings, and keeping the fabric of the church in reasonable shape. In this position a clergyman inevitably made mistakes, and had to live with them – unlike in a town, where alienated parishioners would simply go elsewhere. A country parson enjoyed little stimulus, little encouragement. The bell-ringers would summon people to church and then walk out. The village children might sing in the choir for a few years and then disappear. Church was not an exciting place. It certainly did not figure in my plans for the future, much as I admired the faithfulness of my parents.

As a student at Oxford I found myself involved in St Ebbe's Church, which did a lot for students. The preaching was good, the stance Evangelical. It was packed with people, many of them students of my own age. I could see the value of the minister in such a church, but I had no idea it might be for me. Later on, however, I found myself being drawn inexorably towards ordination. I wrote in an earlier chapter about the struggle I had with this, the guidance I received, and the subsequent confirmation of my decision.

Ordination training

After graduation, I spent two fascinating years in National Service, then started at Ridley Hall in Cambridge, a broadly Evangelical theological college with about 60 students – all male, of course, at that time. I am ashamed to say that I took it very casually. Having got a first-class degree at Oxford, it seemed right to do the postgraduate theological tripos at Cambridge, and this was my primary concern during the two years of ordination training. Thus I had two years' intensive study of the New Testament at Queens' College under the expert guidance of two of the most distinguished professors of the day, Professor Charlie Moule and Sir Henry Chadwick. My official college pastoral training was microscopic. I had no placement in a parish or industry. The one thing I vividly recall was a weekend with the Church Army in London, when an enterprising officer took us out to Hyde Park Corner and put us on a soapbox for a couple of minutes each. We learned a lot in those two minutes! I cannot speak for the others, but it launched me on a path of open-air preaching which has never left me.

Our 'pastoralia' lectures were usually dull and happened on a Saturday morning. I remember complaining about the fact in my final interview with the Principal before leaving. He looked at me with a smile. 'Oh, I am sorry about that ... but I didn't notice you there very often!' Not a knockout blow perhaps, but a definite victory on points for the Principal! My preparation for the ministry seemed primarily to consist of going to chapel (or not), theoretically twice a day.

There were some highlights, but they were unofficial. One was my continued work as an officer at the Iwerne Minster camps, which gave me marvellous experience in evangelism and pastoral care among the schoolboys who went there. The other was the open-air service we used to hold down by a busy waterside pub on a fine Sunday night in the summer. A good few of us young enthusiasts would go down there with a chair, which we set up about 60 yards away from the entrance to the pub. One of my friends would invariably start us off. He was hilariously funny, and got up on the chair and made a delightful fool of himself for five minutes or so. People would come running up to us from the pub, with their beer glasses in their hands, fascinated. We took it in turn to speak, briefly, pungently, to a plan, and often with visual aids. It was plain gospel proclamation with flair and enthusiasm, and the pub's patrons were enthralled. Often there would be a hundred or more people gathered around listening as the evening drew in, and at the end we would make a challenge to follow Christ. Sometimes we had the privilege of helping someone to faith there and then. Sometimes we would book them up to come and see us at Ridley during the following week. A little trickle of new Christians emerged from all this and we, of course, developed our skills in speaking and personal evangelism.

Such was my training for the ordained ministry of the Church of England. During this period Rosemary, by then my fiancée, was working in Cambridge. In December 1957, just three months after our wedding, I was ordained to a curacy at Holy Trinity, Eastbourne. Then I began to discover what parish life was about.

A curate's life

So, what was parish life about? Well, at the end of the 1950s there was still an understood role for the clergyman. He led services in church, taught in school, worked among young people, taught the faith in various ways, visited the sick, baptized, married and buried people. That is what it was all about: a maintenance ministry. Given the changes in society, the role was very much what it had been a hundred years previously.

79

All that was about to change abruptly with the social revolution which happened in the late 1960s and early '70s. No longer would people treat clergy with respect. No longer would they tacitly believe the Christian faith. No longer would they accept a biblically based moral position. No longer would going to church even enter their minds. A social revolution was brewing, and we were blissfully unaware of it.

Nonetheless, I learned lessons in that very happy first curacy which have stood me in excellent stead during and after the social revolution of the 1960s. The Vicar of Holy Trinity was a great big man, shy and warm, called Gordon Sheldon. He had four sons, and there had been no girl in the family line for over a century. He treated Rosemary and me like extra children of his own, and this gave us a marvellous start. We felt loved and wanted. I believe it is even more important for a young curate to go to a place where the incumbent loves him or her, than to go to a place that prides itself on being 'sound'. In all events, we were very happy in our top-floor flat, and threw ourselves enthusiastically into the work of the parish for the next three years. It was an awesome privilege to preach regularly in that vast church packed with people, and it taught me not only to prepare in general, but to word-prepare what I was going to say – and yet not to read it.

One of the first things the vicar asked me to do was to visit a lady in hospital who was suffering from disseminated sclerosis. She was a radiant Christian, and the impact of her life had an enormous effect on her ward. I am certain I did not do her any good, but she did me a tremendous amount, and that is doubtless why Gordon Sheldon sent me there.

Almost the next thing he asked me to do was to visit a road in the parish. In the goodness of God, at the very outset of this project I found a door being opened by a man who was obviously on night shift, and so was around in the afternoon. He asked me in, and we talked about spiritual things for an hour or more. I felt it was a wonderful encouragement to find such a person on my first visit.

Visiting has fallen into disuse these days, in favour of committee meetings and paperwork. This is a great pity. For one thing, it is really impressive if a representative from the church can be on the doorstep of a newcomer to the area with a welcome and a small gift almost before the removal van has left. That shows the church cares. For another, it shows the pastor what the people are like in their homes – who is in their family, what they are watching on television, what their preoccupations are. As a result, sermons can become much more relevant and applied. What is more, it diminishes the alienation between clergy and the ordinary non-churched people in the area. I learned before long how important it was both to visit personally and to equip a team for that sort of work, going to every home in the name of the church and the church's Lord. It is much harder these days, with access denied in many blocks of flats and maisonettes, but with ingenuity a way can generally be found. We need to incarnate the gospel, give people an attractive impression of what a Christian is. Visiting is an excellent way of doing just that.

I loved those three years under Gordon Sheldon. It was a joy to visit the sick, prepare people for confirmation, lead a large young people's fellowship, and start Pathfinders from scratch. Rosemary and I did a lot of entertaining, and discovered that there was a women's College of Physical Education nearby. We had a number of winter supper and games evenings for the young women from the college, with a talk about Christ at the end. Several of them became committed Christians. Rosemary led one of them to the Lord one night and she has spent her subsequent life as a missionary among the blind in Afghanistan. Another became a Christian headmistress, and there were a good many more.

Another initiative I was happy to take was to teach in the local comprehensive school, and draw boys and girls from there for what soon became a flourishing Pathfinder group. In the initial stages we would not have been able to persuade them to go to one of the regular Pathfinder camps. Instead we ran a short camp of our own. They all came, and it was a noisy success. A time away like that not only leads to a few conversions but has a tremendous bonding effect on the group – as well as winning the respect of the parents.

The town had a good many very traditional Christian meetings and we backed these up, but we were always seeking to reach out to those with no Christian commitment. One of the best things that happened emerged because Gordon, seeing me to be a good enough cricketer to play for the town, gave me permission to do just that for an afternoon a week without treating it as my day off. It was very generous of him, and proved to be a marvellous investment. Before long, a cricketing dentist friend, our doctor, a hotelier and myself got together with our wives to put on large supper parties during the winter, to which we invited friends who did not share our Christian faith. We each had a wide circle of friends, not least among the town cricketers, and they were happy to come because they liked and trusted us. We had interesting Christian lay people down to speak on each occasion, and in due course a number of our friends began to follow Christ and are still doing so today. None of this would have happened had my vicar not had the vision and the grace to give me my head.

He encouraged other initiatives, too. There used to be a very old-fashioned open-air service held on the beach after church on Sunday nights in the summer. Hymn sheets were given out by ladies in hats, an ancient harmonium was set up, and prayer was offered by an old gentleman with white hair who removed his bowler hat to do so. We were allowed to update all this. It had been a bold initiative in its day, but had become stale. We did away with the hymn sheets and harmonium, and had prayer in the church before we went out, rather than on the beach. We had a singing group and used testimony freely. We started up humorous exchanges with the people who came past, and prepared gripping visual aids which were progressively unveiled, so that people arriving late could get the gist of what had already happened and were intrigued enough to stay and see what was still covered up. In the late summer we managed to get permission to turn off a section of the lighting on the seafront, and then projected slides onto the lifeboat house. The gap in the lighting successfully attracted the curious. All of this proved a big draw and led to substantial crowds and a trickle of conversions. It was so unusual for an Anglican church to do anything of the kind that we were frequently mistaken for Pentecostals (with whom we enjoyed excellent relations). We duly erected a poster informing passers-by that this was the friendly old Church of England at work!

We also formed an open youth club, with skinheads and bikers coming in for a variety of activities including music, carpentry and boxing. Halfway through the evening we would have a 10-minute spot when we spoke simply and briefly about Jesus. I taught boxing, and I recall sparring with one lad who enthusiastically split my lip, to hoots of approval from his friends. It was clear to me that I would lose the respect of this mob if I did not reciprocate, so I lovingly split his lip in return, and we became the best of friends. The club has not continued, but it worked well for a time and taught me a lot.

Those were some of the areas of ministry I discovered under the guidance of a loving vicar who rejoiced in any small successes that came my way far more than he did in his own. He may not have been as gifted or well known as his predecessor, but he taught me two lessons I never forgot: that good relations lie at the heart of effective ministry, and that one of the main functions in Christian leadership is to equip others for service, not to try to do it all oneself.

After three years in Eastbourne I went to teach in the London College of Divinity, and thus began what turned into a major part of my life. I eventually taught in four different theological institutions, but I will say more about this in the next chapter. It was not an easy decision. I loved parish work, but I was aware that God had entrusted me with a couple of first-class degrees, and I would have to account to him for the way I used them. If I stayed in parochial work, I would probably not make the best use of my education. If I went into university teaching (as I very nearly did), that would limit my pastoral and evangelistic work. I decided that a theological college might be the best of both worlds. I could use my brains to teach the students to the very best of my ability, and I could also help to equip them pastorally and evangelistically for the work of the ministry. With these considerations in mind, Rosemary and I left for the London College of Divinity in the autumn of 1960, with profound gratitude for three very happy years in our curacy.

Some principles for parish ministry

Fifteen years passed before I was in parish ministry again, this time charged with the responsibility of leading St Aldate's, Oxford. It was ironic that, although I had by then trained some hundreds of ordinands for the ministry, I had never been in charge of a parish myself. Now the learning curve became very sharp! St Aldate's was a big church with a large congregation and a hectic round of activity all week long. I did not know what I was doing to begin with, and was graciously guided through the first six months by the two wonderful curates I had inherited – one of whom, Colin Bennetts, has since become Bishop of Coventry.

Rosemary and I, with our four children, spent 12 glorious, demanding and tumultuous years at St Aldate's, and we look back upon them with joy and gratitude. We made endless mistakes, which a generous congregation habitually forgave. The work was complex and much of what we did would not be applicable elsewhere. We were in an inner-city parish of sorts, where few people actually lived. Indeed, we regularly had more people in church on a Sunday than lived in the whole of that small parish composed of shops, car parks and independently-run colleges. We also ran a coffee house, a bookshop, a hostel for overseas students and a decrepit youth centre, of which, to my sorrow, we never managed to make best use.

There were two 'daughter' churches at the time, and a considerable staff. To my shame, at the outset I did very little about collegiality, as I strove to find my feet. However, believing as I did that one of the main functions of ordained ministers in a church is 'to build up the saints for service' (Ephesians 4:12), I soon began to give that priority. That sense of partnership in leadership would never have gained full momentum without the superb colleagues who came to join us, such as Bruce Gillingham and David Prior. Gradually they turned the weekly staff meeting into a place of worship, mutual support and caring, and the agenda seemed to follow on so much more easily from the emphasis on warm, loving relations.

One of David Prior's dicta was that 'good decisions come out of good relationships' and this was something that I, with my goal-oriented mind, was slow to grasp. Yet how right he was. We set out to build the whole church on this principle of relationships. There were Home Fellowship Groups with leaders who had received some specific training. There was a music group that spent much of Friday evening having a meal and offering mutual encouragement and prayer before getting down to the singing practice – and it turned them from crows into canaries. The Beginners' Groups were all run by little teams of leaders who spent time at the end of the evening in mutual accountability and friendship. The same happened with the Parochial Church Council and its Standing Committee. We often had meals together or went away for a night to take broad and relaxed counsel for the church without the tyranny of an agenda. Everyone on the staff had one person to whom they were accountable and another person on whose shoulders they could go and cry, if need arose. I did not chair the Church Council – why should I? There were several lay leaders who had that gift, and I am a better advocate than judge. So others led the council and I was able to put forward my ideas to be accepted or, more often, knocked down by those who possessed a gift of wisdom I did not.

That was the over-riding principle I tried to bring to the parish: equipping the Christians in the congregation for the work of serving the Lord, rather than trying to do most of the ministry myself. It is all about giving away power so as to empower others. I believe that if this principle were more clearly seen and acted upon in our churches there would be far more vigorous church life. People thrive on being given some task and trusted to get on with it. Unfortunately, I see many parishes hamstrung because the vicars cannot and will not decentralize, but want to have the church as the place where they call all the shots.

A second important principle of parish ministry will also have become apparent in what I have just said. We went for a 'fellowship of leadership' in every aspect of parish life. As a result, nobody felt isolated. There was a little team to relate to in the leadership of the Beginners' Groups, among the Sunday school teachers, among the leaders of the Fellowship Groups and the student work. Monarchy is a bad principle for Christian leadership: it leads to the suppression of initiative. So is democracy: it leads to shared incompetence and ineffectiveness. What is needed is a leadership team accountable to God and the congregation; a team which will give a lead and enable each member of the church to achieve his or her full potential and use that in God's service. You need a fellowship of leadership to model that sort of thing and to help it come about.

Had this been a normal way of leadership in the Church of England, we might not be in the parlous position we are in now. Today, particularly in country districts, five, ten or more parishes are grouped together under one incumbent. The minister becomes a sort of medieval mass priest, running round on a Sunday giving Communion in all the different churches, but being quite unable to provide people with the teaching and pastoral care they need. How much better it would be to go the way which John Wesley pioneered with his converts in the eighteenth century. He trained them to become small local fellowships in the villages where they lived, under the lead of a layman, usually a godly farmer. In this way they were not dependent on the ministrations of the circulating minister, but built themselves up and provided a robust Christian presence in each village.

To be sure, under current Anglican regulations that would mean that the villages received Communion much less frequently, unless they went the Methodist route of lay administration or the Catholic route of the reserved sacrament. Nevertheless, had the Church of England travelled this route, it would have led to the solid growth of lively, if small, communities of faith throughout our country. It has not happened from conviction, but we may yet be driven to it by economics. God has a habit of working that way! Lay ministry has received enormous affirmation in recent years, but sadly theology has played a far smaller part in this reformation than shortage of finance.

Where clergy persist in trying to run everything themselves, the church inevitably declines. If members of the congregation are not given responsibility, they do not grow in maturity. Instead, many leave and many more are frustrated, even broken-hearted, because their vicar does not allow them to do any spiritual ministry – not even to lead a Bible study in their own homes. When you trust lay people, however, and give them a lead on the one hand and plenty of scope for initiative on the other, you get a congregation that really begins to function well. Unsuspected talents emerge and enthusiasm deepens. It is no good saying that this is all very well in an Oxford church, but it will not work in the East End. It will, and it does. I recall once being in a church in a desolate part of Manchester where the key leadership was given by an enormous woman publican, to great effect. The talent is there if the clergy will take pains to develop it. That requires three things: (1) competent training courses, (2) a willingness on the part of the minister to take a back seat and become the coach, not the striker in the team, and (3) a willingness on the part of the congregation for things to be less tidy and professional than if the vicar did them. It is, after all, only by trial and error that we grow.

Another principle emerges from this way of being church. If everyone in the congregation realizes they are limbs in the Body of Christ, with their own gifting and responsibility, the whole congregational body springs to life and people discover abilities they never knew they had. Moreover, members of the church come to realize what fulfilling callings the ordained ministry and missionary work are. Consequently, without even trying, a church like this fosters vocations in this country and abroad. Certainly our church in Oxford had a steady stream of ordinands and short-term missionaries going out. We were much weaker on the long-term missionaries, but in due course a number emerged and are doing good jobs in different continents today.

Evangelism in the local church

Throughout my ministry I have tried to give some priority to evangelism, and will be writing about that in a subsequent chapter. At this point, however, it is worth remarking that the church which lives for itself will be sure to die by itself. Far too many of our churches, not least the Anglican ones, seem to have no idea that they were planted to be witnesses to Christ among people who do not yet know him. I do not mind how you do evangelism, so long as you do it. If the church is just a club that likes doing churchy things on a Sunday, then forget it. It has ceased to be what Jesus designed – his counterculture in a world that largely turns its back on God. Our churches have become committed to maintenance, not mission. The result is apparent. Our country has become one of the most godless in the world.

Evangelism is never easy, but the parish setting is by far the most natural location for it. If you have a church which is really concerned for the people in its geographical area, which engages in relationships and activities reaching beyond the church door, then several things happen. People begin to see that Christianity makes a difference to life. A fund of goodwill begins to build up towards the church. A fringe begins to grow, of people who will come to the occasional service, dinner or party put on by the church. That can lead, in due course, to their discovery of Jesus Christ for themselves.

Another advantage is that the local church can never hide. Pretence is impossible: it is seen for what it is. This is not the case with a mission or crusade, led by outsiders. Who knows if they are real? Who knows what they are like at home? Everyone knows what the local churchpeople are like. They are a city set on a hill that cannot be hidden. If they reflect some of Christ's light, it will have an impact, and will lead some people at least to become open to the message of Jesus. Moreover, if the minister is wise, he or she will give a lead in all this. The occasional offices of baptism, marriage preparation, confirmation and funeral visiting can be used to draw people towards Christ. The opportunities are plentiful and are so often missed. Yet they are there, for the minister who chooses to take them. If the minister does so, it will become infectious in the church. The congregation will also begin to look outwards, and see how they can influence their circle of friends for Christ.

At the time of writing, Rosemary and I are about to return to Canada for six months. We spent six years there some time ago, and a pupil I had the privilege of supervising for his Master's degree is now leading a great church. It began with about 30 people in a home, and within seven years grew to some 800. It seeks to build on relationships. People are drawn to the church and then to Christ through warm and welcoming relationships with their Christian friends. Ministers who make evangelism one of their main priorities will face many a challenge but rejoice in many a conversion. They will also see outreach gradually catch fire among their congregation, as it has done in this Canadian church.

Certainly we found that to be the case during our years at St Aldate's. I followed a gifted evangelist in the leadership of the church: he was the one who led people to Christ, in large numbers. By the time we left, however, although I had the gifts of an evangelist, the congregation were clear that evangelism was *their* responsibility too. Sometimes we would end an evangelistic address in church by asking people to stand up and talk to the other people in their pew about what Jesus meant to them. The Christians were thus given the opportunity of helping to an explicit faith the friends they had invited to the service. We had become not just a church with an evangelist as its minister, but a truly evangelistic church. It is not surprising that this had repercussions – in mission teams going out to minister in other parts of the country at weekends, and overseas as well.

Home groups

Another initiative which we found of enormous importance in parish work was the home group. This was a lay-led group of 12 or 15 members, and we tried to base it on the locality where people lived, so that it was in some ways a microcosm of the church. A group like this should meet weekly or fortnightly: if it meets less often, it tends to fall apart. The primary aim should not be Bible reading or prayer, although both will figure prominently. The aim is to express and deepen our *koinonia*, our joint partnership in Christ. There will, of course, be a programme, and there should be food and drink. Supremely, however, it should be the sort of supportive fellowship where someone can drop in one evening and say, 'I feel utterly fed up,' and find that the programme is immediately scrapped and the members attend to that individual's needs.

This utterly open 'being together in Christ' is such a refreshment after a tough day's work. It will lead to new depths of frankness and mutual commitment. It will enable people to discover gifts they did not know they had. They will even dare to try them out in the company of these known and trusted friends. It will probably develop from that point in one direction or another. The group as a whole could go and spend an evening decorating an old person's front room, or they could undertake some ministry within and for their church. Alternatively, they could go out on some pastoral or evangelistic visit to another church, or they could go on holiday together. The small communities of faith represented by these home groups have an immense power to build up their members and attract non-Christians to a quality of life which has its own hallmark of authenticity.

Of course, the leadership of these groups is vital. The leadership needs to be shared, or it can become too much for one person in full-time employment. There also needs to be an annual training course looking at topics such as the basics of group dynamics, leading a prayer time and an inductive Bible study, and offering some help on rudimentary pastoral care. These groups become the primary providers of pastoral care in the church. They can pass on particularly difficult issues to the staff, but provide much of the basic help and support through the life of the group.

Sometimes the number of groups in a church becomes so large that another layer of leadership needs to be put in place to care for the home group leaders. We found that a group of lay pastors, each of whom looked after the leaders of three home groups, became an invaluable resource. The senior staff spent a relaxed evening over a meal with these lay pastors once a month, so that they did not feel isolated and uncared for, but valued and supported. Some clergy have told me that they dare not have these home groups under lay leadership operating in their parish, in case it subverts their own position and makes them feel redundant! I tell them that they will never have worked harder in their lives than when they train and resource the leaders in a number of groups like this. They will be exercising the leadership and training role for which they were ordained.

As will be apparent from all this, the ministry of encouragement is vital at all levels in the church. Unfortunately, in many churches no thanks are given and no mutual encouragement is offered. These things are crucial for the happy working of the Body of Christ. We have few indications in the New Testament that Barnabas was a great preacher, but he was clearly a wonderful encourager. He would never have earned the nickname Barnabas (which means 'Encourager') otherwise – his real name was Joseph. It would be disastrous to have 50 preachers in a church, but marvellous to have 50 Barnabases!

Putting principles into practice

I do not want to close this chapter without alluding to the other main period of pastoral work in which Rosemary and I engaged. It was immediately after the 12 years at St Aldate's. I was appointed as a professor in Vancouver, and told the local Bishop that I would be happy to help in a parish church as well. We landed up in a very small Anglican church with a congregation of 50 or so, all in their sixties or above. We tried to assist the vicar by attempting to draw people into this very traditional service, and some of them came once – but not again. There was little on offer, nothing for children, youth or families. We tried a new tack.

Quite suddenly, the vicar left. I did not attempt to modify the traditional service, which would have alienated the existing elderly congregation. Instead, we started a completely different type of worship at nine o'clock in the morning. We aimed for the non-churchgoers, the people on the street. We wanted to make it accessible, so we did away with the set liturgy, prayer books and robes. We sang contemporary hymns and songs from an overhead projector, used personal testimonies and gave talks illustrated by cartoons drawn by one of the group. It began with a few people encouraging their friends and acquaintances to come along, and I preached my heart out for a few weeks before people broke for the summer.

A dozen or so professed faith and were nurtured in a small Bible study group until the autumn, when we started up in earnest and were joined by the remnant of a nondenominational church which had previously met in the building at a different time. The big question we wrestled with was this: would the principles we had hammered out for a large English church work for a tiny Canadian one?

The answer was an emphatic 'yes'. Clear preaching for conversion produced fruit. Small nurture groups built the newcomers up. Several home groups emerged under lay leadership. The services were participatory, led by a mixture of ordained and lay people. Every-member ministry flourished. The leadership team spent time together for fellowship, planning and setting up training. The principles we had found to be so valuable among many hundreds at Oxford were just as effective in starting literally from scratch and building up a small congregation in Vancouver. Before long, the new congregation was twice the size of the old. Then the taxing task began of trying to blend them together. Today that church has advanced in leaps and bounds. It is one of the leading Anglican churches in the city, and has relocated to a prime site which facilitates further advance.

Parish work is demanding and often frustrating, but it offers the rewards of great joy and fulfilment to those who throw themselves into it with love, prayer and vision.

CHAPTER 6

Theological Education

Humour, as Peter Berger has reminded us, is one of the 'marks of transcendence' in our world. It is one of the characteristics that sets human beings apart from animals, and I am persuaded that humour is part of the divine image in humankind. I think it is hilarious that the good Lord has put me in a position where I have spent most of my working life in theological institutions, although I frankly skived during my own theological education, and retain serious doubts as to whether these insitutions are the best way of training anyone for the ordained ministry.

Theological seminaries or colleges are a relatively new creation. The Church of God got along wonderfully well without them for nearly 1,900 years. Of course, theology was a major part of education in English and European universities, but pastoral work was learned when you became an apprentice to an experienced clergyman in a parish. There is a lot to be said for that. In the middle of the nineteenth century, however, these colleges began to appear. A fascinating brother and sister, Alfred and Keziah Peache, used their wealth most imaginatively to launch some of them. They asked themselves, very properly, whether the good Lord might have chosen other people for ordination who did not have the privilege of attending the ancient universities. Concluding that this was at least possible, they founded St John's College in Highbury, London (adjoining the Arsenal football ground), St John's College in Durham, and Emmanuel College in Saskatoon, Canada. At the end of my curacy in Eastbourne, I was offered a job by the first of these colleges. Somewhat reluctantly, I accepted, and thus began my calling as a staff member in no less than four theological colleges.

The London College of Divinity

St John's had endured several moves during its existence, and when I joined it was called the London College of Divinity and had landed up at Northwood, Middlesex, in a purpose-built property which is now owned by London Bible College. I was asked to teach the New Testament, which had been my speciality at Cambridge.

What a strange world it was. The college was semi-monastic. Women only came in once a year for the annual entertainment, apart from a formidable battle-axe of a lady who was the college secretary. Chapel twice a day was mandatory and adhered strictly to the book. Students were not permitted to go away at weekends, and even the married men had only two 36-hour passes a term. It was worse than the Army! Students wore gowns for lectures, chapel and whenever they wanted to speak with a member of staff. Indeed, it was a cause for rebuke if a student even came to pray with a staff member without his gown. Lecturers were addressed by their surnames, or as 'Sir'. I can recall even now the gasp of shocked surprise in the dining hall when the rugby captain announced a couple of tries that 'Michael' had scored. All meals were taken in hall, even for the married students and staff who lived locally. The staff collected in an anteroom and filed in to the top table once the student body had gathered. Everything was regulated by bells. I suppose I must have been 25 years younger than the other four members of staff. They were godly men, concentrating on their teaching, which was largely by lecture, and totally engrossed in what was a very constricted little world among 60 or so students heading for ordination. They were the last of an era.

The stance of the college was Evangelical and biblical. We taught both for our own college Diploma, which was a recognized ordination qualification, and for the London BD. The two most distinguished students I had the privilege of teaching were George Carey, later to be Archbishop of Canterbury, and Janani Luwum, later to be Archbishop of Uganda and martyr. Despite the restrictions, the atmosphere of the place was happy. There was a lot of sport. I found that playing cricket and rugby for the college teams made a natural avenue into pastoral relationships, and the great majority of the students went on to carry out very worthwhile, sacrificial ministries. I felt it was a good place for me, because I could make full use of both my academic and my pastoral gifts. I longed to send out men who were excited about ministry, well trained and confident in their God. I had turned down a university post before accepting the London College of Divinity, and I never regretted my choice.

There were lots of practical jokes. I recall George Carey and his friend John Battman (later an Archdeacon) managing to get a rocking chair up onto the roof of the main building, and sitting there to observe a soccer match on the field below. On another occasion Principal Hugh Jordan, reverting to his agrarian past, climbed up a ladder in the lofty chapel and wrung the necks of a bunch of roosting pigeons who had cheerfully distributed their droppings all over the chapel seats. The next day the students organized a hilarious funeral for the birds, which were solemnly introduced in a coffin at lunchtime.

The best of all these pranks took place during one of the occasional inspections to which all theological colleges are subject. The arrival of the inspectors usually brings with it a good deal of trepidation, and Hugh Jordan was very keen to have everything just so. Accordingly he set aside a couple of student rooms which would be meticulously tidy, highly polished and prepared to be shown to the inspectors. Little did he know that the students had their eye on a donkey, full of character, which grazed in the field adjoining the college. This animal was very skilled at knocking students off its back by moving at speed under a low branch. Somehow they got hold of the donkey and shut it in one of the rooms due to be on display. Imagine the Principal's face when he said, 'Here is a typical student's room,' and opened the door to usher the inspectors in!

The academic work was dominated by traditional examinations, and we used one week at the end of term for inviting experts in various fields to come and teach on some of the crying pastoral issues of the day. It was not enough, in my opinion, and, as this part of the curriculum was not examined, the motivation was not high. One of the best things at the college, however, was a strong missionary thrust which had continued from the early days back in Highbury. This part of the work was called Vigiles, was led by students or invited guests, and consisted of information and prayer for a particular work or part of the world. It took place twice a week from 6.30 to 7.10 a.m. before morning chapel. One of the results was a stream of men going overseas as missionaries. Two of those men have become bishops in South America, and another was a Dean in the Arctic. I sense that this concern for world mission, and willingness to serve it, is much less prominent in theological colleges today. We have grown more complacent and less sacrificial.

The practical work in those days was slight. There was some exposure to schools, hospitals and churches in the vicinity, but comfortable suburbia was not the most realistic place in which to train ordinands. Eventually, the College Council took the opportunity to relocate.

This was not done without some tension. The previous Principal had been Donald Coggan, and he was now

Archbishop of Canterbury. He was naturally less than thrilled to see the spanking new college, in which he had invested so much effort, being sold. But so it was. Our Council acquired a field in Bramcote, on the edge of Nottingham, which the central church authorities had purchased some years earlier for a hare-brained scheme. They had wanted to build a large graduate college for Professor Alan Richardson to preside over, but the project was ill-fated. How naïve to imagine that the principals of highly independent Anglican theological colleges would release their best students so that someone else could prepare them for ordination. The field remained empty. After much persistence by Hugh Jordan, we procured the field for the college. Then Hugh retired and I was made Principal. We had one more year in Northwood, 1969–70, during which the new college was built in Nottingham and the London Bible College made massive and noisy alterations to the Northwood property. It was an extraordinarily difficult year.

St John's, Nottingham

My tenure as Principal began with the sudden death of an overseas student in his room from an unsuspected heart weakness. This was followed by a student revolt when the architects' plans for the new college were revealed. The students rightly regarded them as impossible. This was embarrassing, since the architects had already gained outline planning permission. They said nothing could be done, especially if the college was going to be built on time. The students said it was 'going to be like Belsen'.

It so happened that at that juncture I was called to lead a university mission in Edinburgh. During the course of that, two very capable architectural students were brought to Christ. I told them my problem, and they immediately replanned the college building to much better effect within the same 'envelope', so that we would not have to reapply for planning permission. Our architects were naturally affronted when I gave them these alternative plans, but it triggered them into replanning the whole thing themselves, and the result is there today as St John's College, Nottingham.

Our problems were not over, however. The architects were determined to build in breeze blocks, which they said were quicker, but the builders in Nottingham had never used breeze blocks and it seemed to freeze or rain all that winter, so we were soon miles behind schedule. It was also clearly impossible to build a new theological college for the same price as you had sold the old one. Moreover, London Bible College had some very acute millionaires on their Board who were expert at driving a hard bargain, but we had no comparable artillery on our Council. As a result we got a poor deal, with all those newish buildings in Northwood going for a song – less than £80,000 on top of the land value.

It was not surprising, therefore, that the architects came to me one day and said that they had cancelled the projected married student accommodation, being unable to do it within our limited budget. We had insisted on the inclusion of 12 flats and two maisonettes for married students, realizing it would be crucial for the future. I told them to reinstate the plans. They asked where the money would come from. 'How much do you need and when do you need it?' I said. They needed £50,000 within two weeks. I instructed them to go and hire the necessary staff for detailed planning, and assured them that they would get their money. This drove me and my colleagues to urgent prayer. We had no idea where the money would come from, and it was almost impossible at that point to raise a bank loan.

Well, I learned a valuable lesson: God pays for what he orders. Through the good offices of the Bishop of Southwell, I was invited to lunch with the Area Manager for Lloyds Bank. This took place in a penthouse, and I had never been in one of those in my life, nor had I enjoyed an executive lunch! We discovered that we had both been to the same school and were both fly-fishermen. As we conversed, ate delectable food and were waited on hand and foot, it became plain to me that it was not the married accommodation project that was on trial, but me.

The matter of the buildings was not even mentioned until well into the coffee. Then the Area Manager looked at me and at the plans, and said, 'Right, I think we can help you. How much do you want?'

I speedily added £10,000 and said, 'We need £60,000.'

'No problem,' he said, 'provided the securities are OK.'

You should have seen the architects' faces when I told them.

There were many other traumas on the way to getting St John's off the ground. The major difficulty became very obvious to me as I made periodic trips up the motorway from Northwood. The job would not be finished in time for the start of the autumn term, despite repeated assurances to the contrary. We had to evacuate Northwood on a fixed date in June, find storage for a couple of months for all the furniture we were taking with us, and then move in for September 1970. Crises happened by phone and mail every day. We were certainly living very much by faith.

On one of my visits I noticed a large house near our Bramcote property, called 'The Grange'. It was advertised for renting at the very reasonable sum of £1,500 a year. I rang up the owners and offered, instead, to purchase it. Surprisingly, they agreed, and set a price of £20,000. I had no money, of course, but assigned a down payment of £3,000 from the funds I had acquired from the bank. The rest was due to be paid at the end of 12 months. That seemed to be acceptable to the owners, and it was a godsend for us. We would have been in very deep trouble had we not purchased this property. It was the only fully habitable building belonging to the college when the autumn term was due to start. We did a temporary job of creating within it three flats for married students, and used the large downstairs room for a dining hall and the adjoining greenhouse for a kitchen.

Meanwhile, five different building firms were working on the college, and none of them finished on time. We had only one unfinished lecture room at the start, and that was lit by a single naked bulb. This was a bit embarrassing when proud parents came to look over the institution to which they were about to entrust their daughters and sons. Nonetheless, it bred a splendid attitude among the students. At the end of the first term the college entertainment centred round the idea of mud, so wet had the weather been. Happily, the arrival of the Prince of Wales to open the college a little later in February galvanized the builders into action, and the actual completion of the work was done in record time, as instant turf and trees appeared overnight.

We were not only building a new college, but were attempting at the same time to make many innovations in terms of theological education. My colleague Colin Buchanan (now a bishop) had a sabbatical during the summer term of 1970, and generously spent much of it building relationships with Nottingham University's Department of Theology and the local social services and churches, so that there was a whole network of good experience available for students once we came into residence. We even bought a house down in a tough area of town and put half a dozen students there, in order to bring something of the fragrance of Christ into the vicinity, to give practical training to the students, and to get away from the old idea of an enclosed monastic community.

We encouraged women students too, and the first of them is now a university lecturer at Oxford. We designed a new vocational degree, the Bachelor of Theology, taught by us and moderated by the university. We also arranged for a two-year BA for graduates, a one-year Master in Theology degree for theological graduates and a new Diploma in Pastoral Studies to be part of the curriculum. We were, I think, the first college to appoint a full-time Director of Pastoral Training. We pioneered the practice of having lay people in to study theology with us, and took ordinands from America and Africa. In all these ways we broke fresh ground, and most of these innovations have subsequently become normal in other theological colleges.

We were certainly making waves, but we had to fight some battles, too. The Nottingham University professor with whom I had negotiated the new Bachelor of Theology degree suddenly went off to be a bishop in Ireland and omitted to share the project with the colleagues he left behind. It all had to be done again from scratch, with a justifiably suspicious university staff and a new professor. The Department of Theology told us that without them we would have no degrees. We told them that without the pulling power we were rapidly developing they would have no graduate students worth talking about. Laughter and agreement followed.

It was not an easy ride within the Church, either. Central Church authorities had been very reluctant to let an Evangelical college buy their precious but unused field in Bramcote in the first place. Eventually they gave in. Then the ordination authorities told me I could not have officially selected women students. I told them I would have women anyway and we would see about their ordination later. That, however, was regularized before long.

Thankfully, the married students' quarters were finished. Married students without children lived on site, while families lived out in a number of small houses we bought or rented. The purchases were only possible because of the very low cost of housing in the area at that time, just before prices soared. The college was different in other ways, too. Gowns and formality disappeared. The new chapel was a multi-purpose room. We incorporated a television studio so that students could see what they looked like when communicating, and a number of programmes were devised there for external use. It was an intoxicating period of trust in God, risk, experimentation, mistakes, and large numbers of students. Ours was seen to be the most imaginative college at the time, and ordinands queued up to come.

We had a wonderful staff team. Among them Colin Buchanan was a key figure on the Liturgical Commission; Julian Charley was an outstanding teacher and very significant on the Anglican Roman Catholic International Commission; Stephen and Pat Travis were both magnificent teachers, he in New Testament and television training, she in schools work. Then there was Dr David Cook, who became a significant figure in bioethics and a regular broadcaster on *The Moral Maze*. John Goldingay, an Old Testament teacher, later became Principal and then a professor at Fuller Theological Seminary in the USA. Gordon Jones was our ebullient Director of Pastoral Training, and the staff also included historian and librarian Noel Pollard from Australia, Charles Napier, a fascinating, polymath ex-Roman Catholic, and Anne Long, a highly innovative and inspiring teacher like all the rest. In addition to being the college Principal, I was on the Doctrine Commission and also acted as a Consultant at the 1968 Lambeth Conference. We were all trying to make some impact in the Church at large and did not confine our attention to the college, although naturally that remained our main focus.

We devised summer placements for students and that, I believe, was another innovation among theological colleges. In addition, all the final-year students were put into small groups and taken out preaching in the vicinity on a Sunday night. A sermon would be prepared carefully, in consultation with a staff member, and then we would go out as a group and one student would preach. Afterwards we all tumbled back for supper in a staff home, where we went through the sermon with critical evaluation. The students were pretty gracious with their comments on the whole, knowing that their turn to be dissected would soon come. This way of training preachers is far more realistic than having students preach to each other in an enclosed college situation.

I was also determined to have tennis courts and a sports field. The former were achieved without too much difficulty, but the latter looked a mess of stones after the graders had been over it. To put this right, we lined up the whole college across the field after lunch one day, armed with buckets, and we cleared the field of stones. It was then sown with grass seed and soon became a passable, if ill-drained, sports field.

We made many other innovations, not least in worship, with the use of modern songs, occasional drama, dance and testimony. Children were catered for, too. We also split students up into fellowship groups, and the appropriate tutor was responsible for their pastoral care and for writing up their final report to the bishop – a task which had hitherto been done by the Principal alone, who did not know the students nearly as well. Instead of doing Morning and Evening Prayer by the book, we varied it considerably. We met together for Morning Prayer once a week, but otherwise worshipped in the small groups. One morning would be a Bible study, one a missionary theme, one a prayer time and one an informal Communion. This seemed to me then, and still does, a much more imaginative and realistic way of worship than the studied repetition of Morning Prayer from the book. That may be helpful to some, but frankly becomes boring for many after a while.

Looking back over those years, particularly my six fast-moving years as Principal, there were obvious weaknesses, and I have alluded to some of these. There were many good things, too. The quality and partnership of the staff team at Nottingham were important, so was the willingness to experiment and take risks, trusting God for big things, including large sums of money, reviewing our teaching to match the changing needs in society, breaking the monastic model and the liturgical boredom, opening up to the charismatic movement, contributing to the Church at large while not losing our Evangelical stance, and learning to relate to a university department. All this and more was invaluable. It was a time of innovation and fresh thinking, and it is a joy to me many years later to see how well those foundations have been developed under my successors.

Regent College, Vancouver

When I became Rector of St Aldate's in 1975, I maintained some theological input there by running a weekly theological seminar, mainly in New Testament studies, to help orthodox Oxford undergraduates who wanted to remain orthodox while reading theology at the university. It was quite an influential gathering, run jointly with Bishop Stephen Neill and the Rev. John Wenham and involving students of the outstanding quality of Dr Martin Davie, who later became a tutor at Oakhill Theological College and then a theological consultant to the House of Bishops. Needless to say, our rogue elephant of a seminar was not always appreciated by the Faculty of Theology!

I did not, however, major on theological teaching again until 12 years later, in 1987, when Rosemary and I made a major move and I accepted a full professorship at Regent College, Vancouver, under the vibrant leadership of Dr Carl Armerding. Loosely affiliated to the University of British Columbia, Regent was broadly self-governing and had been set up some 25 years earlier to provide tertiary education in theology for graduates. It was a visionary institution. Brought into being by Brethren scholars and financial supporters, it soon broadened out into a totally international and interdenominational college in terms of both faculty and students. Drawing as it did on distinguished Evangelical teachers from various countries, it established an enviable international reputation. There was nothing like it on the Pacific Rim. People from Europe and Africa and especially Southeast Asia thronged its lecture courses. Some people gave up their employment and sold their houses to come to a place where there was no college accommodation for staff or students, and the fees were steep.

Regent had enormous strengths. For one thing, it was founded on faith. Faith among the handful of sponsors who put up the initial finance. Faith in James Houston, who left the security of an Oxford fellowship to become Regent's first

Principal. Faith in young men like Carl Armerding and Ward Gasque, who sacrificed their academic respectability to belong to a tiny institution which began with six students, two of whom were killed in a car crash before the first term began. Faith to persevere in seeking to gain recognition from the University of British Columbia, when initially they were comprehensively rebuffed and derided. Faith to operate for nearly 20 years from two small fraternity houses adjoining the campus and with no proper building to call their own, before the present attractive building was developed. Yes, it was founded on faith, and that faith has remained.

I well recall going to lecture at the Regent summer school when they had only been in operation for two or three years. I was directed towards the Vancouver School of Theology, a massive granite building obviously designed to last until Armageddon. Much of the main accommodation upstairs appeared to be unused. They were in deep trouble with numbers: despite having some eminent lecturers, they simply could not draw people with the liberal version of Christianity they were promulgating. At the entrance to the basement I spotted a cardboard notice announcing 'Regent College'. I was amazed by what I saw when I went in. It was seething with people, all passionately keen to learn about authentic New Testament Christianity. The lecture sessions were dynamic, the social life full of fun and interaction, and at night many students were to be found praying together in the community room of Carey Hall, an adjacent Baptist seminary associated with Regent, which provided accommodation for some of the summer school residents. Occasionally I found some of them engaged in open-air witness on the beach. These students were not a bunch of young undergraduates. They were mature people from all walks of life who had come on the summer school to deepen their understanding of their faith. That faith element in Regent College appealed to me strongly. The place was still young enough not to have grown institutionally complacent.

Another great strength was provided by the two Principals I came to know well. The first, Dr James Houston, a geography don from Oxford, had become a very competent theologian over the years, particularly in the area of spirituality. He knew the literature of the subject, wrote on it, lectured constantly, and was a marvellous spiritual mentor to countless students. He has remained at the college ever since, but was succeeded as Principal by Dr Carl Armerding, an excellent Old Testament scholar, a brilliant lecturer, and a real leader who was prepared to take risks and was expert in coaching the best out of his colleagues.

It was Carl Armerding who, over a period of two years, coaxed Rosemary and me to go to Regent at the end of our time at St Aldate's. We were also courted by Fuller Seminary, a remarkable tripartite institution with its own schools of theology, mission and psychology. This, however, seemed such a vast institution that we felt we would be unable to influence it in any significant way, and preferred to go to the smaller and more flexible Regent College, where we stayed nearly six years. We never regretted our decision, for Regent had a warmth and freshness about it reminiscent of an extended family. As the place grew, inevitably that family feeling diminished and structures began to predominate. This was probably unavoidable as the institution expanded. It became more pronounced when Dr Walt Wright, an administrator from Fuller, became Principal at the end of the 1980s. Somewhat regrettably, the adolescence of Regent gave way to adulthood.

Another attraction at Regent was the sense of collegiality among the faculty. Brits such as James Packer, Mike Griffiths and James Houston, Americans such as Gordon Fee, Ward Gasque and Carl Armerding, Chinese such as Edwin Hui, Swiss such as Klaus Bockmuehl and Canadian scholars such as Paul Stevens and Don Lewis made a marvellous set of colleagues. We enjoyed joint teaching, which I had not experienced in England, and we enjoyed each other's company. One of the things Rosemary and I valued greatly was a small group of faculty colleagues and their wives. We all had extensive ministries beyond Regent, and met fortnightly on a Sunday night for dessert, fellowship, mutual encouragement and prayer.

The student body was an enormous magnet, too. They came quite literally from all over the world, and many of them had made tremendous sacrifices to be there. Some of them, although graduates, had a poor educational background, and I was profoundly impressed by their determination to learn, at whatever cost to themselves. Others were highly skilled professionals who wanted to develop their spiritual side so that it was comparable with their professional excellence. Of course, this could degenerate into excessive addiction to book learning and a preoccupation with grades, but on the whole it showed a greater determination to get the best out of their education than I had ever experienced in England.

The greatest of all strengths at Regent was its lay theology. While in other parts of the world a few clergy were writing books on lay ministry, here at Regent it was actually happening. Most of the faculty were not ordained. Most of the students were not seeking ordination. Regent was a genuine and successful attempt to equip nonprofessional Christians with biblical and theological knowledge which they could take out into their everyday lives. For all its talk of every-member ministry, there is an undeniable elitism in the theological training on offer in England. It is offered by clergy for those who are going to be clergy, and any crumbs that fall to the laity are peripheral, if not accidental. At Regent there was a disciplined academic attempt to come to terms with the pressures of marriage, the marketplace, conflict resolution, ethics, interdisciplinary subjects and, above all, the understanding and application of the Bible. Teaching was given in Chinese as well as English, and in addition to the prescribed options offered by the faculty, students could make an agreement with a lecturer to study a subject of their own choice, if ratified by the Senate. Standards were checked by the body which oversaw all North American seminaries, and by the links with the university. I know of no other institution in the world which embodies in practice as well as in theory Regent's preoccupation with lay ministry, equipping God's people for their unpaid Christian ministry in society.

Nevertheless, it seemed to me that there were serious disadvantages to the North American educational system under which Regent operated. There was no residential accommodation for the students. They had to find a garret or a basement somewhere where they could eke out a frugal existence, often working in cafés and so on at night to finance their course and their family. That was a severe blow, for residential training has a great advantage in that it makes you live cheek by jowl with other people, encourages interaction and knocks off the rough edges.

There was also little of the one-to-one teaching which is prominent in leading British universities. It is ideal, but very expensive in terms of money and the instructor's time, so naturally it could not happen. There was not a lot in the way of seminars: too much depended on lectures and final papers. There was too little opportunity to tease out an issue, apart from asking questions at the end of a lecture. Most professors (as the teachers in North American universities are called) relied much too heavily on lecturing rather than on more modern and participatory educational methods. The value of continued lifelong learning, very dear to Canadians, has to be weighed against the fragmentary nature of a degree which could be stretched out over several years, as candidates knocked off one course after another rather than facing a single final examination as an overview of the whole. I found that the system did not encourage independent thought as much as the British one does. Students tended to serve back to you what they thought you would like, and found it hard to believe that a professor could grade them highly if they disagreed with him strongly and gave good reasons for their opinion.

There were three main weaknesses at Regent, it seemed to me. The first was a question of leadership. As the structures became more complicated, the running of the college was dominated by a series of committees. This meant that there was little scope for individual leadership. Matters were decided at meetings to which the protagonists of some projected reform were not invited. By the time we left in 1992, the Principal – or President, as he renamed the office – was not someone who gave a personal lead in the college, but a figure who operated behind the scenes, enabling the different constituent committees and governing body to function properly. That is certainly one way of doing it, but it seems a long way away from the biblical insights on leadership. I do not think Moses would have borne such a system patiently!

The second major weakness was the insularity of the college programmes. A student could spend two or three years at Regent without doing anything that related his or her expanding knowledge to the real world. The head grew, but the feet and arms shrank. Applied subjects were indeed present on the programme, but none of them was mandatory and they were still primarily academic in nature. This large collection of enthusiastic Christians was perched on the edge of a great secular university, yet had almost no impact on the place, apart from whatever initiatives individual students chose to take. That, to my mind, is defective theological education. Knowledge of God should lead to action for God.

The third great snag concerned Regent's emphasis on lay ministry. Each year students reached graduation with the sickening realization that they had no job to go to. They had a Diploma or a Master's degree, but the value of this was not clear either to a potential employer or to their local church, which tended to continue in the normal minister-dominated pattern. There was a large gap between the theory of every-member ministry and the practical lack of opportunity in most churches to put that theory into practice. This often gave rise to a double sense of frustration: the frustration of finding that one's theological insights and achievements were not valued in the local church, and the frustration of having spent all that money and still having no job to go to at the end. That was not a problem for some of the students, who saw their time at Regent as a character-enriching career break, but it certainly was for a good many.

Perhaps as a result, increasing numbers looked towards ordination in one of the Canadian denominations as the next step in their lives. The Master of Divinity degree, the recognized ordination qualification among most of the denominations in North America, became increasingly popular. This was a far cry from the idea of lay ministry for which Regent was founded! I was content with it, however, because I believe in the ordained ministry as well as the lay. My only sorrow was that I was not training members of my own denomination for ordination. The liberal establishment in the Canadian Anglican Church was allergic to the vigorous Evangelicals produced at Regent, and did not recognize the college as a proper place to train its clergy. This was sad for a variety of reasons. Regent regularly had far more Anglican students than the liberal Vancouver School of Theology next door, which was approved for training Anglicans. A good case could therefore be made for the recognition of Regent. Indeed, one year the Diocesan Synod in Vancouver voted to recognize it for training Anglican ordinands, but the bishops reversed the decision. This was short-sighted, because many good men and women with a passionate New Testament faith emerged from Regent, and the Anglican Church in Canada was in sore need of such people. Personally, too, I felt some deprivation at not being able to help train the future leaders in my own denomination.

We did, therefore, find real weaknesses at Regent. Yet, for all that, there was a freshness and a commitment about theological education in Canada which I found most invigorating. I would not have missed it for anything, and we would probably have been there today had not the Archbishop of Canterbury recalled me to England.

There were strengths and weaknesses, yes, and there was also a challenge. Canada is one of the most pluralist nations in the world. It prides itself on the fact. Postmodernity is everywhere. Relativism abounds. Nobody is allowed to say that anything is right or wrong: it is only the opinion of the speaker, and all opinions are deemed to be equally valid – except orthodox Christian claims. This attitude has deeply infected theology, especially in the older mainline denominations. The Anglican Church is in massive, perhaps terminal, decline. It is withering on the vine because of its failure to stand for anything and its passion for political correctness. The same is true of the United Church. A college like Regent which is large, academically able, imaginative and theologically conservative is therefore very unusual. It is a threat to the religion of consensus. It attracts a good deal of scorn and dislike from the liberals, but is academically strong enough to hold its head up anywhere, and its biblical basis is enormously appealing to orthodox Christians. There is no sniff of stifling fundamentalism about the place, but faculty and students alike regard the Bible as trustworthy and normative. Once you have a firm view of the reliability of the Scriptures, of course, you are free to exercise an enormous amount of flexibility in everything else, and that was very apparent at Regent.

Wycliffe Hall, Oxford

The last of my four sojourns in theological institutions came as a surprise. I returned to Britain in 1992 to work for the Archbishop of Canterbury in an initiative called Springboard, designed to promote evangelism in England. This proved to be a four-year contract, and at the end of that time I was of retiring age and would normally have settled down to grow vegetables. Then the Principal of Wycliffe, a Permanent Private Hall in the University of Oxford, invited my wife and myself to come and work there on a part-time basis, helping to train men and women ordinands for the ministry. So we relocated from Nottingham to Oxford, and are once again engaged in ministerial formation. We both do pastoral work among the students, and I do a fair amount of lecturing as well as heading up various mission outreach programmes for the college. It has struck me afresh what a privilege it is to have a hand in preparing the next generation of Christian leaders for a lifetime of ministry.

Wycliffe has a very distinguished theologian as Principal, Professor Alister McGrath, celebrated both as a clear and attractive lecturer and as a theological author with a prodigious output. I have an enormous admiration for him, as a theologian and a friend. He is thoroughly committed to the Scriptures and is orthodox through and through. He is also immensely sharp intellectually. He gained a DPhil in biology at much the same time as attaining his Oxford BD in theology. Indeed, in recognition of his theological eminence, the University of Oxford has accorded him a personal chair, an honour shared by none of the other theological college principals in Britain. Alister is a very disciplined man, and makes the most of every moment in the day. Yet he returns home in the evenings to be there for his family without taking work back with him, and he gets up from his desk immediately to welcome every interruption at his door. As a speaker he combines profound insight with clarity and attractiveness of presentation. He does this in simple, nontechnical language, and it is only in subsequent questioning and discussion that the learned footnotes come out. Such clarity and accessibility are rare among theologians, as is his determination to display his academic building blocks only when called upon to do so. Finally, as a writer Alister does what only great theologians can do: he writes the most massive tomes on Luther, science and religion and so forth, but he also writes simple, illustrated books for people who are feeling their way towards faith or wrestling with initial doubts. In all these ways he embodies what a theologian should be, but frequently is not. It is a great joy for Rosemary and myself to assist a little at his college.

Moreover, at Wycliffe I am struck by the calibre of the men and women who give up attractive and profitable careers in order to offer themselves for ordained ministry in the Anglican Church. I like the way students are expected to do a lot on their own and are not hamstrung by lectures morning, noon and night. I like the Integrated Studies Weeks, which allow all relevant aspects of a subject that will figure large in their ministry to be explored by means of team teaching and praxis. I love the emphasis on apologetics and evangelism. In many colleges, these two subjects are notable for their absence and students are trained as if they are merely to maintain an existing order of affairs. Yet the existing order has changed: Christendom is no more. If they cannot win non-churchgoers to the Christian faith, they are going to have a very small and very frustrated ministry. Evangelism is essential in ordination training, and it is still hardly touched on in many British theological colleges. This is frankly disastrous. So is the absence of competent grappling with apologetics. If young clergy cannot give a good reason for the hope that inspires them, nobody is going to listen. Christianity certainly transcends anything that our human reason could have dreamed up, but it is eminently reasonable and clergy need to be able to contend intelligently for the faith. The essence of the Christian gospel is that it must be shared with others who are at present blind to its appeal. Any theology which does not do that is doomed to irrelevance.

Ongoing concerns

Having been involved in four different theological institutions during the last 40 years, in addition to the one where I was trained, I have noticed many improvements. No longer is there that divide between tutors and students. No longer is it a one-sex society. No longer is the curriculum so narrowly ecclesiastical. No longer are husbands segregated from their wives. No longer are students dominated by university terms:

long practical placements have come in during the summers. All that and more is sheer gain, but serious questions remain.

One of these is whether book learning is the most appropriate training for a people-based ministry. Ministers' fruitfulness is not going to be determined by how well they know the apostolic fathers, but on how well they relate to the actual fathers in the community they serve. The major part of theological training even today is done by lectures, books and examinations. Arguably, that is not the best way to produce Christian leaders. The old-fashioned method of apprenticeship has more to commend it as the main way of training, and it could be supplemented by short sandwich courses at a theological college.

I remember writing a paper to this effect many years ago when I had just been ordained. Today, I am intrigued to note that about half the ordinands in the Church of England are trained in this way, in nonresidential courses with intensive weekends of input. This revolution has not come about because those in authority have recognized the superior relevance of such training, but because it is so much cheaper to have a student continue in his or her normal job, residence and church work, and study in the evenings, supplemented by occasional residential weekends. There is real value in such training. At least, there would be if the best trainers in the Church were leading them. Often, however, these courses are not well taught and the residential occasions are not dominated by the great central themes of the gospel, but by ephemeral, culturally correct issues of the day.

A second weakness of theological education, in residential colleges at least, is the shortage of practical experience. One still hears of students in some colleges being ordained and never having preached a sermon. Many a young minister does not have the faintest idea how to introduce a genuine seeker to faith in Christ, or how to run a nurture group for new believers. Instead, their training has concentrated on how to celebrate Communion with the extravagant minutiae of ritual, or on the avant-garde ideas of some fashionable liberal theologian. We are not yet sending out from our theological colleges men and women who have much practical experience of ministry. In almost all of them practical training is discounted in comparison with academic learning. Often it is not even examined. It is all too easy for students, once recommended for the ministry, to move inexorably towards ordination, however great the practical incompetence they display in their training. The only ways in which a candidate can be dismissed from college are through failing exams or gross immorality – and gross immorality does not necessarily debar a person in these permissive days: there are colleges where promiscuous homosexuality is rampant and is unrestrained by the staff. Nobody trains teachers, doctors or dentists without a wealth of clinical experience. The preparation of ministers languishes a long way behind, not least because many of the teachers lack competence or experience in effective ministry and are academics by temperament who would be most fulfilled in university teaching – if only they could make it.

My final concern is not about what goes on inside colleges, but about how people are selected to enter them. Anglican applicants go through a variety of local hoops and are then sent to a three-day selection conference. Selectors try to assess their devotional life, their education and their pastoral skills. I have read through many hundreds of these reports over the years and I am far from satisfied with the procedure. I am not convinced that they are always selecting men and women for ministry in the twenty-first century. Despite frequent denials, there appears to be considerable prejudice against recommending too many Evangelical and charismatic students, who form the majority of the applicants these days. Sometimes a person is rejected because 'he/she is an evangelist, not a priest'. Since when did the Church not need evangelists? And how does the Church acknowledge and use them if not in the ordained ministry? The gift of evangelism is invaluable for a parish priest. The selectors seem to have a fixation on 'priesthood' in a sense of which the New Testament and, indeed, the Anglican formularies know nothing. A priest must be 'a representative person' to God for the congregation, and for God to the congregation. Now, one can see some force in this, but it is certainly not the central quality to look for in ordinands, and it has little support in the Christianity of the New Testament.

I would prefer to ascertain whether these ordinands actually believe the tenets of the New Testament. Plenty are ordained who do not. Can they communicate the Christian faith to those who do not accept it? Plenty are ordained who cannot. Have they demonstrated in their lay capacity pastoral and teaching gifts which justify their being trained at great cost for the professional ministry? Many are ordained who have not. Are they leaders whom people will follow? Many are ordained who are utterly devoid of leadership gifts. Moreover, no training in leadership is given in most of Britain's theological colleges. No wonder the Church is in some disrepair. I fear that much of the trouble goes back to the selection and theological training of its ministers. Radical reform of theological education is one of the most urgent tasks of the Church if it is to regain its significance in this country.

CHAPTER 7

Writing

I have written many books, but I am an author by mistake. Several publishers seemed to think I had the ability and urged me to write, but I told them I could not do it. I could give reasonably attractive talks and sermons, maybe, but I could not write. Accordingly, until the age of 33, I had written practically nothing: just one article on hypocrisy in *Crusade* magazine, and an attempt at a booklet on the deity of Jesus Christ, which was the only manuscript I have ever had refused. It deserved its fate.

Then, in 1963, a significant event took place. I found myself speaking alongside the gifted apologist Dr Francis Schaeffer at a conference for theological students. At that time he was celebrated as 'the guru of the Alps', having set up shop at Huémoz in Switzerland, where he contended with all comers for the truth of the Christian faith, armed with an amazingly extensive understanding of what was happening in contemporary culture. He may not have been the most profound analyst of that emerging culture, but he was certainly the first to show large numbers of Evangelical Christians what was going on in their world, and how blind they were to it. I owe a lot to Francis Schaeffer. At that time he, too, could not write. He talked incessantly, and the aficionados went around Huémoz wearing earphones, listening to his somewhat repetitive tapes. Consequently, during this conference I took it upon myself to encourage him to write. He told me that he could not do it. I said that I realized his problem, but, if he would give it a go, I would find someone to ghostwrite the work for him. To his endless credit, he did give it a go, and I found a ghostwriter. The result was his first book, an instant success called *Escape from Reason*. At much the same time he produced a more substantial volume, *The God Who Is There*, and these were the precursors of many more which went all over the English-speaking world and have had an enormous influence for good.

At that time I was on the editorial board of the small and struggling Lutterworth Press. I suggested to them that they should publish Schaeffer and predicted that, if they did, they would make a lot of money. They thought about it and declined. Before long, they were out of business and Hodder and Stoughton, who enthusiastically took Francis Schaeffer under their wing, must have made a mint of money out of his books over the years.

Reluctant author

It was at that same conference that I was again urged to write myself. Once again, I refused. My encourager, from the InterVarsity Press, then said something to this effect: 'Look, you've been out to South Africa, assisting Dick Lucas on two university missions in Rhodes and Cape Town. You must have given some reasonable talks then. Why not write those down?'

'Is that all you want?' I asked. It seemed it was. In the following weeks I copied out the talks I had given on topics such as 'Is Christianity Finished?', 'Love – Man's Number One Interest', 'Choose Freedom', and so forth. I was teaching at the London College of Divinity at the time, and I spent the afternoons alternating between writing this book on my old typewriter and playing rugby football for the college. Before long it was done, and I sent it in. It immediately took off.

Two things contributed to the success of *Choose Freedom*. First, David Alexander, at that time the whizzkid of IVP, took a picture of a seagull against the perfect blue of a summer sky and made that the cover of the book. That was most unusual at a time when Christian books were almost produced in brown-paper covers, so dull were they! The other unusual thing was that I wrote just as I spoke – after all, it was merely a matter of turning into print what I had said in live outreach situations. All the illustrations, all the *ad hominem* challenges, found their way into the text. In those days nobody wrote as they spoke. You have only to read *Basic Christianity*, an early classic by John Stott which was widely read at the time, to see that it has a far more literary style than the one I adopted in *Choose Freedom*. Nowadays many authors write as they speak, but in those days it was unheard of.

For those two reasons, *Choose Freedom* flourished. Yet it was a very bad book. It did not have any discernible theme. It was simply a few reasonably imaginative and lively evangelistic talks thrown together with a final chapter on growth in the Christian life. It was also helped by the title. When speaking on 'Choose Freedom' one night in Cape Town, I had discovered to my surprise that it evoked an enormous response, for which I was quite unprepared. I had not then cottoned on to the fact that the freedom motif was capturing the world, and was certainly sweeping all over Africa. Once I did realize that, I found myself frequently speaking on the theme of freedom for a couple of years, and discovered that it was indeed the appropriate way to explain the Christian gospel at that time. Having said that, however, I am not proud of that first book. It really was not very good, but surprisingly it stayed in print with edition after edition until the 1990s.

Writing for two audiences

Having discovered that I could, perhaps, write after all, I then embarked on two very different books at the same time. The fact is worth mentioning, since I have always been somewhat schizophrenic between the academic and the applied aspects of my Christian faith. I am incapable of writing anything, however slight, without seriously thinking through its doctrinal content. Equally, when I am addressing a serious academic issue in theology, I am incapable of writing about it in an unapplied way. It has got to be of some use to the Church. Such is the position I have adopted from my earliest days of writing. That is why I resolved not to write too many contributions to journals. Although that is the normal avenue for academic approval and progress, much of it seemed to me to be sterile: so often one scholar put forward a position, only to be shot down by another scholar in a journal which had a small circulation and no influence on the Christian public at all. I felt that any time I had for writing would be better employed in doing something for the Church at large, so I determined to write books. I have not had occasion to regret that decision.

That schizophrenia of mine between the academic and the applied has meant that my books have fallen into two categories. They have been designed either to point people who are not yet Christians towards commitment to Christ, or to build Christians up into maturity. Although perhaps subconsciously, I found myself doing that from the start. I used the college vacations to write a serious book on salvation, a topic that was much debated at the time and was of great interest to someone like myself who had a heart for evangelism. What is the biblical understanding of salvation? What does it really mean in Old Testament, intertestamental and secular literature, and supremely in the New Testament? And how does it relate to profound issues like universalism, perseverance, healing and the like?

The book occupied a good deal of my study time, and when it was finished I was encouraged by Professor Moule, my friend and erstwhile supervisor, to throw it in for a Cambridge higher degree. If one has a first in the Cambridge tripos, as I had, it is permissible to put a book in for either a Doctor of Philosophy or a Bachelor of Divinity degree without giving previous indication of intent or needing to have a supervisor. You simply submit the finished work. The book, *The Meaning of Salvation*, was indeed finished. I was, however, in a quandary about where to publish it. To my surprise, SCM Press, SPCK, Hodders and Lutterworth all wanted to put it out. I decided to go with Hodders, and thus began a very happy partnership with them that has lasted until today. I also decided to submit it for a Bachelor of Divinity degree, which is senior to the PhD at Cambridge.

The degree was awarded, but I am still not sure whether I should have gone for the PhD, whose significance is widely understood, rather than the BD, which can be a pass degree in some universities and higher than a PhD in others! I was persuaded, I think, by the prospect of submitting a further learned book later on which might change the Bachelor's degree into a doctorate. I did, in fact, make that submission a few years later, when I had written *Evangelism in the Early Church*, and it narrowly failed to get the DD. The New Testament assessor deemed the New Testament standard to be adequate if it supported the Patristic, and the Patristic assessor regarded that standard as adequate if it supported the New Testament! I had to wait many years before being awarded a DD. Nevertheless, I had tried to fulfil one side of my abilities, by writing a serious work of Christian theology. Later on, I wrote several more.

At the same time I was also working at a very different level. After *Choose Freedom* sold 20,000 copies very fast, the publishers suggested to me that I ought to write a 96-page book which concentrated on a single topic of my choice, in contrast to the somewhat disparate nature of the earlier book. They wanted something lively, contemporary and in the same rather racy style. I asked myself what would be most useful. What would take the reader to the very heart of Christian distinctiveness? It seemed to me that the resurrection of Jesus

Christ was the subject to work on. As I reflected on it, it occurred to me that the resurrection, while being absolutely central to the Christian faith, suffered from two unfortunate tendencies when people wrote about it. Either they tended to give many somewhat dry reasons for crediting the fact of the resurrection, or else they concentrated pietistically on the presence of the risen Christ in their lives. I asked myself if I knew of any book which wrote compellingly about the evidence for Christ's resurrection on the one hand, and equally compellingly about the significance it has for our world and our individual lives on the other. I could not think of one.

That observation determined the shape of the book I was about to write. It would be on the resurrection of Jesus Christ, the most amazing and best attested fact in ancient history, and it would be concerned to relate that resurrection to the lives of both those who were Christians and those who were not. You could almost say that the theme was 'Is it true and does it matter?' I was helped in preparing the book by a number of testimonies from friends in different countries concerning the difference the resurrection had made in their lives. That apart, I found that the book almost wrote itself. I completed it in roughly six days, during which I worked so hard that I imagine I was not very good company. There was a short period of revision, and then the book was done. The title *Man Alive* was, I am mildly embarrassed to say, pirated from a popular television programme of the time.

The publishers did a splendid job. When the book published in 1967, they got it reviewed in the daily papers as well as the religious press, and had it in all the WH Smith bookshops. It had an immediate and far-reaching circulation, not only spreading round the English-speaking world, but being translated into some 40 languages. It was read for divinity lessons in countless sixth forms and was much in evidence in the universities. It had enormous sales in New Zealand, too, where a distinguished liberal theologian was busy denying the resurrection, and my book was used in debate with him.

Indeed, he and I took the matter further in personal correspondence. I found in the years that followed that many people who had been converted through that book were moving out into missionary service and ordination in different parts of the world. I was amazed at the book's impact, and I still am, but I think books tend to succeed if they touch the mood of the moment. At that time people were wondering if the Christian faith could stand up to critical examination. They still believed in truth in those days, before postmodernism struck, and people wanted to know if the gospel story was true. *Man Alive* made a strong case for the central tenet of the Christian faith, and also for its significance in areas of personal concern like loneliness, defeat, guilt and fear of death. The 1960s was a period of massive cultural change and profound questing, and the book fitted easily into that atmosphere.

Man Alive has gone through various revisions since then and has been put out by various publishers, but it has never gone out of print and is available today under the somewhat infelicitous title *Christ Is Risen – So What?*, published by Sovereign World. It would never make the splash today that it did when it first published. The climate is different. The concern for truth has given way to the concern for relevance, and people are less inclined to stand up for strongly held convictions. It would not make much impact today, but it certainly did when it first emerged – greatly to my surprise and that of my publisher, Ronald Inchley of IVP. Curiously enough, I hear that it has just been published in Macedonian and their President has eagerly bought a copy!

By now Ronald realized he was on to a good thing! *Man Alive* was at the top of the bestseller lists. He therefore commissioned me to write another book, looking sharply at other apologetic issues which were central to the credibility of the Christian faith. This time I wrote a somewhat longer book, but in the same racy and challenging style. It was called *Runaway World*. The idea arose from a critical question: was it the Christians who were wilfully blinding themselves to the evidence about God and Jesus Christ, or was it others who were anxious to keep out of God's way, and therefore were only too glad to argue that he did not exist?

The first chapter was a careful writing up of the historical, literary and archaeological support for the life, death and resurrection of Jesus Christ. The person of Jesus has always been the most compelling argument for the existence of God, and the evidence about Jesus is strong, early and convincing. As a classicist and a New Testament scholar I was familiar with the material, much of it hidden in learned journals and not widely known. As a writer I had learnt by now how to produce that material attractively and forcefully. This first chapter caught the imagination of a wide spectrum of people and made them look hard at the question of the historicity of Jesus and the challenge which that presents. Indeed, it was not only taken up on radio and televison programmes, but was given a substantial and approving review in the *Daily Mirror*. That newspaper was not famous for reviewing any books, let alone a Christian one! I understand that they had only reviewed two Christian books since the Second World War – John Robinson's *Honest to God* and my *Runaway World*. It was all very surprising.

I recall Ronald warning me not to expect again the success I had enjoyed with *Man Alive*. The subject matter was more demanding in this new book, and he felt it would not have the same wide circulation. He was wrong. The book went all over the world, and was translated into a great many languages. My friend and ex-pupil Taffy Davies, the clergyman/cartoonist, designed a marvellous cover for the book featuring an ostrich with its head firmly hidden in the sand. That cover remained on most of the translations, and I vividly remember seeing it on one of the Chinese language versions. I suppose I will never have any true idea of what that book did. It was, once again, a tract for the times, although I did not realize it until afterwards. I was greatly moved by the number of people who wrote in and told me how that book had led them to Christ. I would receive little carved animals from countries like Hungary and Russia with a note in broken English explaining that the book had helped someone to faith whom I would never see.

This was astonishing to me, but the thought was not quite new. I had previously heard from a friend travelling in South Africa that a Zulu chieftain had been converted through reading *Choose Freedom*, and so it had begun to dawn on me that the pen is often mightier than the spoken word. It certainly gets to places the spoken word cannot reach. Now, however, I was being flooded with stories of people brought to faith through reading my books. When I was chatting some time later with the Orthodox Patriarch Metropolitan Anthony, he told me of a recent visit he had made to Russia, during which he had discovered an underground press where illicit copies of *Runaway World* were being printed and distributed. He had even concealed a few copies under his cassock for secret distribution! Needless to say, no contracts were ever struck between these Russian entrepreneurs and the UK publishers.

I believe that *Man Alive* and *Runaway World* had the good fortune to be published at just the right time, and that they were the most widely influential books I wrote for many a long year. None of my later evangelistic books equalled them in impact, with the possible exception of *Why Bother with Jesus?* and *You Must Be Joking!*, of which more in due course.

Keele and Lambeth

Meanwhile, I found myself writing on a very different topic and for a very different readership. The greatest Evangelical leader in twentieth-century Britain was undoubtedly Dr John Stott, and by the early 1960s he was planning a National Evangelical Anglican Congress. It took place at Keele University in 1967, and was a major rallying point for

Evangelical Anglicans, who had tended to be defensive, disorganized and scorned by the rest of the Anglican Church. Keele changed all that. It rapidly became apparent that the despised Evangelicals had great vitality, were bound into a new unity, had clear ideas derived from Scripture and the Church fathers on many areas of contemporary debate, and were determined to commit themselves henceforth to the social as well as the evangelistic aspects of the gospel – something they had neglected for several decades. Moreover, they determined to contract into, rather than sit back from, the structures of the Church, in an endeavour to make their weight count. Anyone who has studied Anglican history in the past half-century will know that Keele was a turning point for Evangelicals. From then on they were a major force in the councils and parishes of the Church of England.

I had the privilege of reading a paper at the Keele Congress in 1967 on 'Christ's sacrifice – and ours', relating the cross to Holy Communion. I also spoke at the Nottingham NEAC Congress 10 years later, on 'Mission and ministry', in which I examined and applied New Testament principles for church life today. Both congresses were extraordinarily influential.

Part of the effectiveness of Keele was the meticulous care devoted to preparation. The speakers were very carefully briefed by John, and their contributions were published in *Guidelines* to coincide with the Congress. Earlier on, however, John Stott had also got together 20 competent Evangelicals and commissioned them each to write a short book in what became known as the 'Christian Foundations' series. It was designed to influence the forthcoming 1968 Lambeth Conference. Copies of these books were sent to every diocesan bishop in the Anglican Communion. I was asked to write on the topic of Christian ministry. At that time it was a highly disputed area, with questions about apostolic succession and sacrificial priesthood figuring large. Stott gave me the outline of the book, and I wrote it. As far as I recall, he gave all of us outlines! His knowledge and vision were phenomenal, and so was his attention to detail. I shall always be grateful for his friendship and guidance over many years.

Some books in that 1964 'Christian Foundations' series made little impact, but others were very influential indeed and I suppose my own *Called to Serve* (written at the same time as *Choose Freedom*) was one of these. Not only is it still in print (with some modifications), but I was invited on the strength of it to be one of the handful of Consultants at the 1968 Lambeth Conference, held throughout August in the steamy heat of London. It was a fascinating experience. I think we Consultants had the best of it. We were able to go and join whatever committee of bishops we liked or were asked to attend, while the bishops themselves had to stay in their one group. In any event, it became clear to all and sundry in positions of influence in the Church that there was a strong and informed Evangelical voice that refused to accept the commonly held views on sacrificial priesthood and apostolic succession. Today you hear little enough in favour of these two doctrines, but they were very influential when I was ordained.

Called to Serve also stressed the fact that all Christians, not just some, are called to serve the Lord, and that there is no distinction between clergy and laity in their standing, although there is in their spheres of ministry. That was radical stuff in those days, although it is accepted everywhere today. The book had a lot to say about lay ministry, which again was regarded as avant-garde at that time, although now it is universally recognized. *Called to Serve* therefore turned out to be rather important. None of the authors made any money out of that series, I am amused to recall. The idiosyncratic chief executive of Hodder and Stoughton had struck a bargain with John Stott, giving him £50 for each author!

Biblical commentaries

I continued to teach for university and theological college courses, and I wrote a number of books as the years went by.

Being primarily a New Testament scholar, I naturally concentrated on biblical themes. Sometimes they emerged from speaking invitations. Thus *Reflections from the Lion's Den* is a study of some of the book of Daniel, based on four Bible studies I gave at Spring Harvest one year. Sometimes they were running commentaries, like *Matthew for Today* and *Acts for Today*, applying the biblical text to the contemporary scene.

Both these latter books originated in a lecture series and I had thought of writing a whole series on the four Gospels and Acts, but this was never carried through for a number of reasons. One was that there were already many much more detailed commentaries in existence, and an excellent applied series edited by John Stott, 'The Bible Speaks Today', was already appearing and covered the whole New Testament. Another was that the two books were very different in treatment. While I had done a running commentary through the whole text of Matthew, I felt there were many good commentaries on Acts, so I had extracted particular themes to comment on and apply – themes such as church-planting, evangelistic preaching, guidance, the Holy Spirit and leadership. The clinching reason for not taking the series idea further was that the sales did not justify prolonging it. All was not lost, however. IVP are proposing to reissue a revised *Acts for Today*, and I have heavily revised and rewritten *Matthew for Today*, which is now the commentary on Matthew in 'The Bible Speaks Today' series.

The other biblical commentary I wrote around that time requires a little more explanation. While I was engaged in postgraduate New Testament work at Cambridge, I became a member of the Senior New Testament Seminar there, which met weekly under the chairmanship of the Lady Margaret Professor of Divinity, Dr Charlie Moule. Usually a member would read a short paper and discussion would follow. On one occasion somebody summarized a recent paper by the distinguished radical New Testament scholar Ernst Käsemann on 2 Peter, dismissing it as a worthless pseudo-Gnostic attempt to revive enthusiasm about the discredited doctrine of Christ's Second Coming sometime in the middle of the second century. I found myself totally at odds with his presuppositions, methods and conclusion, and asked if I might read a paper to controvert his position at a later meeting. Given the weight of scholarship gathered in that room, I knew it needed to be good. I worked hard on it, and in due course produced an address which was later written up in *2 Peter Reconsidered*, a Tyndale monograph.

On the whole the Seminar members were impressed rather than persuaded, but one man who wholeheartedly agreed with me on the early date and apostolic authorship of 2 Peter was Dr John Robinson, later Bishop of Woolwich. He was a brilliant and original New Testament scholar, and subsequently produced a controversial book arguing that not only 2 Peter but all the documents in the New Testament were written before the fall of Jerusalem in AD 70. In those days it was regarded as almost eccentric or, worse, fundamentalist for a New Testament scholar to believe in the early date and apostolic authorship of 2 Peter, but nowadays further discoveries and major commentaries have made that an eminently tenable position once again. For some years, however, I was known among Seminar members as 'the man who believes 2 Peter is authentic'.

In the light of the work I had done on the epistle, I was asked to write the Tyndale New Testament commentary on it. The Tyndale series has attracted a large readership around the world, combining as it does competent scholarship with a reverent attitude to the text. It was originally based on the King James Version of the Bible, but has subsequently been reissued in the New International Version, which gave me an opportunity for revision.

Books about evangelism

During my years at the London College of Divinity and St John's, Nottingham, I developed a growing concern for evangelism. It seemed to me that, if the gospel was true for anyone, it should be true for everyone and Christians should make every effort to spread it. I tried to do so through my books in two ways. One was to write evangelistic books. The other was to write about evangelism.

My first popular attempt in this latter direction was *Evangelism Now and Then*, a book based on the Acts of the Apostles, comparing and contrasting the way the first Christians and their modern descendants in the West went about evangelism. It originated in a conference in Miami at which I addressed the top leadership of the United Methodist Church of the USA, and examined the motives, message, methods and spiritual power of the first Christians. The book was challenging and well illustrated by contemporary examples, and it stayed in print for several decades.

Some years earlier, however, I had set about writing a major book on the subject, a careful examination of the growth of the early Church in the first two or three centuries. It was called *Evangelism in the Early Church*. In preparation, I read all the surviving patristic literature that was relevant, and gained a good understanding of the massive evangelistic achievement of the early Christians. Of course, much of the book dealt with the biblical material, particularly the Acts, but it did not stop there. It went on to examine the developments in the next two centuries. The book was published in 1970 and has remained in print on both sides of the Atlantic ever since. In the States it is one of the basic books on evangelism in almost all the universities and seminaries. This seems to be partly because it is written with passion, partly because it is thorough (it has 100 pages of footnotes!) and partly because there is not much else in print which covers evangelism in the early Church. There is Harnack's *The Mission and Expansion of Christianity*, C.H. Dodd's *The Apostolic Preaching and its Developments* and Roland Allen's *Missionary Methods – St Paul's and Ours*, but that is about all. Undoubtedly it is the most significant academic book I have written.

Twenty years later, I followed it up with *Evangelism through the Local Church*, another large book which was designed to help Christian leaders with the task of evangelism in our own day. This, too, had a very generous reception in many countries. The first part of the book looked at Christianity and other faiths, and the propriety or otherwise of evangelism in our multifaith culture. It also looked at some of the qualities that need to be present in a church if it is to be effective in evangelism. The second part of the book was devoted to apologetic issues – the existence of God, the deity of Jesus Christ, the truth of the resurrection, miracles and suffering. The third part was concerned with various ways of evangelism today, including preaching, personal evangelism, nurture and both single-church and multi-church missions. A final and very practical part of the book was a series of appendices, jointly written with Jane Holloway, my personal assistant for 14 years who had vast experience of setting up mission ventures. We wrote on topics like running groups for agnostics, outlining the contents of an eight-week course for Christian beginners, appropriate music in evangelism, evangelism and sport, leading a mission team, setting up a town-wide mission, and the interplay of spiritual and social aspects in evangelism. The book proved useful, but it would have been considerably improved had I paid more attention to postmodern issues in the section on apologetics.

I have also written a couple of shorter books on evangelism. When I returned from Canada in 1992 to join the small Springboard team which the Archbishops set up as their own contribution to the Decade of Evangelism, I was approached by Shelagh Brown to write something on evangelism for the (largely Anglican) Bible Reading Fellowship. The result was *Good News is for Sharing*, and it was a composite work. I did the selection of Bible passages relevant to evangelism and wrote the commentary on them. Shelagh selected prayers and questions for group study to go with them. How much good the book did I have no idea, but I was glad to write it, both because my wife Rosemary is a regular and popular writer of Bible Reading Fellowship notes and because Shelagh was such a character. She revived the fortunes of the BRF almost single-handedly and it was a sad loss when she tripped down the stairs and lost her life while going to let friends in at her front door. You can gauge something of the flavour of the woman when you know that in her will she directed that the mourners at her funeral should be provided with the best champagne to celebrate Jesus and his risen life which she had gone to share.

The other book I have written more recently on evangelism came from a suggestion by my wife. She noticed that years ago there were plenty of books on how to do evangelism – some of them, it has to be said, rather wooden and unimaginative – but in recent years there has been a big swing away from rigid 'how to' books towards an emphasis on the importance of relationships. It is almost, though not quite, true that you can only evangelize friends, and 'friendship evangelism' has been the parrot cry for some time. Often it seems to be more friendship than evangelism, but the idea is sound. The net result of this swing, however, is that many people have little or no idea how to introduce a friend to Christ, once that friend is keen to find out. I wrote *How Can I Lead a Friend to Christ?* – or *One to One*, as the US edition is called – to try to rectify this. The book is in no sense a dogmatic manual of instruction, but sets out to offer help with motivation, building bridges of friendship, possible ways of starting the conversation, knowing the good news, becoming the 'midwife', handling the variety of possible responses and offering aftercare. There is a final chapter on avoiding some of the mistakes I have made over the years! A girl once gave a wonderful testimonial to a friend: 'You built a bridge of friendship to me, and in due course Jesus came and walked across that bridge.' This little book is an attempt to show how bridges can be built and how we can help people welcome Jesus across that bridge.

Evangelistic books

Writing books about evangelism is one thing; writing evangelistic books is quite another. I have noticed with sorrow that few Christian writers set out to write books for those who are not yet Christians. David Watson did, C.S. Lewis did, J. John does, but not many other names come to mind. With the experience of *Choose Freedom*, *Man Alive* and *Runaway World* behind me, I did not need much persuasion to continue to write evangelistically, especially as I was continually getting letters from people who had been helped to faith through those books. The next one was *Jesus Spells Freedom*, and it was based on a series of evangelistic addresses I gave in Cambridge at the university mission I was asked to lead. The mission was very fruitful, and I had thought that the book would be also, but its sales were only moderate. Although the freedom issue was still very much in the air, the book clearly did not catch the public's attention in the way *Choose Freedom* had done, although it went into several impressions.

A couple of small books may be worth a mention. Both were put out by Eagle Publishing, and are lavishly illustrated. One called *My God* has had a very large circulation; the other, *Jesus*, was published much later and will probably do less well. My daughter Jenny took the photos which figure in *My God*, and the thrust of the book is clear on the cover from the three questions: Does God exist? What is he like? What can he do for me? Part of the attractiveness of this book is its very cheap price, just 99 pence, so people can give it away as a gift without breaking the bank. Eagle organized an extensive network of other nationalities to co-publish these books: they retained our photos and translated the text.

I also find *Come, Follow Me* a helpful evangelistic booklet to use after preaching. I wrote it in the early 1980s to answer some of the initial questions people often have at the point of commitment to Christ. Does it matter? Will it make any difference? What will it cost to follow Christ? How can I be sure

I belong? How do I begin? What next? My experience is that, if used on its own, a booklet like this is rarely effective, but if it is used as a follow-up to an address that has moved someone, it reinforces and clarifies the challenge of the sermon. It is also nice to be able to offer the hearer something I have written myself. It continues the link with the preacher.

There are three evangelistic books that perhaps merit a less cursory glance. The first is *Why Bother with Jesus?* It arose in an interesting way. I had been preaching evangelistically at St Aldate's, where I was Rector at the time, and among the people who came to see me after the service was one who asked if I could recommend something for an apathetic friend to read. I searched our extensive bookstall to no avail. Then I checked with the bookshops, but could find no book designed to arouse the indifferent. So I decided to write one. We had a bit of holiday coming up in a borrowed cottage on the Yorkshire moors. When it was fine, I went out on long walks with the family. When it rained, I wrote this book. It had deliberately short, hard-hitting chapters, each giving a pungent reason for bothering with Jesus. It was not difficult to do one of these short chapters in half an afternoon, and before long the book was finished. It has proved very popular. Something like a quarter of a million copies are in print, and it has gone through several editions since its first publication at the end of the 1970s.

My fondest memory of that book is from a mission I was asked to lead in Victoria, the capital city of British Columbia. The local ministerial was keen on an ambitious plan to place an evangelistic book in every home in the city. They asked me if they could use *Why Bother with Jesus?* for this purpose, providing I could secure good terms for a bulk order. Hodder and Stoughton came up trumps, producing 150,000 special copies at 18 pence each, if I remember right, and the book went right round the city. When I invited people to respond to Christ on the first night of the mission, one man who must have read and been converted through the book came to the *great/funny!*

front and, not realizing who I was, urged me to read the book and get right with God!

Who Is this Jesus? is another evangelistic book of mine that had an interesting history. I recall the day when I took the manuscript of *Evangelism through the Local Church* into Hodders and found their senior management discussing the recent visit of two bishops. It was 1990, the start of the Decade of Evangelism. These bishops had asked Hodders what they proposed to put in front of the enquirers who were expected during the decade. There was not very much on offer that was nontechnical, arrestingly written, theologically reliable and designed to engage with the doubts and questions of the non-aligned. They immediately asked me to write such a book and wanted to give me a contract then and there! I declined. It is not easy to write a book that is not cluttered with footnotes and yet can stand critical appraisal by fellow New Testament teachers, and that can at the same time grasp the attention of agnostics and draw uncommitted people to the faith. I did not know if I could do it.

I had a sabbatical term coming up from my employers at Regent College, however, and I spent it in an isolated shack in Hawaii, where I ate the local fruit, revelled in the sun and surf, and wrote *Who Is this Jesus?* When I am writing I rarely cross out anything, but I revised this book repeatedly. It did not come easily. I am glad that I wrote it, though. I gave it to a businessman who had only been a Christian for a few weeks, and he could not put it down. That was the encouragement I needed, and it was only then that I took out a contract with Hodders. The book begins by reflecting on why the name of Jesus Christ should be used most often as a swearword – we do not shout 'Allah!' or 'Buddha!' when something falls on our toe. Then a number of short chapters address specific questions: What was he like? What did he teach? What did he claim? Why did he die? Was death the end? Can we meet him? What about the Church? There are also two carefully constructed apologetic chapters entitled 'Footnotes for the

Curious'. One deals with the secular evidence for Jesus, the other with the Gospels and whether we can trust them. It was one of my major contributions to the Decade of Evangelism, and I often meet people who were converted through it.

The final evangelistic book worth mentioning here is *Strange Intelligence*, a brilliant piece of imaginative publishing by InterVarsity Press, at the instigation of one of its senior editors, Colin Duriez. He asked if there was any possibility of my writing something as a preparation for the Oxford University mission which I was to lead in 1997. The Bible Society had agreed to put up half the money for the production, and I was able to find a generous sponsor for the rest. The idea was to write a book, attractive to Oxford students, which could be delivered personally to every member of the university. Half the book comprised some fast-moving material written by me, with testimonies and photos of Oxford converts, while the other half consisted of St Mark's Gospel, to which I added an introduction and a challenging postscript – may I be forgiven! If you picked the book up one way, you read my *Strange Intelligence*. If you picked it up the other way, you read *Men Like Trees Walking* – our Oxford-like name for Mark's Gospel.

The book was given out to every undergraduate at the end of the 1996 Michaelmas Term, so that students could read it over Christmas. It prepared the way for the mission which was held the following February, and it seems to have been very effective. One man read it through five times, completely missing all the mission addresses, and arrived for the last of the follow-up meetings proclaiming that he had been convinced and converted. Another read it through the night he was given it, and immediately entrusted his life to Christ. It is events like this which make me feel it is important for Christian writers to direct some of their work beyond the Christian circle. I would love to see more artists, film-makers and cartoonists doing the same thing.

Nurture

Evangelism is no good without proper nurture. From time to time down the years, I have tried to provide something to nurture Christians in general and new believers in particular. The most useful is undoubtedly *New Life, New Lifestyle*, first published as long ago as 1973 and still very much around today, having gone through several revisions. At that time David Watson and I were doing a good deal of evangelism, and we were both looking for something useful to put in the hands of new believers. There was nothing on the market except a very old book by Hugh Evan Hopkins which had long passed its sell-by date. We each sat down and wrote a suitable book, without realizing that the other was doing the same. We were very amused when we found out! Both books came to be much used. *New Life, New Lifestyle* takes a bird's-eye view of the Christian life as new believers seek to reorient themselves and begin the walk of discipleship with Christ.

Other books of mine in this category include *On Your Knees*, a study of the prayers of St Paul, *After Alpha*, and *New Testament Spirituality*. The first of these arose from my own devotional life, the second out of the phenomenal success of the Alpha programme (I deliberately put the book out with the Alpha publisher, Kingsway). I kept discovering that many people had been through Alpha once, twice, and perhaps a third time, but had no idea what to do next. So I wrote *After Alpha*, not in any way as a sequel to that admirable course, but to help people who had been through it to see where they could be useful in their local churches and how they could use the skills and experience they had gained in Alpha. I also had in mind the clergy who did not know how to make best use of the members of their congregation who had erupted into new life through their involvement with Alpha. I dare to hope that the book has been a help to both categories.

New Testament Spirituality was a joint publication by Dr Paul Stevens and myself. As fellow members of the faculty at

Regent College, we could not help being impressed by the gripping lectures on spirituality given by our colleague Dr James Houston. Much of his teaching centred on the desert fathers and the medieval mystics. It occurred to us that, if we offered a joint lecture course on New Testament spirituality, it might be a useful complement, and this is what we did. We repeated the course on a second occasion and it was much appreciated, so we turned it into a book. It takes various aspects of New Testament spirituality, beginning with a strong Trinitarian emphasis and seeing Christians under the three images of Abba worshippers, Jesus people and temples of the Holy Spirit. It then moves on to examine prayer, obedience, healing and deliverance, faith, hope, love, and the sacraments.

I do not know whether my book *Baptism*, published in 1987, should be included here or with the books I wrote on apologetics. It was designed both to build Christian believers up in the understanding of what their baptism into Christ implies, and to handle some of the very difficult issues that keep coming up. Should baptism be administered to adult believers only, or also to children? What about those whose profession of faith turns out subsequently to be false? What about rebaptism, and baptism with the Holy Spirit? What about the relationship between baptism and conversion? I fully expected to get hammered on all sides for this book, but instead it remained for months at or near the top of the best-seller list, and at least one Baptist minister read it and then baptized his young children!

Apologetics

Apologetics has always been a concern of mine. How can we commend the gospel intelligently to those who do not believe it? Naturally apologetics cannot drive anyone into the kingdom of God, but it can remove some of the roadblocks on the way. It therefore has a real, though subordinate, place in the whole Christian enterprise. In fact, reason and revelation often march together (not surprisingly, since both are God-given), and the arguments for the Christian faith are much more impressive than those against it. Potentially, therefore, the thoughtful Christian is on strong ground when he seeks, in St Peter's words, 'to give an answer to anyone who asks a reason for the hope that is within him'. Accordingly, I have attempted to write in this area too.

The first such attempt was *You Must Be Joking!*, with the subtitle 'Popular excuses for avoiding Jesus Christ'. It was carrying on the thrust of my earlier *Runaway World*, since both are not only apologetic but evangelistic. Over the years since 1976 when it was first published, this book has led many people into Christian faith. At most of the meetings where I speak, someone comes up and thanks me for one of these thoughtful evangelistic books, because it has started them on their Christian journey. The privilege of hearing this again and again is incalculable and humbling. The plan of *You Must Be Joking!* is simple. I took some of the well-known chestnuts thrown against Christians and said in effect, 'If you tell me you believe that stuff, you have got to be joking!' It was written as a friendly but hard-hitting exposé of the shallowness of saying things such as, 'You can't believe in God these days,' or, 'All religions lead to God,' or, 'Jesus was just a good man,' or, 'It doesn't matter what you believe so long as you're sincere,' or, 'When you're dead, you're dead,' or, 'You can't change human nature.'

As I said in its preface, the stimulus for the book came from Friedrich Hänssler, head of the German publishing firm Hänssler-Verlag. The idea and title emerged as I lay in bed with meningitis under the care and imaginative friendship of Dr John Hill. The chapter headings came from the many jokers who have tried the excuses out on me. As I returned by plane from the Durban hospital where part of the book was written, I discovered that I was at least addressing the right topics. A wealthy businessman sitting next to me produced at least three of these well-worn excuses, and I murmured to myself, 'Chapter 3, Chapter 1, Chapter 5!' The answers I gave in the book may not have been conclusive, but the questions were obviously spot on – and for many people they still are. That is, I suppose, why it continues to sell.

My next venture into apologetics came when *The Myth of God Incarnate* hit the headlines. Published in August 1977, the silly season when there was no hard news, *The Myth* created a sensation. Here were a group of liberal scholars deconstructing all the main tenets of the Christian faith. Moreover, the book was put out by Hodder and Stoughton, a respected Christian publisher (although publication was strenuously opposed by their religious department), and launched in St Paul's Cathedral. I managed to get a copy of the book, which had just been devastatingly reviewed by Professor John Macquarrie, by the expedient of resurrecting it from his dustbin! It was enough to enable me to edit a rebuttal of the book, in partnership with some distinguished theologians, Dean Brian Hebblethwaite, Professor John Macquarrie, Bishop Stephen Neill and the Roman Catholic Bishop Christopher Butler. Hodder's religious department did the unthinkable and published *The Truth of God Incarnate* within six weeks of its inception, and it contributed very greatly to the debate aroused by *The Myth*. Amusingly, it also far outsold it. Yet it seemed sad to me that it was necessary to use apologetics to controvert the writings of professed Christian scholars who, in fact, had allowed secularist presuppositions to cloud their Christian understanding.

In the late 1980s I joined with Gordon Carkner, a thoughtful Canadian Inter-Varsity worker at the University of British Columbia, in producing a small pocket book called *Ten Myths about Christianity*. He had some superb posters contrasting the sayings of Jesus with those of famous opponents of God, and he and the students were using these in outreach on the university campus. The rough accompanying handout he had was not brilliant, so we agreed to write this short book together, giving 1,500-word answers to ten of the common questions about the Christian faith found in student circles. The resulting delightfully illustrated book was published by Lion, and sold in large quantities for 20 years and more. It led to at least one amusing incident. I was speaking somewhere in Western Canada and I noticed a distinguished-looking man waiting to talk to me after the meeting. He told me he had been a lifelong atheist, and was married to a Christian woman whom he took great delight in mocking for her faith. Seeing a copy of *Ten Myths about Christianity* in a bookshop one day, he bought it, intending to use it as an opportunity to heap yet more derision on his long-suffering wife. To his great credit, he read it first – and it led him to faith. He had come to thank me!

Some years later I joined with Professor Alister McGrath in writing another book of apologetics. Called *Springboard for Faith* in England and *How Shall We Reach Them?* in the States, this book addressed some of the topical issues of the 1990s such as relativism, pluralism, scepticism and reaching people who cannot read. Finally, I also tried to write not so much a book of apologetics as an evangelistic book which took postmodern concerns very seriously. *Critical Choices* was put out by IVP in 1995, and the contents stand in sharp contrast to those of *You Must Be Joking!* from 20 years earlier, which was addressed to modern rather than postmodern concerns. There are chapters on aloneness, identity, story, extra-terrestrials, stress, freedom, love and choices – a very different agenda for a very different age, but enshrining the same gospel.

Series editor

Before closing this chapter, I should mention three series of books which I was commissioned to edit by Hodder and Stoughton. The first emerged when Edward England, their most brilliant Senior Editor and board member, came to see me at Nottingham for a night in the early 1970s. He was trying to persuade me to write a one-volume commentary on the whole Bible. I refused for two reasons: I do not believe in one-volume commentaries, as they are almost bound to be shallow, and I was not competent to write on the Old Testament, although I was on the New. With characteristic flexibility, Edward changed tack completely. We talked about the theological confusion that was prevalent at the time, and we agreed that I would edit a series of thoughtful books entitled 'I Believe'. Edward undertook to get the books published in the States as well as in the UK, and I undertook to find the authors. They were a distinguished crowd, and included George Carey, David Watson, Howard Marshall, Michael Harper, John Stott, David Wenham and Max Warren.

My own contribution to the series was *I Believe in the Holy Spirit* (1975), a careful, biblical, theological and contemporary examination of the subject that took full account of the emerging charismatic movement – which had already begun to change my own Christian life. I also wrote a second volume, called *I Believe in Satan's Downfall* (1981), outlining reasons for belief in the devil, sketches of the way he grips human life, his defeat on the cross and future annihilation. It was not an easy book to write. There is a powerful anti-God force, and he does not like being unmasked. I believe C.S. Lewis had a lot of personal trouble when he was writing *The Screwtape Letters*. I know I found this the most difficult book I have ever written. Eventually the job was done, however, and it is still in print and in demand. That was the last book in a series which had a great deal of influence.

Some years later, I edited the 'Jesus Library' for Hodders. Here again we had an influential group of authors. Here again we were concentrating on one of the missing emphases of the day, the person and achievements of Jesus himself. I contributed one volume to the series, *The Empty Cross of Jesus*. Written during a sabbatical in South Africa in the mid-1980s, this book seeks to hold together, just as the New Testament does, the cross and resurrection of Jesus Christ. Too often they are put in different doctrinal boxes and examined separately. That impoverishes both. It is the Jesus who died on the cross who is alive for ever more. Michaelangelo once broke out in protest against his fellow artists who were forever depicting Jesus in his death on the cross. 'Paint him instead as the Lord of life!' he cried – but failed, in each of his *Pieta* statues, to take his own advice. I tried in this book to set the balance right by looking at the cross in the light of the resurrection. The death of Jesus Christ on the cross turned the symbol of ultimate shame into the elixir of cosmic hope. 'If you are going to buy one book this year on theology and its impact on modern man,' wrote *Librarian's World*, 'this would be an excellent choice.'

The third series which Hodders asked me to edit was much smaller and less ambitious. It arose by accident. I was doing a tour of major Canadian cities, speaking on evangelism with my friend Canon Harold Percy, the leading Anglican evangelist in Canada. I brought with me a series of cartoons for overhead projection, created for our Springboard work by my old friend, the artist Taffy Davies. When he saw them, Harold said to me, 'Man, you should make them into a book.' So I did, and the book was called *Evangelism for Amateurs*. It embraced all Taffy's cartoons and consisted of a series of short, contrasting chapters about evangelism. It is not activism, but prayer that matters. It must not be dominated by clergy, but owned by the laity. It is usually not a crisis, but a process. It is not more activity that is needed, but more training. And it must not be an occasional raid, but consistent congregational life. Such was the flavour of the chapters.

Curiously enough, I was not at all sure that I was on to something, so I did what I had never done before: I submitted the book to five publishers at the same time, and asked their advice. They all wanted it! That at least gave me the go-ahead, and Hodders duly published it in 1998. They also decided that they wanted to make it part of a little 'Amateurs' series. Thus we have had Alister McGrath on *Theology for Amateurs*, Jane

Holloway on *Prayer for Amateurs* and Tom Wright on *Holy Communion for Amateurs*. I have contributed two further volumes, illustrated by Taffy, called *Churchgoing for Amateurs* and *Bible Reading for Amateurs*. It is too soon to assess the value of the series, but it certainly has been different and fun. We hope it may attract a new clientele.

I am aware that I have commented almost exclusively about my own writings in this chapter. I am a little embarrassed to have done so. Writing is not, in fact, something I value very highly in my ministry, and I do not much like doing it. Yet many people all over the world have read my books, and I thought those people might like to know what lay behind them, or what circumstances led to their creation. Other parts of my life and ministry seem to me to be more important, but God has called me to write, and I have tried to be obedient. I dare say that, when I am dead, this may seem a not insignificant part of my Christian service.

PART 3

FAITH AND OUTREACH

CHAPTER 8

Postmodernism

We are living at a fascinating time – at one of the great watersheds of human thought, one of the highly significant shifts in civilization. The philosopher-theologian Diogenes Allen observed in his book *Christian Belief in a Postmodern World*, 'A massive revolution is taking place, that is perhaps as great as that which marked off the modern world from the Middle Ages.' In *A World Split Apart*, the great prophetic thinker Alexandr Solzhenitsyn went further, both in analysis and prescription:

> If the world has not approached its end, it has reached a major watershed in history, equal in importance to the turn from the Middle Ages to the Renaissance. It will demand of us a spiritual blaze. We shall have to rise to new heights of vision, to a new level of life where our physical nature will not be cursed, as in the Middle Ages, but even more importantly our spiritual nature will not be trampled upon, as in the Modern era.

I have lived through this massive change, and am struggling to understand it more fully so that I can proclaim the gospel more effectively. If we fail to root ourselves in Christ and the

Scriptures, we shall be tossed around with every whim of contemporary thought. Yet if we fail to root ourselves in the culture of our society, we shall be utterly incapable of sharing the gospel of God with others. The herald of good news must have two horizons: that of his message and that of those he hopes to awaken to it.

The pre-modern period

Let me backtrack a little. At the risk of oversimplification, it can be helpful to analyse Western thought in three great periods, the pre-modern, the modern and the postmodern. From the rise of Christianity until the time of the Renaissance and the Reformation in the sixteenth century, Europe was dominated by a Christian mindset. Christian faith and values held sway. This does not mean, of course, that the majority of the population were believing Christians. Evil flourished. Nonetheless, the accepted background of society was a Christian world view. The supernatural was taken for granted. Truth, goodness and beauty were valued. Heaven and hell were the ultimate realities. God was recognized as the architect both of the universe and of humankind, and the Bible provided a firm foundation for science, morals and belief. The early scientists saw God's handiwork in nature and his Word in Scripture. Both came from the same divine source. Morals were dominated by the commandments of God in the Old Testament and the example of Jesus in the New. Belief was based not upon human speculation but upon divine revelation. Here was a solid framework for society.

Europe, as Lesslie Newbigin observed, is distinguished from Asia primarily by these remarkable features: the creative mix of Christianity on the one hand and Graeco-Roman classical culture on the other. The Christian influence had been the greater of the two in the first 1,500 years of our era, but with the capture of Constantinople by the Turks in 1453 the full glory of humanist Greek thought and literature burst upon the educated centres of the West, and enormously influenced art, medicine, the beginnings of science and, above all, the way people thought about the world. The Renaissance, a new period in European history, was born, and it placed much greater emphasis on the non-Christian element in Europe's cultural heritage. This tendency was much accentuated in the eighteenth century, and so began what is normally known as the modern period.

The modern period

The Renaissance, and to a greater extent its product in the eighteenth-century Enlightenment, made things difficult for orthodox Christianity. Agnostic about God, it put human reason in his place – reason which claimed to unveil a natural religion common to all humanity, a universal morality in which everyone was supposed to seek the greatest good of the greatest number, human rights which were possessed by one and all, in a society held together by a social contract (replacing the concept of the fatherhood of God and the brotherhood of man). All of this operated in a universe which resembled a great machine, intricate and self-sustaining. Human nature was essentially good, and unlimited progress was assured. Those Enlightenment convictions made increasing impact on the educational system and the cultural assumptions of the next two centuries, and certainly rendered evangelism a great deal more problematical.

The subsequent growth of scientific materialism and its associated technologies provided a massive challenge to the Christian way of understanding the world. The success of the empirical methods adopted by the natural sciences is undisputed. None of us would want to change it. Yet God is not subject to the same sort of empirical verification as a scientific experiment. He does not get caught in the wide mesh of the scientific net which people increasingly assume is the only reliable avenue to truth. We have only to reflect on the influence of the three giants of the nineteenth century, Darwin, Marx and Freud, to see the enormous new hurdles they erected for the Christian evangelist to surmount. The gospel was becoming again what it had been at the very beginning – an outsider.

Urbanization has provided a further challenge. When you concentrate people in great urban wastelands, when you sever them from the soil and from their ancestral lands, family ties and mores, you inevitably create a moral and social maelstrom in which anything is acceptable and the weakest go to the wall. Crime multiplies. Anonymity is the order of the day. Relationships become more brittle. Alienation and disbelief in God are only two of the side effects of the urbanization which is proceeding apace throughout the world. The universal tendency is for churches to move out to the suburbs where the wealthier and more rooted people live, leaving the inner city to its own devices.

These trends have been evident for a long time. One might have thought, therefore, that the Church would have set its best minds and most committed commandos to confront the situation. Mission and evangelism, one imagines, would have been in the forefront of the life of the Church and the training of her ordinands. Not so. Old habits die hard. From about the sixth century, the face of Britain has been divided up into parishes, which theoretically embraced every yard of soil and every single individual in the land. What need, then, of evangelism? The only religion known to the majority was Christianity. All were deemed to be Christians by virtue of their baptism or their membership of Christendom. The clergy had no need of apologetic skills, or a knowledge of the varied approaches to evangelism or the priority of mission. These things were not taught in the theological colleges – indeed, for the most part, they are still not taught. The clergy were expected to take the services, teach the faith and offer pastoral care to the congregation. Maintenance, not mission, was the watchword of the Church, and in a great many parishes still is.

That was certainly true of the ministerial training I received in the late 1950s. It was broadly true when I joined the staff of the London College of Divinity in 1960. Few theological colleges in those days gave effective pastoral training and fewer still did anything about equipping students for mission in an increasingly non-Christian society. We used to take students out on evangelistic forays from time to time, but we did not major on it, and to churchmen of a different stripe it seemed bizarre and un-Anglican. Was this not still a Christian country? Did we not just need to train men to serve as clergy? Later, in the robust days at the end of the 1960s, the Evangelicals were almost alone in standing out against the fashionable 'death of God' theology and confronting contemporary unbelief with a reasonably imaginative presentation of New Testament apologetics. We did not then understand that 'the times they are a-changin''. We failed to appreciate the real significance of the 1960s. We did not realize at the time that we were part of a major culture shift, as significant as the change from the Bronze Age to the Iron Age, from the Middle Ages to the Renaissance. As the British Chief Rabbi Jonathan Sachs put it, 'The old era is dying: the new is waiting to be born.'

We did not realize that the modern age was passing away, and that postmodernism was already afoot. We did not see that all the familiar landmarks would soon be changing. The Enlightenment profoundly influenced all subsequent intellectual, moral and religious life in the West until around the 1960s. Then came the cataclysmic change.

The convictions of Enlightenment thinking can be summarized very simply, without serious distortion. There were six basic beliefs.

- Belief in humankind: we, not God, are in charge of our world.
- Belief in science: it will prove the key to all knowledge and advance.

- Belief in progress: we are evolving towards a better future at all levels.
- Belief in facts, empirically verified: values, including faith, are anyone's choice.
- Belief in freedom: especially from Church, dogma and empire.
- Belief in human goodness: we all have hearts of gold.

Those were the pillars of the Age of Reason. But during the past 30 years or so they have come under heavy attack. It is almost universally recognized now that this 'modern' world view was ludicrously optimistic. We are living in a time of massive cultural change, and it is not change for the better.

We are destroying the environment – the ozone layer, the seas, the rainforests, the land itself. We possess the capacity to destroy the world with a nuclear holocaust, and more and more nations are joining the nuclear club, thus intensifying the risks. We have AIDS, the most potent scourge since the Black Death, but will we change our selfish, hedonistic sexual habits? No: we put our faith in fallible condoms. We are witnessing the increasing breakdown of community as individualism and violence run riot. There is no restraint today. Our fundamental problem is how we can manage to live together in this global village without destroying each other like rats in a trap. We like to believe we are free; in fact, men and women everywhere are in chains of different sorts. The myths of the essential goodness of human nature and the inevitability of progress have worn remarkably thin, especially in the light of two world wars and the Holocaust.

The postmodern period

The whole package derived from the Age of Reason has become suspect. The crisis in the modern world view has prompted a strong reaction. The cry of today is one of 'post' everything: postcolonialism, postliberalism, postmodernity.

Nobody knows what will come. We only know that we have left behind the accumulated world view of the past three centuries. We are 'after' all that. It has outlived its shelf life.

Today, in the aftermath of the perceived demise both of Christendom and of the Enlightenment, there is great suspicion of all 'meta-stories', all attempts to find an umbrella to erect over our fragmented experiences. There is no big story of the world for us to believe, so we are told, only a mosaic of little stories, yours and mine included. In the absence of a widely accepted framework, we must all make our own choices. Choice is the key to it all, whether in the supermarket of food or of ideas.

Accordingly we find ourselves in a highly relativizing climate which denies all absolutes, despite the logical fallacy of making so absolute a claim. It is an age which distrusts all authority figures and structures: Nietzsche's postulate of the naked 'will to power' has come of age with Nazism, Communism and the multinationals. There is deep cynicism about institutions: the law, the monarchy, the police, the Church, parliament, industry and education are all viewed with distrust. Morality has no norms: make up your own concept of what is right for you, but don't you dare try to inflict it on anyone else. Scorn of the past is matched by loss of hope for the future. The cry is for 'instant' everything. Live for now, live for self. It is a one-dimensional life, but that should not surprise us. If past and future are discounted, all we are left with is the present. If other people do not matter, you had better take care of yourself. Needless to say, it is an age of visual, not written communication, a culture of the worldwide web, not of the book. Information is communicated in sound-bites and slogans. Consistency is at a discount, as is linear thinking. Even the law of noncontradiction is rejected.

It goes without saying, therefore, that in the last 30 years, while these massive cultural shifts have been becoming increasingly apparent, evangelism has become very different. In some ways it is easier, in others more difficult. Less often do Christian apologists have to be preoccupied with the issues which were so challenging in the modern age, such as evidence for the existence of God, the possibility of miracles, or the resurrection. The goalposts of debate have shifted wildly, and they have to seek to build a house of faith when all foundations are denied them. Armed with no objective truths, no moral norms, no rational arguments, they have to attempt to swim against a flood of subjectivism. It is not an easy situation, especially for traditional linear thinkers. What is the Christian to say?

Towards a Christian response

Before I say anything about a possible Christian response to postmodernism, there is an important point to make. The moderns may no longer make the intellectual headlines, but there are plenty of them still around. Despite the seductions of advertisements and films which imply or proclaim the deconstruction of all truths and the subjective nature of all value judgements, a great many people today are unimpressed by the cult of virtual reality, the preference for image over substance and the supposed collapse of truth into relativism. They still believe in the law of noncontradiction, and in an objective substructure to morals. The bulwark for this commonsense realism is the natural sciences. You will not persuade the physicist that truth claims are merely power games, or that the laws of nature are a subjective chimera. Richard Dawkins said, 'Show me a cultural relativist at 30,000 feet and I will show you a hypocrite. Airplanes built according to scientific principles work.'

In a world so dominated by the empiricism of scientific thought, a large section of the thinking population will dismiss postmodernism as so much fashionable nonsense, a passing phase on the periphery of human thought and behaviour. Consequently, Christian apologists who direct all their powder and shot exclusively towards dealing with postmodernist concerns are going to miss out on a lot of ordinary people, and will be foolish to do so. When I conducted a mission at Oxford University in 1997, I had three sets of people in mind as I prepared each address. There were the scientific modernists, followers of Richard Dawkins and his brand of atheism; there were the postmodernists, whose current viewing was films like *Trainspotting*; and there were the cheery hedonists, who were just out for a good time and did not think too deeply about anything. Contemporary apologetics and evangelism has to take account of at least these three types of people. They will be represented in any gathering.

Nevertheless, it cannot be denied that the wind has changed these days, and the prevailing direction from which it now blows is postmodernism. If we are going to be able to connect with it at all, we would be wise to begin by trying to rip away some of the masks from its basic assumptions. Here are two important approaches, in which the late Lesslie Newbigin has given the lead.

In the first place, we need to reiterate constantly that during recent centuries humankind has pinned its faith on the scientific method, on the power of observation and reason to establish truth. Valuable though this empirical approach is, it cannot be a comprehensive method of discovering reality. Observation can never enable us to grasp purpose. It is one thing to learn in great detail of what life and our universe consists, and science is brilliant at that. It is quite another to know what the meaning and purpose of life is. Science is necessarily silent on that topic, but it is at least as important a quest. I should know very little about the meaning and purpose of a great painting if I only analysed the nature of its paints.

Newbigin gives a powerful illustration of this point in his book *Proper Confidence*. Suppose you were to notice a concrete-mixer in an open space, surrounded by piles of bricks and steel. From observation you rightly infer that a building is about to be erected. But will it be a church? A school? An office block? You cannot tell. There are only two ways to find out. One is to wait until it is complete. The other is to ask the architect. He will reveal his plan, and you will believe him. Revelation and faith are by no means incompatible. Now, if the 'building' we are talking about is the whole cosmos, the first option is not available to us. We cannot wait until it is complete to see what its purpose is. We have to ask the architect to reveal his purposes to us, and that requires revelation on his part and faith on ours. Revelation can only be received in faith: to pit faith and reason against one another is a category confusion. There are many things we can know by observation and scientific enquiry, but others we can only appreciate if we are content to accept divine revelation. Reject that, and we have no means of knowing the purpose and meaning of our lives and our world. The lack of that knowledge is having a very deleterious effect on postmodern people. What is life all about? Who am I? Is there any overarching purpose in life? These are frequent questions to which neither modernity nor postmodernity offers any answers. Modernity ruled questions of meaning and purpose out of court, while postmodernity is very sensitive to the pain these difficult questions bring.

In the second place, we need to bring home to people that, if you exclude consideration of purpose from your discussions, there is no frame of reference for calling anything good or bad. Our society has made precisely that mistake. In the marketplace of ideas we have declined to countenance any discussion about the purpose of human life, although we have been dogmatic about its origins and constituents. This stands in sharp contrast to the pre-modern days when, for example, the catechism asked, 'What is the chief duty of man?' and the expected reply was, 'To know God and enjoy him for ever.' Not everyone will agree with the answer, but the question is crucial.

We shall never understand what is meant by a good action or a good life until we discern the purpose and meaning of the action. It goes without saying that a thing can be good for one purpose but bad for another. A pen is good for writing but useless for painting. A pulpit is good for standing in but useless for locomotion. If there is no public discussion of the purpose of human life, then we cannot properly use words like 'good' and 'bad' to describe human actions. All we can do is express our opinion. The fact is, however, that people do not think they are just expressing an opinion when they declare murder bad and generosity good. They believe – yes, even postmodernists believe – that they are saying something more categorical. Judges certainly believe that they are not merely expressing a private opinion or preference when they send murderers to prison.

I think Newbigin was right in saying that these are two vital unmasking operations which cut deep at the roots of post-modernism. They constitute an effective form of apologetic even when the traditional methods have been undercut in this 'age of no foundations'.

My friend Dr Os Guinness has long been an exceptionally acute critic of culture and defender of truth in the face of rel-ativism. He recently published a short but devastating book called *Time for Truth*, aiming to show the folly and inconsis-tency of postmodern relativism and to offer helpful ways of confronting it. His first suggestion is a negative one: it is a good strategy to relativize the claim of the relativizers. He gives a superb example, culled from G.K.Chesterton, of a pes-simistic don promulgating his depressing theories about the miseries of life and the benefits of death. Yet this man cannot maintain his position with a pistol pointing at his head in the light of a glorious dawn. Truth has broken in. The young student holding the pistol explains what he is trying to do: 'I am holding a pistol to the head of modern man, but I shall not use it to kill him, only to bring him to life.'

The apologist, like the student in the story, has a positive aim for an apparently negative approach. He is driving the rel-ativist to the logical end implied in his position, and showing him that he cannot bear to live there. Much the same thing happened to a number of guilty people brought before the

Peace and Reconciliation Commission in South Africa in the wake of apartheid, and in Germany after the Nazi abominations. In the end, the intolerable consequences of Nietzsche's 'will to power', untrammelled by any moral considerations, were shown up by the whole world's revulsion at Auschwitz and the Holocaust. Truth does have the last word.

Guinness owes much to his mentor Peter Berger, one of the foremost writers in this area. Berger has pointed out that relativism and scepticism are rarely comprehensive: relativists tend to apply it to others but not to themselves. The Christian needs to find an opportunity to bring this painful and well-concealed point home. Guinness gives a superb example of this approach when he records a conversation he once had in a train with the logical positivist A.J. Ayer. During my undergraduate days, Ayer caused a tremendous stir. In his *Language, Truth and Logic* he argued that only what could be tested by the five senses could be regarded as true, and therefore the whole of religion and metaphysics was not only misguided but quite literally nonsense. As others were not slow to point out, however, Ayer's verification principle had a fatal flaw: it could be turned against his own position. Logical positivism could certainly not be verified by the five senses! In their train conversation Ayer admitted to Os Guinness that it had been a blind alley, and that 'any iconoclast who brandishes a debunker's sword should be required to demonstrate it publicly on his own cherished beliefs'. The Christian apologist should be alert to make gentle but firm use of this negative weapon. C.S. Lewis made brilliant use of it. So did Francis Schaeffer. He called it the modern preaching of hell: it takes the roof off an opponent's position and allows the hail of truth in.

Berger has a positive point to make, too. In his book *A Rumour of Angels*, he indicates various 'signals of transcendence' in our world, phenomena which occur in the natural world but appear to point beyond it. Hope, order and humour are among such signs which are hard to account for on naturalistic premises, as is the argument for damnation – the rationale for people regarding the actions of some tyrant as so evil that even death is deemed insufficient penalty. How could this concept arise if there is no afterlife?

In *Time for Truth* Guinness gives a classic example of this positive break-in of transcendent truth when he tells of the conversion of W.H. Auden to Christianity. In an early film of the Second World War, Auden saw Germans screaming for the slaughter of Poles, howling for blood. At once he realized that his liberal view of human nature as basically good was hopelessly shallow. These people were denying every humane value. If he was to say this, however, he had to have some norm by which to make the judgement. There had to be an absolute standard by which inhumanities could be judged. His subsequent quest for that absolute standard led him in due course to Christ. I am grateful to Os Guinness for pointing out so clearly both the negative and positive ways of confronting postmodernist relativism. I have often used similar methods, and have found them to be effective.

Let us now pursue this apologetic approach from another angle. One of the essential faces of postmodernism is pluralism – the assertion that there are many equally valid ways to reach any conclusion. Truth is a chimera: you have your view, I have mine. It does not matter, so long as we do not inhibit each other's freedom to express our private values and follow our private beliefs. None of them is absolute. None can lay claim to 'truth'. Accordingly, there is no one way to God. All religions could lead his way, just as all spokes of a wheel lead to the hub. This untenable view is very widely held today.

There are two rather important facts to note. The first is that this relapse into pluralism arises not primarily from the resurgence of other faiths or any perceived failure in Christianity, but from the collapse of modernist convictions about universally valid accounts of the world. There is, according to postmodernists, no overarching truth in religion or morals. We all have to find our own way, and one way is as good as another.

The second fact is that, despite claims to the contrary, such pluralism is not new. It was the essential cultural background against which the drama of the Old Testament was played out. Pluralism was everywhere in the environment of ancient Israel: they were called to stand out against it and worship one God, with no runners-up. What is more, pluralism was no less prevalent in the background of the first Christians. Their message of one God who had revealed himself and rescued humanity exclusively in and through Jesus Christ was anathema in the Roman Empire, which was welcoming to a variety of faiths and made a virtue of pluralism. The intransigent attitude of the Christians invited persecution, and got it. Yet they stood firm and in due course they prevailed.

Pluralism is not new, therefore, and we are not to succumb to it. As Visser t'Hooft, the first General Secretary of the World Council of Churches, rightly observed, 'It is high time Christians should rediscover that Jesus Christ did not come to make a contribution to the religious storehouse of mankind, but that in him God reconciled the world to himself.' Of course a claim like that will be highly offensive to postmodern pluralists, but I think it is possible to persuade them that pluralism has some very strange assumptions. Here are three.

The first is the assumption that, because there are so many religious views in the world, they ought all to be regarded as equally valid. There is a deep-seated fallacy here, namely the attempt to deduce what ought to be from what is. There are diverse religious faiths, yes, but that says nothing about the basis on which we evaluate them, and it certainly does nothing to deny that one of them may be right and the rest inadequate. There may appear to be many ways out of a maze, yet all but one of them may be dead ends.

Another strange assumption is that all religions lead to God. That sounds wonderfully liberal, but it is nonsense just the same. How can all religions lead to God when some of them, such as Buddhism, do not believe in a personal God at all, while others, such as animism, believe in many gods? Some believe in an inscrutable deity who cares nothing about the world he set in progress, while others maintain that God is personal, loving and has come to rescue us from our alienation from him and from each other. The whole idea of 'God' is utterly different in these contrasting viewpoints. The notion that all religions lead to God is ludicrous.

The moral dimension of postmodern pluralism is equally defective. As Professor Alister McGrath has forcibly pointed out, even the most tolerant pluralist has difficulties with that aspect of Hinduism which justifies slavery by insistence on a fixed social order. There is no less difficulty in justifying the Hindu practice of forcibly burning alive a widow on her late husband's funeral pyre. This used to happen. Were the British wrong to put an end to this practice in the nineteenth century? On pluralist principles, they were. Can you believe that?

Yes, there is a place for apologetics even in this postmodern age, but it is a restricted one. Your average relativist is no more likely to change colour in the light of what I have written above than in the face of the self-evident absurdity in the claim that there are no universal truths – this, of course, being set out as a universal truth! We are not going to progress very far by logic. Here are some approaches which may prove more promising.

First, we need to recognize the force of postmodernism's reaction against power structures in society. Royalty, government, police, teachers, parents and the Church all come under heavy suspicion. All have come out with strong moral imperatives. All have at times been oppressive and dominating. The history of the twentieth century bleeds with the oppression of regimes – Victorian parents, Nazism, Communism, repressive Church structures – which marginalized those who did not go along with them. The Christian Church has rightly earned censure for its moralistic ethics, its zealous repudiation or suppression of other faiths in the course of its missionary advance, its restrictions on human sexuality and its ambiguous attitude to freedom. The Church must face up to failures in these directions which have rightly attracted the criticism of postmodernists. We must also point to the crucified Saviour at the heart of the Christian faith, the one who emptied himself of power in order to be available for the powerless. We need to point to him and live like him. There will be great power in weakness like that. It will have the appeal of Jesus.

Second, we must recognize that one of the great concerns of postmodernism is the hunger for community: not community in some vague, idealistic form, but tightly-knit communities of black people, gays, teenagers and so forth. Today's breakdown of the family and the mobility which removes us from human contact down our street tend to isolate people and breed a great longing for community. The Church has got to become the community which welcomes one and all with the unjudging love of Jesus Christ if it is to have any pulling power in today's fragmented society.

Third, we should understand that our society has become rootless. We have access to immediate knowledge about almost everything through the worldwide web, and yet generally have little understanding of what our community has stood for. Any sense of history has been eroded by the latest wave of fashion. Our postmodern condition is very unstable. People feel insecure. Many are scarcely able to cope with the stresses of modern life. Hence the current preoccupation with tarot cards, horoscopes and the Lottery. It is all part of an attempt to make the future secure. Not surprisingly in such a climate, there is considerable appeal in Eastern religions, which have a cyclical notion of time rather than the Judaeo-Christian linear view of time, in which the beginning and end are secure.

It would be all too easy for the Church to collude with this contemporary existentialism, and be bewitched into offering people the latest fashionable innovation, instead of helping people to root their security in the historical coming and dying and rising of the God who passionately cares about the salvation and eternal security of his creatures. There are abundant opportunities for the Church to advance in this transitional age of postmodernity, provided we are willing to proclaim the way of the cross with sensitivity and relevance, and to offer genuine community to people, while majoring on the story of what God has done for us within human history.

This leads on to a major thrust in Lesslie Newbigin's method of approaching postmodernism in seminal books such as *Foolishness to the Greeks*, *Truth to Tell*, *The Gospel in a Pluralist Society* and *Proper Confidence*. He does not merely ask the unmasking questions to which I have referred above. He is also very clear how we should proceed: we need to tell the Christian story in a fresh way. This is not simply our subjective story, attractive though that is these days. No: we may dare to present it as the story of humankind which has such power and yet such frailty, the 'meta-story' which could prove acceptable to postmodernists because it does not oppress but rather invites.

What a story it is! We have a grand story which does not attempt to force belief, but offers itself humbly as the best means of making sense of ourselves and our world. It tells of the triune God who is not an absolute potentate, such as Nietzsche reacted against, but a communion of persons ceaselessly offering themselves in self-giving love, joy and service. In this intensely person-oriented age, the Christian doctrine of the Trinity appears more relevant than it has been for centuries. We shall get nowhere if we present God, on the model of Aristotle and Aquinas, as the prime mover in the universe, sheer power bringing all into existence. Naked power like that is precisely what postmodernists are reacting against. Rather, the world was called forth by the undreamed-of love of God and responded to his call. When God said, 'Let there be...' there was. Creation has a history, as science emphasizes, and the human family is meant to cultivate the earth with mutual consideration and in co-operation with God the giver. In this way, some progress will be made towards leading the world to its true glory, which is to be a worthy theatre of all God's self-disclosure, a worthy counterpart to his undying love. That is a story which cannot be proved, but which makes sense and can speak powerfully to the heart of the postmodern environmentalist, while being entirely true to the teaching of the Bible.

Of course, the story does not end there. We must not conceal the terrible account of how we refuse that life of loving trust in God, how we insist on the rape of our environment and on our own determination of what is right and wrong, 'the knowledge of good and evil'. By our declaration of independence from God we have set in motion a rebellion which has corrupted the whole world and the course of every human life. And God comes to us, as Genesis so poignantly puts it, with his cry to Adam, 'Where are you?' It is an agonized cry, a cry of frustrated love. Here is a parent who so loves his child that anything which threatens that child's well-being and security evokes strong passions of love and wrath: they are, after all, the obverse and reverse of the same thing. So the story continues through the Bible, finding its climax in the coming, living and dying of God himself. Its supreme glory is his self-sacrificial involvement in our human predicament, drinking the cup of human suffering and wickedness to the brim. He stood in our place so that we might stand in his. The task was accomplished: he cried, 'It is finished.' What a message of comfort, assurance and invitation to the bruised postmodernists who have grown to distrust almost everyone and everything. Here is someone who loves us unconditionally and profoundly. He has shown he is worthy of our trust, however suspicious and streetwise we may be.

Is that the end of the story? Not at all. The resurrection followed. But can we believe so momentous a possibility? Might it just be conceivable that a life of such unique quality could not be liquidated for ever by the power of death? There were no independent witnesses to the resurrection, were there? Actually, that is not the case. All the witnesses were independent unbelievers in the resurrection until the risen Jesus met them. Why, though, was the resurrection not public in the same way that the crucifixion was public? Well, had that been so, it would have meant the end of everything. There would have been no more room for the believer or the unbeliever; no more room for disobedience or freely-given loyalty. God deliberately did not bring all things to a conclusion at that point. Instead, he committed the reality of Christ's victory to the company chosen to be the bearers of it – the Church. They give testimony to a truth which is still hidden from public demonstration, so as to leave people at liberty to respond to it in the freedom of faith. Our God looks not for forced surrender but for allegiance willingly given in love. That is something that has the capacity to move many a postmodernist soul.

Such is the heart of the great story which we have to communicate and in which we stand. We Christians are a part of the story, and that is why we need to proclaim it without embarrassment and to live it with enthusiasm. We will never be able to compel conviction, but we can bear testimony to the hidden reality which changes lives. I recall Lesslie Newbigin, whose friendship meant so much to me, using a memorable illustration for this point. An X-ray shows a bone structure which is invisible to the naked eye, but without which the body would collapse. The Church is called to be that X-ray plate – something which makes it possible for people to discern a reality which is not visible to the naked eye, but without which the world would collapse. This is the fact that God reigns: his kingdom is a present, if hidden, reality and awaits a future consummation.

It is therefore vital to realize, and to demonstrate by our way of life, that the Church is the community of hope. So much in our society tends towards despair. We in the Church must be a shaft of hope, living in the light of the resurrection and in anticipation of the day when all will be made plain and complete. This community of the Church is ultimately what draws others to Christ, or alienates them further from him.

There is no intellectual argument which enables us to prove our story. Aquinas and later Descartes tried to do precisely that and failed. Yet we can humbly bear testimony to it through a community living by faith, love and service. Moreover, once a person has submitted to the claims of Jesus Christ, they have the inner 'proof' in themselves. It is not a mathematical certainty, but it is an unshakeable conviction that, amidst the shifting sands of ideological debates and lifestyles, they have found reality, a rock that will not crumble. Real Christianity is a state of existence, not a state of mind. When that life is lived with joy and holiness, it has a tremendous appeal. After all, postmodernism is a joyless state. It began in disenchantment, following the failure of the 1960 student riots in Paris to change the world. That disenchantment continues in the view that truth and morality are chimeras. You cannot survive for long on that diet. Postmodernism will not last. It is a vacuum waiting to be filled.

The inability to clinch our case by argument alone should not dismay us. If ultimate reality were merely a series of disparate events which have no purpose, then observation and demonstrable truth would be the way to show it. If, however, the universe does not simply consist of a series of random events and atoms, if it has a purpose and if we have been given a glimpse of that ultimate purpose and that final reality through the Word made flesh, then there is no way we can expect others to come to know the truth except by faith – that is, by responding with a grateful 'Yes' to God's disclosure of it. That is a decision which we cannot force and they cannot avoid.

Accordingly, none of us is exempt from the risk of taking personal responsibility for the stance we adopt on these great matters of life and death, truth and falsehood. There is no spectator's gallery in the world from which we can coolly observe the follies and struggles of humankind. We are all on the ground floor together. There are indeed many stories on offer, many accounts of ourselves and our world, but we

Christians must not allow this fact to cow us. It gives us the chance to stake our claim with humility but confidence. Nowadays we have an unparalleled opportunity to gain a hearing if we bear testimony to what we have found. To be sure, we are a minority – but so what? This is the day of revolt against the big battalions. It is the day for the marginalized and the despised to state their case. Let us state ours boldly, and see if it stands up.

This call to witness is one of the most crying needs in the post-Christian West. Believers tend to keep themselves to themselves, to keep their heads down below the parapet, to be unwilling to stand up and be counted. They are afraid of being marked out as Christians, afraid of being shot down in argument. That fear is reasonable enough in debate: it is all too easy to get destroyed. There need be no such fear with testimony. You are not arguing a case when you give testimony, you are announcing a discovery. Others may not have found it, or may not be willing to seek it, but nobody can controvert your experience. It stands like a blazing torch in the darkness. Testimony is extremely powerful. It is saying, 'Life may seem a maze, but I believe I have been shown a way out. Come and try it for yourself.' I am distressed that in the West so little of this Christian confidence is displayed in daily life. It can have an enormous impact. It raises the question, 'Could that person be right? Could they have found something vital that I have missed? I must watch them to see if it rings true.'

I cannot exaggerate the need for testimony. Over the years, the Church has done a bad job in its preaching, and people greatly dislike being preached at. Testimony is a very different matter. There is a note of joy and confidence about the ringing cry, 'I have found...!' and the warm invitation, 'Come and see...!' Such testimony is regular and natural in the Two-Thirds World, where dynamic Christianity is growing fast, but it is not yet a characteristic of the West. It needs to be. There is nothing imperialistic about testimony to infuriate the post-modernist, nothing hierarchical, authoritarian or traditional.

It is a cry of joy, of light in the darkness, of a discovery so good that it must be shared. It speaks of experience, and experience is one of the highways to the heart of the postmodernist.

We are all called to bear witness to what God has shown us in Christ, and to do so joyfully, naturally, in normal language and non-churchy situations. We are called to bear witness to it as a truth we both proclaim and live by. People will rightly be watching to see if life and lip are consistent. We will not be able to prove our position. It will be spoken against and attacked, as it has been throughout history. Yet what a marvellous privilege it is to be called as witnesses, knowing that our account is not demonstrable, but knowing also that it is one of God's chosen agencies by which he breaks into other lives and embraces them in his love. It takes me back to the very pre-modern days of the first century, when St Paul was acutely aware of being engaged in a cosmic battle. He maintains that 'the god of this age' blinds the minds of unbelievers to keep them from seeing the glorious light of the gospel of Christ, who is the image of God. By way of contrast, God Almighty is striving to open blind eyes, and Paul cries out in confident testimony, 'The God who said, "Let light shine out of darkness," has shone in our hearts to give the light of the knowledge of the glory of God in the face of Christ.' How was this illumination, this advance of the gospel, achieved? By Christians renouncing disgraceful ways, commending themselves to everyone's conscience in the sight of God, being their servants for Jesus' sake, and preaching Jesus Christ as Lord. Such was God's way then, and it remains the same today.

I must add a word about 'preaching Jesus Christ as Lord'. Despite nervousness among some clergy and apologists, the fearless, relational proclamation of the gospel does transform postmodernist lives today as effectively as it has done in any period of Church history. It is simply not true that people will not listen to good preaching. They will. One should not say, 'I am telling you this from a position of greater knowledge or authority,' but, 'Listen to this and see if it doesn't speak to your condition.' God has called me to be a preacher of the gospel and I find that people respond today just as readily as they did in the days of modernism when I began my ministry – although the packaging of the unchanging gospel is radically different nowadays, because it is shaped towards very different needs and presuppositions. The contemporary Church's craven flight from preaching is unjustified, and the proof of the fact is the large number of conversions in those parts of the worldwide Church where there is strong biblical proclamation.

Of course, that makes us countercultural. You cannot escape it if you are going to bear witness to the Christian gospel, which has always flown in the face of human expectations, challenged human arrogance and far exceeded human hopes. There is no way we can agree with the postmodernists that there is no such thing as truth, that morals are essentially relative and that there are many equally valid paths to God. We must insist on truth and morality, and that will make us stand out like a sore thumb. Yet is that not always the position the Church has had to adopt when it has been true to its Founder?

Gene Veith makes an interesting observation in his fine book, *Guide to Contemporary Culture*. In the days of the Roman Empire, the Church claimed to possess exclusive truth. This affronted the cultural and religious relativism of the day, which affirmed the validity of all religions (so long, of course, as everyone burned incense to Caesar). The Christians were persecuted, at times to extinction, because they claimed to possess *the truth* in the midst of this relativistic morass. Nevertheless, the gospel grew.

It was much the same in the days of the Enlightenment. Many in the Church chose conformity with the Age of Reason. They surrendered to its rationalism. They jettisoned belief in miracles and reinterpreted Christianity without reference to divine revelation. This was the first version of liberal Christianity. Yet, in that very same century, one of the most extensive and powerful revivals of all time took place, with the Great Awakening led by Jonathan Edwards in America and the Evangelical Revival led by Wesley and Whitefield in England. Here were Christians prepared to be countercultural, prepared to stand against the trend of their times. God honoured their witness to the truth of his revelation, and vast numbers were convinced.

Twentieth-century existentialism and subjectivism have affected the Church very strongly. Most of the mainline churches in the West have surrendered to this tendency and are currently in decline, but in America the fundamentalists have grown and become the mainstream, while in Britain the Evangelicals and the charismatics are currently leading the way. In wartime Germany it was not the State Lutheran Church but Bonhoeffer's Confessing Church that had the courage to stand against Hitler – and to prevail. Polish Catholicism undermined Communism, and Eastern Orthodoxy outlasted Soviet domination. The Church is always called to be a 'sign of contradiction' in the world. As such it will be spoken against and reviled, whatever the prevailing philosophy. Yet it will also bear humble but firm witness to the truth and, however much people rail against it and proclaim that there is no such thing, truth will prevail. It always has, and it always will.

CHAPTER 9

Evangelism

Evangelism is in my blood. I think it has been ever since I made the discovery of my life, back in my teens, that Jesus Christ was alive and available. I began sharing this discovery by inviting other boys to the house party at Iwerne Minster which had meant so much to me. Several of them found Christ for themselves, and I shared in their joy. When I went up to university, I at once started to talk to my friends about Jesus Christ whenever it seemed appropriate, and once again had the sheer delight of seeing many lives changed by that same encounter which had revolutionized my own. Apart from personal conversations, one of the great ways of helping people to faith while I was at Oxford was to invite them to an evangelistic address which was given every Sunday during term-time. This may seem old hat now, but back in the 1950s and '60s it was highly effective.

After Oxford, I discovered that the impact of Christ could be just as great in the Army. I had two years of National Service from 1953 to 1955, and spent some of it as an ordinary gunner, some as an officer, and the last year as assistant adjutant of my regiment, which meant I was able to make some small impact on the structures.

I well recall my first night in the Army. Basic training deliberately set out to break you, and we were a miserable 30 men crammed into a barrack room, 'bulling' boots as Radio Luxembourg blared out its raw music. It so happened that I entered the forces with a Christian friend, and with much trepidation we knelt to pray on that first night, to the raucous mirth and derision of our comrades. I don't think our prayers were very profound, but at least we made a stand. Next morning the man in the bed opposite said to me, 'Can yer 'elp me, mate? I've got wife trouble.' Well, I did not even have a wife at that stage, but it was a start! Before a week had gone by, half a dozen of us were praying publicly in the barrack room and had discovered a friendly sergeant's room where we held Bible studies. The first night we were let out on the town, I joined in with a Salvation Army open-air event and spoke at it. Back in the barrack room, people were beginning to be interested. We Christians did not seem to be driven to despair by the system, tough though it was. We seemed happy in uncongenial circumstances. Why? It is very easy to explain the gospel in such a situation, and we saw a number of our colleagues in the squad become Christians.

After I was commissioned as an officer, outreach took a different form. A subaltern was responsible for 30 men, and the way those responsibilities were discharged gave ample opportunity to demonstrate the gospel. Once I was assistant adjutant of the regiment and had constant daily contact with Brigade Headquarters, it was not difficult to get permission to have a Billy Graham relay in the Garrison Theatre. This was in the days when Dr Graham's mission addresses were widely dispersed through telephone lines terminating in a little black box placed on a table – the ultimate refutation of any charge of emotionalism! We trained counsellors. We invited the colonels of the four regiments and gave them front-row seats. We had the regimental sergeant majors organizing troops to fill the place with chairs. Many soldiers came, and civilians as well. There was a substantial response, and some of those who became Christians on that occasion are exercising a lively witness in the area to this day.

What fun it was to mobilize the Army for the cause of the gospel! Christian homes, too, had a real part to play in helping people discover a living faith. There was a home in the adjoining town to which I would often go for Sunday lunch, taking with me someone I was hoping to introduce to the love of God. The impact of a home that overflowed with such love was remarkable and made conversion seem natural, almost inevitable. A true Christian home can be immensely attractive.

The love of this Xian home made evang. easy

A model for evangelism

After the Army came Cambridge, and within a couple of years I was ordained and launched into a ministry of pastoral work, teaching, leadership and evangelism. At that time the most gifted evangelist in Britain was John Stott. His church, All Souls, Langham Place, adjoined the BBC in the heart of London's West End and soon became the flagship for evangelism. It was he who embodied the truth that the regular life of the parish church, not the occasional evangelistic invasion, is the prime agency in mission.

There are many qualities needed in a church which seeks to be engaged in continuous evangelism, and Stott's church had most of them. It was warm and welcoming, despite being so large. That is essential. An evangelistic church is, in a sense, a maternity ward and maternity wards must be warm. The love which is so essential in a church was nurtured in home fellowship groups. These are normal now, but were much more innovative in those days. The church was deliberately organized under the Word of God. They did not make their message up as they went along, but anchored it firmly to the testimony of the New Testament – 'the faith once and for all delivered to the saints'.

The innovative Christian initiatives that sprang from All Souls are too numerous to mention, even if I knew them all. They emerged from a radical openness to the Holy Spirit. It is God's church, not the Rector's, and the Spirit must be allowed to have his way. That is one reason why prayer is so important. Nothing of substance is achieved without it, and it is through prayer that the mind of the Spirit is discerned. The midweek Prayer Meeting at All Souls became a major institution for the congregation before most churches in Britain had got round to having one at all. An evangelizing church must inevitably be a praying church, for the very good reason that God alone is the evangelist. We human beings cannot bring anyone to faith in Christ. Only the Spirit of God can do that. In prayer we confess as much and cry to him to do his sovereign work.

Another vital quality if a church is to be effective in evangelism is every-member ministry. The congregation must get deeply involved, and not rely on the pastor to do it all. This is something that Stott pioneered in England, and it has become a recognized quality in active churches. He refused the temptation to be a prima donna, as it were, and surrounded himself with a team committed to equipping the congregation for their witness to Christ. Training therefore became imperative, and under John Stott's leadership a superb training course was put in place, with the successful candidates being commissioned by the bishop. Churchpeople are not going to be vocal about their faith unless they know what they are talking about. Stott set out to train people at a depth which would enable them to hold up their heads in the midst of the surrounding scepticism. He had an equal determination to reach the mind and the will. 'Your mind matters,' was one of his emphases, and he worked to fill the minds of his congregation with good biblical teaching and competent apologetics.

There were two other characteristics of All Souls which stood out in those days. One was the creation of nurture groups for new Christians. You might think that this is absolutely obvious, but no. Stott was the first to follow through an evangelistic address with a course for new believers, called a Nursery Class, which lasted for three months. Nowadays, when there is so much emphasis on the journey of faith rather than the moment of commitment, the nurture group is fundamental. We take it for granted. Then, however, there was much poor evangelism which appealed for an immediate response and then left people to their own devices. The Nursery Class was a repudiation of this bad practice.

The other feature that struck me has not been so carefully followed elsewhere. All Souls had a passion for excellence. There was great attention to detail, and everything was done to the glory of God. Whether it was the bookstall, the music in worship, the leading of prayers, the training of lesson readers – everything was given the utmost attention. It was a mute but powerful message. It said, 'Our God is great. Nothing but the best is good enough for him.'

One has only to rehearse these qualities to see how much they have affected whole sections of the Church in subsequent years. Yet many of them were brand new at the time, because Evangelicals had not done well in the first part of the twenti-eth century. They had become a beleaguered few, with a fortress mentality, defending minutiae of doctrine and practice while people perished from spiritual famine. John Stott's church showed that things could be different, and encouraged a whole generation of clergy to expect great things from God and attempt great things for God.

Those were some of the qualities John Stott sought to incul-cate in his church. Now for some of the evangelistic outreach-es he initiated. One of these was the guest service. A guest service is simply a service that is totally subordinated to a single aim: helping those who do not know Christ to find him. That one aim governs all the publicity, the personal invitations, the visiting beforehand, the choice of music, the nature of the address, the use of testimony, the challenge to commitment and the introduction of nurture groups. It is a well-tried procedure which has been spawned all over the country since then, but it was very new in the 1950s – and it began in All Souls.

At the opposite extreme from the guest service was the one-to-one conversation between Christian and non-Christian, and John Stott gave a lot of care to training people in this respect. Another thing which he took over and revamped was the running of missions in different parts of the country, aided by a team that could work closely with the local church and get alongside people who had been affected by the mission talks. It was All Souls which took the initiative in running Agnostics Anonymous groups, generally built around food, where those who did not share a Christian faith were exposed to an intelligent and warm-hearted encounter with those who did. There is no preaching in a group like this. The Christian leader responds to the particular difficulties the agnostics have, and it has proved a very effective form of ministry. At around that period, David Watson's *Jesus Then and Now*, a high-quality video dealing with a number of common objections to Christianity, became an invaluable tool in those Agnostics Groups.

John Stott is a convinced Anglican, and was quick to grasp the opportunities afforded by the occasional offices of baptism, marriage, confirmation and funerals. His book *Your Confirmation* became the most widely used tool for confirmation preparation, and nobody was presented to the bishop for confirmation at All Souls without a personal interview with the Rector to see if they had a real faith to confirm! As someone who was prepared for marriage by him, I know that he used such occasions to press the claims of Christ gently but firmly on the couples with whom he met.

A further area of outreach which was enthusiastically grasped by John Stott was ministry towards specialist groups. One of these was the medical fraternity. Harley Street was in the parish and they used to have a tremendous service on St Luke's Day, taking a major theme of interest both to the church and the doctors. He also appointed a chaplain to the big London stores and initiated a chaplaincy in the London Polytechnic, which was situated in his area. Clearly most churches will not have such specialized areas for ministry available within their parishes, but if they are alert evangelistically, they will spare no effort to make appropriate inroads with the gospel wherever opportunity offers.

The media often appear to have little time for the church, but John Stott achieved a position of honoured trust in the BBC. They used his church to record their daily radio service, and he was frequently a guest on their programmes. Writing is another form of media work, and Stott achieved widespread outreach through the production of an immensely influential booklet called *Becoming a Christian*, as well as his larger book, *Basic Christianity*. Not every parish will have the BBC within its boundaries, or a minister of the calibre of John Stott as a writer – but all have pen and paper, and all have some form of regular publicity which they could use much more imaginatively. Stimulated by John Stott's example, many have learnt to do just that.

Stott could not contain his passion for the gospel within the parish of All Souls, and he began to respond to the many invitations to speak in universities. He saw what a critically important area it was to address, for from these universities would emerge some of the future leaders in Church and State. He became one of the first and most effective missioners in the triennial missions put on by the university Christian Unions. His mixture of clarity, intellectual rigour, spiritual power and willingness to challenge people for decision had an enormous effect, and many students at Oxford, Cambridge, Durham and overseas institutions such as the University of British Columbia profited from these missions. Not only did John Stott lead these himself, but he inspired a whole new generation of missioners to do likewise.

Two other of John Stott's initiatives in those early days at All Souls stand out, and have greatly affected not only the Evangelical community but the Church at large. One was extensive ministry among overseas students. All Souls supports many missionaries overseas, and it might have rested content with that. It did not. It set about actively befriending through its members the many visitors from overseas who lived nearby. They realized that a mission field was all around them, and they went out to make friends with them, not with any hidden motive but simply to embody the unconditional love with which Jesus has loved us all. Many Christians in that period used to bewail the fact that they could not go to 'the mission field', but were oblivious of the mission field all around them.

The final ministry to which All Souls gave great attention was work among the disadvantaged. It would have been all too easy for a large, fashionable, wealthy, middle-class church in the West End to go on its way oblivious of the seamier side of life represented by the adjacent Tottenham Court Road, but John Stott took on that challenge too. The Clubhouse was specifically designed to minister to the unchurched and under-privileged youth of the neighbourhood, and it became one of the most rewarding and exciting of All Souls' initiatives. When, at the Keele Congress in 1967, the Evangelical con-science at large became sensitive to Britain's crying social needs, there was already an outstanding example of imagina-tive, practical, nonjudgemental social outreach in place.

A changing perspective

If John Stott at All Souls gave the lead in this new and many-textured type of evangelism some 40 years and more ago, many churches learned from his example, and thus began the current resurgence of Evangelical Christianity in the Anglican Church in England. One of Stott's creations which helped in this resurgence was Eclectics, a regular gathering of young Evangelical clergy for study, fellowship, planning and prayer. Eclectics grew and developed chapters in different areas of the country, through which the new vitality, ideas and confidence in the gospel displayed by Stott and his colleagues became widely disseminated. Many young clergy learned what had never been taught them in college and what they had not experienced in the older Evangelicalism to which they were accustomed: how to lead guest services, how to nurture new believers, how to run lay leadership courses, how to lead missions and preach for decision. I was one of them.

Yet evangelism was not easy then, any more than it is now. It is always costly, for it springs from personal involvement in God's own costly self-giving for the unreached. It is always difficult, because evangelists have an imperfect understanding of the good news they carry – it is far greater than themselves and their insights. It is difficult, too, because the Church is an imperfect expression of what Christian life should be, and in consequence tends to obscure the truth it proclaims. And it is difficult because the human heart is a rebel, and men and women are reluctant to surrender their prized independence to the great Lover. Evangelism has never been easy.

Moreover, in the 1960s and '70s a massive revolution in thought was taking place. It made us re-evaluate our whole approach to evangelism. The context in which we were called to operate was no longer dominated by the rationalism which emerged from the Enlightenment, but was influenced much more by the existentialism which followed the Second World War and developed into the postmodernism of today. I looked at this in some detail in the previous chapter. It was a massive change of perspective with which we are only now beginning to grapple effectively.

The essence of the modern world view had been its conviction that there is one single principle which undergirds all knowledge – namely reason. That hypothesis is no longer convincing to a great many people in the postmodern period in which we now live. It began to be undermined by Darwin's theory of natural selection, Freud's psychological assertions, and Marx's economic theory. None of them left reason unscathed as queen of the intellectual world, although the deconstructionist conclusions which destroyed the foundations of truth, morality and meaning were not explicitly drawn until the 1960s. Today there is great suspicion of all 'meta-stories', all attempts to find an umbrella to erect over our fragmented experiences. Accordingly, we find ourselves in a climate which denies all absolutes, despite the logical fallacy of making so absolute a claim. It is an age which distrusts all authority figures and structures. There is deep cynicism about institutions. Morality has no norms. Scorn of the past is matched by loss of hope for the future.

There is, however, one unexpected feature in this deconstructed society, and that is the hunger for spirituality. 'One of the great ironies of our time,' wrote Dr John Drane, 'is the way Western churches are declining at the same time as the sense of spiritual search in the community is increasing in intensity and power.' People are not looking to the churches to quench this irrepressible hunger: they do not believe the churches have much spirituality. Yet you see it in the appeal of alternative medicine, the occult, astrology, the New Age, drugs and the plethora of new cults and superstitions.

It goes without saying, therefore, that in the last 30 years, while these massive cultural shifts have been becoming increasingly apparent, evangelism has become more difficult than ever. Three of the classical routes by which people used to enter into Christian experience and discipleship have a great deal less appeal in postmodern society.

Belonging to an institution, the Church, has little appeal. This was the characteristic Catholic way of Christian incorporation. Nowadays many dismiss it as part of the hierarchical, institutional life against which postmoderns react.

Believing in dogma is anathema to postmoderns. Who is to tell them they need to repent? Who is to tell them what to believe? They accept no authority but their own, and regard truth claims as merely other people's power games. That does not help the traditional Evangelical approach to evangelism.

Intellectual argument leaves postmoderns cold. For one thing, it has a rationalistic smell about it. For another, connected abstract argument is a nonstarter. That makes it hard for the sweet reasonableness of the best liberal apologetic to cut any ice. Perhaps those most likely to impact postmodern

society are the Pentecostals and the charismatics. They put a
lot of emphasis on experience, and that accords well with
postmodern concerns – but they are liable to get the response,
'I'm delighted that Jesus helps you to get fulfilment. I get mine
from my channeller.'

These are difficult days. No part of the Church enjoys easy
success in the evangelistic enterprise. As a result, there has
been a great deal of hard thinking in recent years, as Christians
have sought to reappraise their evangelistic approaches. Here
are some of the provisional conclusions that are winning wide
acceptance among those (of whatever theological position)
who have a heart for evangelism.

There is a clear trend away from the big crusade meeting as
the main method of evangelism. Crusade evangelism and personal evangelism used to be the two main ways of reaching
non-Christians 40 years ago, but that is no longer the case.
There is less and less appeal in the crusade model. Customers
are increasingly wary of coming to be shot at by anyone other
than Billy Graham. Who can blame them? In any case, the
fallout from this kind of evangelism was unacceptably great. It
has become clear that the local church is the proper place for
ongoing, culturally appropriate evangelism. During the
Decade of Evangelism leading up to the millennium, practically all churches began to put evangelism on their agenda. At the
very least they began to discuss it, even if they did not get
round to doing any! No longer is it a taboo subject that must
not be mentioned in polite company. In one way or another,
local churches in the West are making determined efforts to
reach out to people who do not go to church and do not know
Christ. Evangelism is now recognized as being far too important to be left to the Evangelicals, or to enthusiastic para-
church groups. It is seen as a primary part of the life of the
local church, not an optional extra. That is sheer gain.

Equally, there is a clear change of emphasis from crisis to
process in evangelism. There are several good reasons for this.
One is that people today are far more ignorant of the gospel

than they used to be, and need to hear it a good many times before they respond. Another is that bringing the challenge of Christ to people through a warm, friendly process like an Alpha course allows them to find their own level and make their own response when they are ready. This is much more natural than having an evangelist fulminate for instant conversion at the end of an address. It also enables cautious enquirers to watch others responding to Christ, to make their own response in due time, and to see that initial response flowering into discipleship in the company of others in a similar situation.

A further reason for the current emphasis on process is the contemporary reluctance, particularly among postmodernists, to become committed to anything. A course gives them the courage to do this. Naturally, there is still the need for crisis: you cannot drift into the kingdom of God, but it is crisis within a process. That is why courses such as Alpha and Emmaus have had such spectacular success in recent years. In the year 1998/9, more than 400,000 people were added to the Church through Alpha alone. Worldwide, well over 2 million have become Christians through its agency.

When I started out in evangelism, there was a good deal of emphasis on technique. Nowadays there is much less of this – perhaps too little, because a great many Christians have no idea how they can actually help their friends to faith. As I said earlier, it is almost true that we can only evangelize friends, and without question we must all earn the right to speak. There is a lot more relational evangelism around today than there used to be, and a large number of modern converts would attribute the main factor in their new life to relations or friends who loved them and persevered with them. Personal relationships have always been more important than evangelistic methods, and the most effective witness among everyday contacts comes from natural, relaxed, loving and unembarrassed Christian workmates.

Another trend making itself felt today is the shift from speaking to listening. It can go to extremes, of course, as if we have nothing to declare, and as if listening was a gospel therapy in itself. Nevertheless, in an age when thought forms are so confused and disparate, and when people's situations and needs are so diverse, it has become more necessary than ever to listen to where people are before charging in with the gospel message. As in medicine, diagnosis is essential before treatment.

I also notice a change from indiscriminate to more focused outreach. Instead of general evangelistic events, there is more emphasis on reaching a particular sector of society in a way that is appropriate for it. Children, young people, professionals, sportspeople, working men and women, all respond much better when they are reached by an approach which is specifically geared to their situation and concerns. While the celebrated 'homogeneous unit principle' is heresy if applied to the Church (that most heterogeneous of all entities), it is a wise and helpful way to evangelize particular groupings in our culture. Fortunately, evangelists are becoming more aware of that fact.

If we are trying to reach different slices of the social cake, it is wise to approach them where they are most relaxed. There is, accordingly, in much of the best modern evangelism, a shift from operating on our turf to theirs. Instead of expecting people to come to church, where we feel most comfortable, it is much better to go to them in the place where they feel most at home. It may be in a bar, a home, a restaurant, a sports hall – almost anywhere other than church property, from which most people today feel a real sense of alienation. We are being driven back to the way in which the first Christians spread their good news. They did not own any buildings: they made use of common ground to proclaim Christ.

A further shift is discernible in the light of postmodern developments which are more concerned with feeling and experience than with dogma. We are seeing in much of our evangelism a gradual shift from emphasis on doctrine to emphasis on spirituality, from things that must be believed to the God who must be encountered. Many churches and Christian Unions which used to be most severe in ensuring that there was little in the way of worship at an evangelistic event, for fear of putting words into the mouths of the visitors which they might not mean, now recognize the power of worship in evangelism. There is a new willingness to expose people to a passionate body of men and women worshipping God with all their heart and soul. It draws people in. They are intrigued and attracted by encountering something much bigger than themselves.

Of course, there is danger in this if we rest content with experience. The gospel is good news about what God has done, and therefore we can never evacuate a strong doctrinal element from evangelism. The Word without the Spirit can easily dry up. The Spirit without the Word can all too readily blow up, however, and there is plenty of evidence to prove it. Nevertheless, it is wise, as well as biblical, to approach people at the point of their experience and help them to discover the Lord as he relates to that, however limited the rest of their understanding may be. The dying thief had very little concept of the gospel, but he made saving contact with Jesus. I have found that Christ's words, 'I have come so that you may have life, life in all its fullness,' have a great resonance with today's spiritually hungry young people. In the 1960s we were clear that believing Christian truth preceded belonging to the Christian community. Nowadays it is not so tidy. Belonging, albeit in the guise of enquirer, often precedes believing, and our evangelism needs to take account of that.

There is an associated postmodern trend which is also discernible today. A lot of effective evangelism places less stress on declaration than it does on celebration. This is all the more significant because it is so widely believed that Christianity is killjoy and dull. Here again there are obvious dangers to avoid: there is pain as well as celebration in the service of Christ. Yet so much of his invitation in the Gospels is cast in celebratory mould that it would be foolish to dismiss it.

Everyone loves a party, and the kingdom of heaven is precisely that, a party thrown by God himself. Many thousands discover Christ in the exhilaration of a celebration like Greenbelt, Spring Harvest, New Wine or, in another key, Taizé. I find I do more and more of my evangelism at dinners, breakfasts, parties and on holidays. Jesus is the one who made more than a hundred gallons of wine at Cana. He is not against celebration!

Today's society is perplexed about truth. Many doubt whether there is any such thing, so to hammer the gospel home as 'truth' may be counterproductive, and to some postmoderns could seem rather like intellectual fascism. On the other hand, our society is profoundly concerned with issues of personal identity, meaning in life, happiness and purpose. Who am I? What am I worth? How can I cope? Where am I headed? These are the sorts of questions that simmer away under the surface of a great many apparently happy people. I have seen evangelism concentrate more and more on such topics in recent years. It is probably not wise to begin with 'sin' today, although people are sinners, just as they always have been. They misunderstand the word, and the concept of an absolute standard which they have broken goes against all their postmodern instincts. Instead, a topic like loneliness, alienation, frustration, stress, the Lottery, even the millennium, will be a much more fruitful way to gain their attention and help them to see how the gospel speaks to their felt needs. Aim to stimulate their hunger: that is the key strategy. Then is the time to point to our rebellion against God as the deepest source of our human malaise. There is unquestionably a move from the search for truth to the search for identity and purpose nowadays, and the wise evangelist will follow that trail – without for a moment surrendering the truth dimension. It may simply not be the most profitable entry port.

Another change is more welcome. Evangelism is seen in the most vital circles today not as the function of the preacher so much as of the living community. When you encounter a church which buzzes with life, love and laughter, you are inevitably drawn towards it. It becomes a positive honey pot. This is not to denigrate the role of the preacher: it is simply to contextualize it. I think I have realized this for many years. Certainly, I made a point of taking teams out with me on evangelistic enterprises. At St Aldate's, we did a lot with teams. Every September we would conduct a carefully planned outreach in a city where most, if not all, the local churches agreed to take part. Our team – staff, a few church members and the rest students – was usually around a hundred in number, and we would pour ourselves into the lives of the church and community for two full weeks. We would do dance and drama in the open air, sometimes even congas in the main street, and it certainly made an impact. We would send teams daily into all the schools, run concerts for teenagers, visit old people's homes, do drama and proclamation at the railway station in front of commuters, engage in any and all church activities, and put on special events, dinners, breakfast meetings and the like.

If you bear in mind that the average age of our team members was about 21, you will realize that their effectiveness did not spring from a great depth of Christian experience and theological acumen. It was the note of joyful celebration that made such an impact. They all had a lively faith in Christ. They all knew his touch on their lives. They had all learnt to tell of the difference he had made to them. Most of them were able to lead an enquirer to Christ. The result was marvellous. People were at first cynical, then impressed, then often converted. Frequently a hundred or more local people were drawn into the Christian community by these student missions. They were struck by the freshness, the sincere joy and celebration, the sheer sense of discovery shown by these young men and women. It was very attractive. We did not understand in the 1970s that 'celebration' was a key way in for the gospel, but we just did it and found it to be so. Needless to say, it still is. Parties, dances and meals are prime contexts in which people can relax and consider the claims of Christ.

I have noticed, moreover, a real change in recent years from the rather imperialist churchly independence of the late 1960s to a newer, humbler, more co-operative way of doing evangelism. It is now not unusual to find a whole town or a complete Anglican deanery joining together for a major evangelistic outreach across all the barriers of denomination and churchmanship. They are prepared to sink a good many of their tribal loyalties in order to come together and make Christ known in the locality. This welcome change is on the increase. I have been involved in many such missions, embracing Christians of every stripe, and I find it enormously exciting that we can unite on the massive weight of things on which we can agree, rather than concentrating on the few which divide. The future clearly lies in transdenominational partnership. Why should God honour denominational insularity in his gospel of reconciliation? Interestingly, the large numbers of young people who come to Christ these days are totally disinterested in denominations. They will go where there is life, whatever the label of the church. Ecclesiastical authorities abhor such an attitude, and it can certainly lead to shallowness in allegiance. Nonetheless, if the old wineskins will not be flexible, the new wine will find new wineskins – as the rapid growth of Vineyard Churches in Britain during the past decade abundantly shows.

There is perhaps also just the glimmer of a change from activism to intercession. In the West we have been besotted by methodology, but have hardly begun to tread the path of serious intercession, which is the hallmark of the massive church growth in Africa and Asia. There are signs, however, that we may be beginning to wake up to the priority of prayer. It is through sustained and costly intercession that the gospel has spread in Korea, from nothing a hundred years ago to the current situation where it embraces more than a third of the nation. It is through prayer that the gospel has made such inroads in the urban wildernesses of Argentina, as Harvest

Ministries have demonstrated. It is estimated that at least 170 million Christians worldwide are committed to praying daily for world evangelization and spiritual revival. There are now citywide networks and national prayer networks in all four countries of the UK. Some 50 million people are praying regularly for a breakthrough in the Muslim lands of the 10/40 window. The international day of prayer for the persecuted Church normally has 300,000 people praying in more than a hundred countries. Prayer is coming into its own, even in the prayerless West. Prayer is always going to be the most important part of evangelism, for in prayer we confess that it is not our ability and expertise which achieves anything, but God's. In prayer we express our utter dependence on him – and, when his people cast themselves on him alone, God is free to act.

Special initiatives

I cannot close this chapter on evangelism without mentioning several important initiatives which have taken place in Britain in recent years. Perhaps most significant were the repeated crusades of Billy Graham, at Harringay in 1954 and in the years that followed. It is hard to exaggerate the effect of these. To begin with, the Church hierarchy was very scornful of them, while journalists, debutantes, pop singers, prizefighters and jailbirds got converted. Later, when Billy Graham became 'respectable', bishops were only too pleased to sit on the platform when he was speaking. I was working in a theological college during most of those years, and it was thrilling to see ordinand after ordinand coming to the college, having been brought to Christ through Billy Graham. We will never be able adequately to show our gratitude. It was through Dr Graham that a new appreciation of evangelism began to emerge in Britain. It was due to him, under God, that hundreds of thousands of men and women in the bleak postwar years turned to the living God. Other evangelists like Luis

Palau, great though they were, never had an influence in Britain that was remotely comparable.

Nowadays, in J. John and Steve Chalke, we are growing our own brand of evangelist who can speak both to the media and to the big rally. Let us thank God for them, and pray for more like them. The average man or woman in Britain pays almost no attention to the Church and the pronouncements of its clergy, who appear to belong to a bygone era. When a distinguished politician, sportsperson, singer or entertainer becomes a passionate and articulate ambassador of Jesus Christ, however, people do sit up and take notice. I am so thankful for Billy Graham, and I pray that God will raise up others after him to carry the torch, but I long just as earnestly for skilled Christian scriptwriters to emerge. We need such creative people to help write the soap operas which increasingly provide not only the nightly entertainment but the main understanding of life, relationships and morals for countless thousands. That might prepare the way for a major spiritual breakthrough in this country, and open the ears and hearts of our people to the gospel which they currently reject.

I have already touched on one of the most effective of all modern methods of evangelism, at least in the West – the Alpha course. It is immensely appropriate for the postmodern world, catering as it does for the inchoate hunger for spirituality, the questing intellect, the longing for community, the investigation of life and what it is all about. Nobody in an Alpha course pontificates with an air of authority: the teaching sessions, of the highest technical quality, are open for discussion and disagreement. That appeals. So does the day or weekend on the Holy Spirit, which gives members a real opportunity to open themselves up to God the Holy Spirit and experience his reality and power in their own lives. There are so many other ways in which Alpha speaks to our times: lightness of touch is one of them. They recently produced for mass distribution a special 'millennium package', including a corkscrew (for celebration) and an invitation to an Alpha course (for edification). The sheer imaginativeness and professionalism of Alpha is awe-inspiring.

I find it amusing, and even a little pathetic, that some central churchmen and Anglo-Catholics complain that there is too little about the sacraments and too much about the Holy Spirit in Alpha, while the Roman Catholic Church has no such problems, but takes Alpha on board in a big way. We may be very thankful that so broadly unitive a course has won such general recognition across the world, binding together Catholics, Baptists, Anglicans, Methodists and Pentecostals in an introduction to basic Christianity.

There are several other initiatives which deserve a mention in this context. One is the formation of the College of Evangelists. It was launched in October 1999 by the two Archbishops after more than a decade of debate, evasion, procrastination and objection. I am delighted. It is so valuable to have a list of gifted evangelists made available to the whole Church. Male and female, ordained and lay, those who have well-established evangelistic gifts and track records are (after due scrutiny) invited to become members of the College of Evangelists, and it goes some way towards rectifying a distressing lack of recognition for evangelists within the Church for many a long year. Hitherto, as far as the Anglican Church was concerned, you could only find 'evangelists' within the ranks of the Church Army. Excellent though that body of men and women is, it does not exhaust the evangelistic potential of the Anglican Church! The foundation of the College of Evangelists may, in the coming decades, be seen as a small but important step in recalling this country to God. Some 30 or so evangelists were recognized in the first year, and the numbers are being added to annually, as gifted evangelists emerge and are recognized.

While this is happening at the official level, something which could turn out to be even more significant is taking place at grass-roots level. For some years the Rev. Dan Cozens, the leader of an evangelistic organization known as

Through Faith Missions and one of the Six Preachers at Canterbury Cathedral, has been leading 'The Walk of 1,000 Men'. These walks gather together many hundreds of men who go out to where people are and bring the gospel to them. Six massive missions have now taken place in different parts of the British Isles, and more than 3,000 team members have been trained in personal evangelism and evangelistic speaking. They do most of this in one of the hardest locations, the pub. That is where you meet men; that is where they are relaxed and ready to talk – so that is primarily where you find team members, who give up their summer holidays to go on these Walks. I have been with them, and it is thrilling, challenging work.

Whereas some of these lay evangelists have been ordained and others have become overseas missionaries, the vast majority are waiting to be used not just for a couple of weeks in the summer but on a regular basis. That is why Dan Cozens is inaugurating his transdenominational Order of Evangelists. He plans to put full- and part-time evangelists to work in struggling urban and rural churches. There they can become catalysts for outreach and the reversal of the Church's numerical decline. He and his colleagues at Through Faith Missions are putting a thoughtful course of preparation in place, and will offer moral and, if necessary, financial support to these evangelists when they are in the field. This is an astonishing initiative for a single clergyman to undertake, with no official resources or backing behind him. Yet it is precisely the sort of thing God has blessed and multiplied down the ages, and it would be just like him to do it again! It could be very important to 'watch this space'.

The other significant initiative was the launch of Springboard in 1992, with a considerable fanfare of trumpets, in St Paul's Cathedral. This was the vision of George Carey, the Archbishop of Canterbury, who longed to make a personal contribution to the Decade of Evangelism in the final decade of the twentieth century. Despite initial scepticism from some of the bishops, Springboard gained the support of the Archbishop of York, who became a joint sponsor, and before long it was on its way. Indeed, it seems to have been almost the only substantial initiative actually undertaken by the Anglican Church in the Decade of Evangelism. To be sure, there was a discussion forum on evangelism among the various denominations, put together by the Board of Mission, but they decided only to review what was going on and declined to initiate anything. Springboard did initiate a lot. It consisted of Bishop Michael Marshall, recalled by Archbishop Carey from America, my wife Rosemary and myself, recalled from Canada, and Martin Cavender. Martin is a most gifted and gracious lawyer who left his safe post as a Diocesan Registrar for the thankless task of mobilizing this small Springboard team across the country, wherever the bishops invited us.

The whole Springboard initiative was very near to the Archbishop's heart. Though not primarily an evangelist himself, he contrives to do the work of an evangelist by holding no less than six teaching missions a year in his Diocese of Canterbury. What previous Archbishop has done that? By getting together a body of donors keen to see England re-evangelized, he raised well over a million pounds for Springboard and other outreach initiatives, knowing that, if he waited for Synod to fund them, he would wait a very long time. This enabled him to offer Springboard as a gift to the Church. We could give our services free, because our salaries and expenses were paid by the funds which the Archbishop had raised. You do not often get something for nothing these days, and that gesture of his has been enormously appreciated. He spent quality time with the team members four times in the year, monitoring and encouraging us. Springboard would never have happened without him. I remember his predecessor Archbishop Runcie once bewailing to me his inability to get Michael Marshall and myself back to Britain to give a lead in evangelism. What Runcie bewailed, Carey achieved.

We quickly gelled as a team, and set out to hold together, embody and teach evangelism, spirituality and apologetics, as if they were three legs of a single stool. We found our main work to lie in conducting Travelling Schools among the clergy in different dioceses, helping them to start operating effectively in evangelism. We also took great delight in offering specific teaching on outreach to the Parochial Church Councils, whom nobody seemed to have taken pains with hitherto. Predictably, we had mixed (although largely favourable) reviews among the clergy, but the laity loved it and showed their gratitude in no uncertain way.

Many new experiments in outreach resulted. We not only taught about evangelism – we did it, as an integral element in the Travelling Schools, and we invited clergy to take part or observe. We did it at dinner parties, in churches, in pubs, in the open air, in schools and in many other places. Our only stipulation was that the opportunities should be carved out for us by the diocese or local churches. In this way they not only experienced some modelling of evangelism, but exercised ownership. We took clergy and lay people with us in teams to do urban and rural missions as invited, and this gave them practical experience of evangelism. Such team work continues to this day, and has been widely copied throughout the country. We also found that we could take things further by inviting gifted clergy to come on a Long Course on Evangelism, lasting 10 days or so and involving much theory and practice. It transformed the ministry of some, and gave others the tools for continuous effective outreach. There has also been a considerable overseas dimension to the Springboard work, in South and North America, Canada, Malaysia, Singapore, Australia, New Zealand and elsewhere.

After four years most of the original team were put out to grass, and a younger and very able team of replacements were recruited, still under the overall direction of Martin Cavender. It is very exciting to see the impact that Springboard is making wherever it goes, its increased appreciation among the clergy, and the way it works across the different strands of church-manship in Anglicanism. Many diocesan bishops who were sceptical in 1992 are now lining up to get Springboard to come and operate in their neck of the woods.

Evangelistic initiatives continue to multiply. Here are three, taken almost at random. The first is the crucial matter of church-planting. The distribution of churches in Britain does not correspond at all closely with where the current population is living. As a result, some areas of the country have far too many churches and other parts have none at all. Church-planting has, accordingly, been undertaken by various denominations, and even the Church of England is planting about one church a fortnight. This does not necessarily involve the purchase of a property or the ordination of a minister. A lively church sets up a church plant in an appropriate pub or community hall – the kind of location which enables unchurched people to give it a try without great embarrassment. Hiring the property gives the flexibility to change, if need be. The informal location and the lay initiative allows the church plant to dispense with unhelpful traditions, dress and furniture which belonged to a bygone age but are treasured by those who have been in church circles for a long time. There is an annual Conference on Church-planting in Britain, and it constantly grows. I find that a very encouraging development. It was certainly not there a few years ago. Worldwide, church-planting is the fastest and most effective growth strategy of the Christian Church.

Another initiative is the cell church, where Christians gather not in a church building but in a small home cell which subdivides once it reaches 20 or so members. This is very warm, relational and informal, and has a great deal going for it. To be sure, it is very small in Britain at present, but I fancy it will become one of the main methods of Christian advance in the next 50 years. It is, as I hope to show in Chapter 15, a particularly effective way of spreading the faith among a network of friendships and acquaintances who have hitherto had no experience whatever of church life. In Asia it is proving exceptionally valuable in doubling and even trebling membership of the Church, and it is beginning to take root in Britain.

The third initiative I want to mention is no less visionary. Called 'On the Move', it is the brainchild of an able and godly Christian named Martin Graham. He recognized that for a long time Christianity in Britain had been imprisoned within the walls of the churches, thus excluding a vast number from its influence. On the other hand, such Christian open-air work as existed was crude and tended to carry a high cringe factor. Yet he sensed there was an area here which needed to be explored afresh. Until he resigned in 1998, he was head of the Kent Chamber of Commerce, and was responsible for a multimillion-pound annual budget. He gave it all up and gladly embraced financial insecurity in order to follow the vision God had given him and launch On the Move, which essentially offers people free barbecues.

Starting small, Martin used his administrative and ambassadorial skills to get together teams of ordinary church members in a locality, often from a variety of churches, and give them some very basic training. They move out onto the crowded high street or shopping area and, as the crowds go by, they see a worship band joyfully praising God on the street, with guitars, trumpets, double basses, etc. Then, a bit further down the street, they meet another band, and then another. The impact of two or three such bands is tremendous, and creates the atmosphere of a fiesta. In the light of the goodwill which this creates, team members go up to passers-by and invite them to a free barbecue. Hundreds accept. They have never seen the Church in so vibrant, relaxed and generous a mood!

Meanwhile, another group has been preparing barbecue lunches in an attractive open-air location. The food is customarily donated by a large store such as Marks and Spencer, or is sold to On the Move at half-price. That shows how impressed some of the big institutions are with Martin and his idea. At the barbecue there is another worship band, and every now and again someone says a few words at the microphone about the essential meaning of the Christian gospel. People listen for quite a while because they are in a queue waiting for their lunch. The team members sit with their contacts at picnic tables, borrowed from a local pub whose landlord, too, thinks this is a great idea. They play host to the visitors, who are amazed at the free hospitality. Why is the team doing it? Such questions make it very easy to speak of God's generosity to us all. Team members have a simple and attractive handout called *Yes* (which is God's attitude to us), with a tear-off portion people can fill in to link up with local churches.

I have worked with On the Move myself, and was amazed first by the numbers who came to the lunch, second by the interest displayed, and third by the many who opened up on spiritual issues and wanted to join an Alpha course, or even to commit themselves to Christ on the spot. Independent research has shown that the vast majority of those who responded become regular worshippers.

Finding this to be such an effective means of outreach, Martin and his team have undertaken intensive initiatives in eight of the largest cities in England (apart from London, which is slated for a later year). In these cities, some 3,000 team members drawn from over 400 churches have fed 100,000 people. Of that number, some 3,000 gave their names and addresses because they wanted to be linked up with the local church, and almost 1,000 professed conversion. The stories which emerge from these contacts on the streets are extremely moving and show that there is a hunger in the human heart which the regular activities of the Church are not touching, but which enterprises such as On the Move are beginning to satisfy.

All these initiatives at the start of the new millennium remind us that evangelism is gloriously possible today. We may have to learn new approaches and empathize with mindsets we find uncongenial. We may have to learn new lessons in courage and taking initiative. Yet there is a hunger out there which was absent 50 years ago. As the great evangelist St Paul said, in the words which became the motto of St John's College, Nottingham, where I served for so long, 'Woe to me if I do not preach the gospel.' I want to keep doing it until my dying day. There is no greater joy in the world than helping someone to come, as Paul put it, 'from darkness to light, from the power of Satan to God'.

CHAPTER 10

Leadership

At the end of a mission I recently led in Canada, the team gave me a delightful wall-hanging about leadership. It featured a Canadian bald eagle soaring high, and these words from Charles de Gaulle: 'A true leader always keeps an element of surprise up his sleeve, which others cannot grasp but which keeps his public excited and breathless.' Anyone can see the truth of that in the life of de Gaulle himself. He was enigmatic to his observers, infuriating to his allies, a hero to his countrymen, and always produced something unexpected from up his sleeve. True leaders are not dull, predictable, operating always by the book. They are exciting, imaginative, inspiring people to trust and follow them.

Bad leaders

I have seen many leaders in my day, but in this chapter I will confine myself to Christian leaders. There tend to be two kinds. First there is the petty dictator. Many parish priests fall into this category, although they would be shocked to be told so. Nothing can happen in their parish – no lay initiatives, no new ideas – without their knowledge and goodwill. Sometimes, of course, they are working with the Parochial

Church Council, or the equivalent in churches other than the Church of England. Sometimes they simply call the shots themselves. If people in the church do not like it, they either have to put up with it or move elsewhere. In Anglo-Catholic and Roman Catholic circles, there is a tacit agreement that 'Father knows best'. In Evangelical circles, everyone is clear that 'we had better go and check it out with Bill first'. Different nomenclature, same disease. Synodical government has done something to rectify this clerical paternalism, but in parish after parish it persists. I have long ago lost count of the lay people, full of ideas and initiative, who are frustrated by a vicar who will not allow them room to exercise their ministries. Everything is dictated by the clergy.

That is a tendency so reprehensible and so far from the teaching of the New Testament that I have fought against it long and hard. In particular, I spoke about every-member ministry and shared leadership on many significant occasions in the Church of England, in days when it was very unfashionable to do so. I made a particular assault on restrictive priestcraft at the National Evangelical Anglican Congress at Nottingham in 1977, and I had done so very pungently some years earlier in the book I wrote for the 1968 Lambeth Conference, *Called to Serve*.

I had seen people's lives broken by what was really tyrannous church leadership. I had seen a South African bishop who disliked Evangelicals vowing that he would rather have a church left without a minister than put in an Evangelical. I had seen a bishop in Gambia banish into the interior, far from wife and family, a gifted clergyman who was very loyal but whose abilities threatened the bishop. It is a very ugly side to leadership and unfortunately it is not rare, because all power tends to corrupt and absolute power tends to corrupt absolutely. I have known a bishop and his lawyer in British Columbia summon a clergyman and tell him that he would either be sacked (in which case there would be no other clerical job in Canada open to him), or he must resign on the spot. I have seen a bishop in that same diocese tell the Synod that he personally created all the rules of the Synod, and that if he did not like what a delegate was saying he would simply turn the microphone off. That was my first, astonished introduction to the Synod of the Canadian Diocese of New Westminster! The tyranny of authoritarian leadership in the Church can be a cancer.

When I went to work in Canada in 1987, however, I encountered an equal and opposite distortion of leadership. I discovered the committee which sits in privacy over an issue and simply releases its decisions – rarely accompanied by the reasons for them, let alone the opportunity for those decisions to be challenged. I even found that the membership of these committees was kept private.

'The committee has decided,' I was told.

'Why has it made that decision?' I would ask.

'We are not at liberty to release what went on in private discussion,' would be the reply.

'Well, who is on the committee?' I would persist.

'The names of the membership are not on general release.'

It was enough to make me wild! That is not leadership. It is a dereliction of leadership.

Jesus, the model for leaders

Neither autocracy nor hiding behind a committee decision is the right way to lead. We have a superb example of true leadership in the person of Jesus Christ. Think of him for a moment not as the Son of God, but as the most distinguished leader who ever lived. He totally eclipses Napoleon, Alexander the Great, Eisenhower or Montgomery. None of those have many millions of people following them centuries after their deaths. On any showing, Jesus is the greatest leader who ever existed, and I am very grateful to my friend Dr Leighton Ford for writing an outstanding book on *Jesus, Leader of Men* in the 'Jesus Library' series which I edited. He shows how, for 50 years and more, discussions of leadership have centred round a transaction, an exchange. The leader gives a reward in exchange for performance. Yet there is another kind of leader to which he draws attention: the kind of leader who transforms the situation – a Pope John Paul or Mother Teresa in religion, a John Kennedy in politics.

Transactional leaders work within a situation. Transforming leaders change the situation. Transactional leaders accept what can be talked about. Transforming leaders change what can be talked about. Transactional leaders accept the rules and values of their organization. Transforming leaders change them. Transactional leaders talk about payoffs. Transforming leaders talk about goals.

Jesus is the supreme transforming leader of all time. Two thousand years after his death, a third of humankind professes to follow him. And remember, he lived in a small village, had no home and little formal education, never wrote a book and was executed at the age of 30. Some of his characteristics should mark any leader worthy of the name.

First, he knew who he was. He knew he was God the Father's only Son, and spent time with him. What he did throughout his career proceeded from who he was. He had a very solid inner core to his being, so he was not constantly tossed about by the vagaries of public opinion, the attacks of enemies or the pressures of friends. He exemplified the truth that who we are is a lot more significant than what we do. If we are always wondering what people will think of us, we cannot lead. Our true identity is in our relationship with the Lord, not in our job. We have all seen people so wrapped up in their work that they fold up when they are stripped of it at retirement. If you are going to lead others, you have to be very sure about who you are.

Second, Jesus had a very clear vision. Karl Marx concluded his Communist Manifesto with the words, 'You have a world to win,' and he was right. Jesus had that same clarity of vision, and he subordinated everything to it. He had come to found an alternative society, the kingdom of God in the midst of the political kingdoms of the earth. Justice, integrity and community were among his goals, along with the greatest of them all – reconciliation to God. Mere managers want to do things right. Real leaders want to do the right thing, and they have the vision and the courage to go for it. When General Slim took command of the 14th Army in the Second World War, he enunciated three principles which transformed the morale of the soldiers. First, there must be a great and noble aim. Second, it must be essential to achieve it. Third, every man must feel that what he is and does is important for achieving that goal. Jesus uniquely embodied that clarity of vision.

3   Third, the example of Jesus the leader was magnetic. People listened to him, followed him, laid down their lives for him, because he genuinely practised what he preached. He taught, 'Love your enemies … forgive your persecutors' – and he did precisely that. He taught that nobility consisted in serving rather than being served – and he washed his disciples' feet. He taught that the greatest love one could have was to lay down one's life for one's friends – and then he did it for his enemies. The point is clear: unless people see leaders modelling what they teach, they will give them scant respect. Charisma without character is a catastrophe.

4   Fourth, Jesus was the servant of all, although he was the Lord of all. Real leadership springs not from asking, 'How many people will help me?' but, 'How deep is my commitment to serve others?' When that is in place, people will follow a leader through hell and high water.

5   A fifth vital quality of a good leader is the determination and ability to equip others. Jesus refused the role of the manager behind the big desk and preferred, if anything, the principle of the inverted cone. He concentrated first and foremost on three men in his inner circle. Then he poured himself into a group of twelve men, and to a lesser extent into 70 others. It was brilliant leadership. He did not dominate them, but enabled them to discover and use their gifts. He poured

himself into those disciples, and he was ready to move aside and let them get on with it when they were ready. It is interesting to notice how he prepared them for their future ministry. He had them along first to watch him at work. Next, they were allowed to give him a little help, as when the 12 sat the crowds down at the feeding of the 5,000 and cleared up the broken fragments afterwards. They were, you might say, junior partners in the enterprise. Then he entrusted them with an assignment of limited duration on their own: when he sent out the twelve and the 70, they reported back to him at the conclusion of their task. Finally, they were ready to carry the work forward and become his successors. The Acts of the Apostles shows how well such training paid off. One of the great weaknesses of many leaders is that they do not equip others. They have illusions of their own indispensability. Nobody could say that of Jesus, the supremely great leader and equipper.

A sixth notable feature in Jesus as a spiritual leader is his loyalty to Scripture. He saw it as the authority for his ministry, and he lived to fulfil it. He was far less influenced by tradition, political correctness and expediency than he was by the Scriptures. 'It is written' formed his clinching argument time and again, and all his major initiatives, all his core teaching, all his self-understanding, sprang from that source. That is not a notable feature among some Christian leaders I have known.

A further characteristic of Jesus the leader is that he was radical and challenging. Nowhere else do you find such a radical appraisal of human nature, and such a radical remedy for it. Think of his willingness to touch lepers – something unheard of in his day. Moreover, he dared to challenge people. He challenged the rich, the prostitutes, the demonized, the political and ecclesiastical leaders. This was never done to show off or to provoke an argument, but always to serve the truth. We need leaders like that.

An eighth quality which I see supremely modelled in Jesus is the willingness to sacrifice. That is essential in a great leader.

It is costly to endure despite the knocks, to be unjustly attacked without hitting back, to endure pain rather than inflict it, and to be totally committed to the welfare of your followers whatever the personal cost. Jesus did all that – and endured the excruciating agony of the cross as well. Well might he say, 'The Son of Man did not come to be served but to serve and to give his life as a ransom for many' (Matthew 20:28). Leaders who, like Churchill and Garibaldi, offer their followers 'blood, toil, tears and sweat' and are prepared to give a lead in facing it – these are the leaders who change the world.

9 Finally, Jesus was vulnerable – vulnerable to exhaustion, loneliness, criticism, betrayal, pain and death. When others see us shed our masks of invulnerability and come over as the frail human beings that we are, albeit strengthened by God's grace, they will love us the more deeply and respect us more. That was true of the followers of Jesus. It is universally the case.

Whether consciously or unconsciously, the outstanding leaders I have met all exhibit some or all of the characteristics of Jesus Christ. They have tended to adopt these crucial characteristics from their Master. I would love to see these qualities more required of ordination candidates, but, on the whole, little training is given in the area of leadership in most theological institutions. Perhaps that is why the American journal *Leadership* has such a wide readership. Pastors realize how neglected leadership was in their training and are keen to rectify this. Theological college students in the West are trained to do the things that churches normally do, but they are not trained to strategize for growth.

What has struck me about the ordinands in Africa and Asia is that they may have much less technical knowledge, but they have much more in the way of possibility thinking. Much of the failure of the Church in the West to grow is due to impossibility thinking. By contrast, the Third-World Christians, with far fewer resources and less experience, and for the most part in an equally hostile urban environment, seek leaders who expect God to act and are prepared to make great sacrifices and expend great commitment in order to see the vision taking place. They have a clear goal. Perhaps it is geographical – reaching a block of flats with the gospel. Perhaps it is genera-tional – a church for and run by teenagers. Perhaps it is repro-ductive – to double the number of cell groups each year. Whatever, there is a clear delineation of goals, then a whole-hearted commitment to prayer, abundant love, human contact, witness-bearing, conversion and nurture. The Christians in Africa and Asia seem to believe in growth before they see it. God honours faith and leadership of that quality.

Outstanding Christian leaders

I would like to give some examples of Christian leaders from whom I have learnt much. The first of them was the Rev. E.J.H. Nash, a gentle, self-effacing clergyman who was uni-versally known as Bash. He was a wise and enthusiastic Evangelical who built up the influential Iwerne Minster house parties, which I described in some detail in the first two chap-ters of this book. He was a man of remarkable single-minded-ness, as most great leaders are. With a few able and deeply committed clergy friends like John Eddison and Philip Tompson, he set up the house parties for public schoolboys aged between 14 and 18. In wartime they embraced a fair amount of simple agriculture to help the war effort. In peace-time they concentrated much more on leisure activities. The boys had a superb holiday, with congenial colleagues, out-standing entertainment and activities, and a strong and care-fully organized Christian induction.

The effect of this built up over the years. In almost all the leading public schools, groups of boys who had been to Iwerne Minster began to have a weekly meeting during term-time in their own schools, and if one of the Iwerne officers taught in the school, he would look after them. These officers were constantly replenished by university graduates who had either come into the Iwerne system as schoolboys and worked their way up, or been recruited as undergraduates and initiated in a service role – helping to make the meals, wash the dishes, mow the lawns and so forth. In due course most of them became officers.

The man who kept all this in place with the gentlest of hands was Bash. Many of the officers had far more charisma, yet Bash proved himself the outstanding leader. I think this was partly due to his deep spirituality, coupled with some most endearing idiosyncrasies, and also to his unobtrusive organizational skills and gifted decentralization. He also had an uncanny knack of winning and retaining the loyalty of people who were much more obviously gifted than himself. Above all, however, he was the most talented spiritual director I have ever met. He always gave the talk on personal commitment to Christ himself, and he was brilliantly simple and powerful in doing so, but his greatest effectiveness lay in the pastoral care he gave to countless individuals. He would take someone off for a walk or to a café and see right through them. I know, because he did it to me time and again. I could never hide anything from him. He read me like a book. Although he was quite uncompromising, he was so warm and encouraging that it stimulated me and many others to try to put Christ first in our lives and make the necessary changes in our lifestyles.

Very much an Evangelical, he would have hated to be described as a 'spiritual director', but that is what he was. This astonishing gift of gentle insight and wisdom from God made him the most outstanding spiritual guide I have ever encountered. I am privileged to have known him and to have been trained by him during those formative years of my mid-teens and early twenties. I owe more than I can say to Bash and his work at Iwerne Minster.

The second leader who made a great impact on me stands in stark contrast to Bash. Gordon Sheldon was the Vicar of Holy Trinity, Eastbourne, where I served my curacy, and he would be very surprised to be included in a list of people with outstanding leadership ability. That is not how he regarded himself at all, and it is not how some others regarded him either. He was compared somewhat disparagingly with his predecessor at the church, Canon Warner, who was a preacher of some note – which Gordon was not. Yet I found him a marvellous leader.

He was just right for me. He gave me my head as a young curate, but he exercised a gentle and loving advisory role. I loved the man and would willingly accept his advice, even if I did not agree with it. He had a real talent for holding a large, diverse congregation together, and that is no small feat of leadership. He showed tremendous warmth towards me, and that made me grow in confidence. He had a great gift of encouragement, and he spent regular quality time with me, discussing, praying and dreaming dreams. He taught me how important it is for leaders to give people their head, to encourage and love them, to advise them from time to time, and to spend quality time with them. These may not seem very distinguished gifts of leadership, but for lack of them many leaders fail to impact and equip their colleagues. I thank God for the start I had under this loving and wise man.

The third leader I want to mention is Dr John Stott. I once heard Archbishop Runcie describe John Stott as 'the most distinguished Anglican since William Temple', and I am sure he was right. He was one of the many gifted people brought to faith by Bash and faithfully pastored by him – I believe Bash wrote to him every single week for many years. I know Bash hoped that this able young man, who had been head boy at Rugby and had greatly distinguished himself with a double first at Cambridge, would become principal of a theological college and in due course Archbishop of Canterbury. It was not an unreasonable expectation. Stott's abilities, achievements, theological insight and leadership skills eclipse all sorts of mediocre men who have become bishops. Yet he was intent upon a very different path. Instead of preferment in the Anglican Church, John aimed at usefulness to the universal

Church. He has been a loyal Anglican, but his influence has far outshone the Anglican Church arena. It is worldwide, and he has travelled the world preaching the gospel. In recent years he has concentrated on teaching the faith to clergy in particular, many of whom had neither his theological understanding nor his experience as a pastor.

Possessed of a very sharp mind, he declined the spires of academia, but instead has subjected all his teaching and writing to the most severe academic scrutiny before allowing it to go out. I recall raising with him many years ago a few minor background points where I thought he was mistaken in one of his earliest books, *Men with a Message*. I was amazed that he asked me to come and see him, went through the points with a fine-tooth comb, accepting some and rejecting others, and was obviously determined to get all the details right even in such a small paperback. This precision and discipline has governed all his work down the years. Married to other qualities such as enormous preaching skill, clarity of expression, strong evangelistic gifts, linguistic skills, a strategic mind, a deep love for people and a great deal of personal warmth, it adds up to a phenomenal mix. John is the most complete world Christian leader I know.

I owe him a lot. It was he who prepared my wife and myself for marriage. It was he who had me to sleep on his study floor the night before my wedding, and I noted with awe the early hour next morning at which he was closeted with his Bible. He preached at our wedding, at which my father officiated, and we have kept in touch down the years, occasionally speaking at the same conferences. An example of this was the first, and indeed second, National Evangelical Anglican Congress. This was his brainchild and enormously influenced the future direction of the Church of England and the Evangelicals in particular. He not only included me in his team of speakers at both congresses, but on the second occasion, in 1977, he commissioned us all to write our contributions down for publication before the Congress. This greatly enhanced the nature of the Congress, for the prior publication of the books (published by Collins in three volumes as *Obeying Christ in a Changing World*) meant that the delegates all had a chance to read them beforehand. Their comments were fed back to the respective speakers, who, when it came to their turn to speak, were able to respond to the comments that had been made about their written paper – and thus carry the debate forward to a level never reached in an ordinary conference.

I have shared more recent platforms with him, too. In Germany we both spoke to a major gathering of students under the aegis of the International Fellowship of Evangelical Students. I recall John observing that the IFES was without question the most significant evangelistic body in the world today, although it has been in business for only 50 years. As I have moved around the world and seen what has been done by that organization in country after country, I am bound to agree with him. Not only has this student work spread like wildfire worldwide, but it has produced enormous numbers of church leaders who owe their souls and their early training to its ministry.

Even more recently, John Stott, Alister McGrath and myself had a fascinating day in Oxford with a large audience, looking back on developments, opportunities missed and grasped, and directions taken, particularly by Evangelicals, during the past four or five decades. Much of this was totally unknown to the theological students who formed a substantial part of the audience. It was fun to watch the amazement on their faces! John delivered a tear-jerking address, directed as much to the heart as to the head, in which he expressed his longing for the faithfulness of his audience to Evangelical truth, and the emergence of gifted younger leaders to take up the torch. He used some of the material from his recent book, *Evangelical Truth*. I think he saw it as a sort of last will and testament, rather as the apostle Paul gave to Timothy in his Second Epistle – appropriately enough for someone who was approaching 80 and had achieved so much.

Just reflect on what John Stott has accomplished: the Eclectics groups, the Church of England Evangelical Council, the Langham Foundation, the Evangelical Fellowship of the Anglican Communion, major congresses in the UK and abroad, a massive international teaching ministry sustained over many years, 'The Bible Speaks Today' series which he inspired and edited, his own extensive writings, his evangelistic missions, his distinguished Rectorship of All Souls, Langham Place (and the whole vision for guest services, overseas student hospitality, lay ministry and training which he developed there) – all this and much more emerged from the fertile spirituality of this remarkable man, who remained single so that he could accomplish more for God. It is a marvel. The story is being recorded in Bishop Tim Dudley Smith's two-volume biography. All I can say is that it has been a great privilege to have known such a great leader.

Another man in the same league is Billy Graham, and it has been my privilege to know him too. We have not met very often, but it was often enough for him to have had a considerable influence on my life. Of all the American evangelists who have achieved prominence, he is by far the greatest, and one of the few to have remained uncorrupted by sex, drink, pride or money – the bane of many a famous person. His humility is undoubted to anyone who knows him, and he owes that to a deep and sustained walk with God. He is untroubled by drink because he is a teetotaller, and he goes to great lengths to remain irreproachable in the area of sex – his secretary, for example, never stays in the same hotel as he does. He is careful to ensure that he does not fix his own salary, but is paid by the Board of the Billy Graham Evangelistic Organization.

Many people who know him only as a famous preacher would like to know the man personally. Even his autobiography does not tell us that much about the real person, although it faithfully chronicles his ministry and influence. I can at least supply a few details which enable us to see through the famous persona to the humble man of God. One such glimpse was

Where it all began – Shenington Rectory, Oxfordshire.

My mother – and me!

My father, Rector of Shenington with Alkerton for 35 years.

Five years old,
and my first fish!

Clifton College
Fencing Team, 1948.

Commissioning at Mons Officer Cadet School, 1954.

The day we got engaged.

Rosemary
as I first knew her.

Wedding in the rain,
September 10, 1957.

St. John's College, Nottingham.

HRH Prince Charles opening
the College, 1970.

St. John's College, Nottingham, as it is today.

Print, 1836, of
St. Aldate's Church
and Pembroke
College (where
George Whitefield
was converted).

Rosemary, Michael,
Jenny, Sarah, Tim
and Jonathan in
Oxford days.

Street ministry – in the olden days!

Street ministry – today.

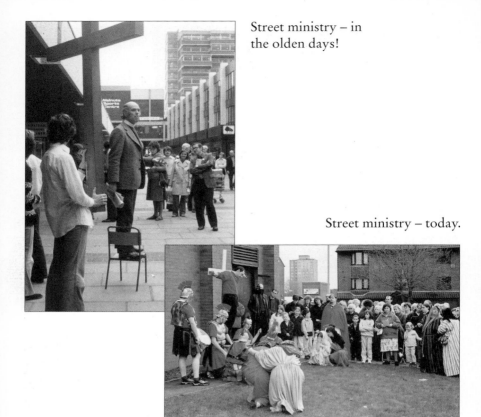

In 1973 at the Billy Graham Rally, Durban, which, along with the accompanying Convention, ignored apartheid laws.

Catholic and Evangelical – with Bishop Michael Marshall,
Springboard Missioners 1992-96.

With grandchildren
David and Sarah.

Fishing – more ways than one!

Rosemary and Michael – a joint ministry.

'My joy I give to you!'

given me at the first conference embracing black, white, Indian and Coloured Christans ever to be held in South Africa under the apartheid regime. The South African Cabinet only allowed it because Billy Graham had been invited by the organizer Michael Cassidy, and they would have lost so much international credit if they had barred his entry into the country. He spoke at the big public rally which packed the Durban rugby ground with more than 80,000 people and had such a profound influence that they ran out of counsellors and counselling materials.

Billy heard me giving a Bible study on the morning after the rally, and immediately grabbed me and took me to his hotel to talk. His concern was to go deeper with God in theological understanding, and he felt that perhaps I had something to offer him there. He told me that, if he had his time over again, he would have followed the same career but would have given more time to theological study before starting out. That is a very humble thing to say for a man as deeply versed in Scripture as Billy Graham. After a while, we went out for a walk. He disguised himself with baseball cap and dark glasses – but not well enough to fool a poor Indian woman who came up to us and begged us to pray for her unbelieving husband. So there on that beach we stood, the three of us from very different countries and backgrounds, praying for this woman's husband. I was so impressed that a man who had spoken to 80,000 the day before now had time for the concerns of one needy woman.

On another occasion, he came to Oxford to lead a short mission in the university. I was in charge of the team, so I saw a good deal of him. He is a large man and it was difficult to squeeze him into our small car, but we succeeded. I was struck by a number of things during his time with us. He had suffered a fall in London just before coming and had broken a couple of ribs. I had to take him to the hospital on his first night and I was amazed to find that the Egyptian registrar on duty was thrilled to see him because he had been present at one of Billy's crusades in Egypt. The next day, we received a prophetic utterance about the healing of those ribs and the relief from pain that God would give him. I do not think Billy was used to this sort of spirituality, but he received it with joy and gratitude and, sure enough, from that point on he was set free from pain. He also impressed me greatly at a reception laid on by the Lord Mayor. He moved around everyone, expressing genuine interest in each person. He did not attempt to preach or to turn the conversation to Christian channels unless it moved there naturally, but he showed the concern of his Master for every person present. That had a great impact. It was not what people had expected.

It was wonderful, too, to have him in the staff meeting each day, fine-tuning the plans for the evening's meeting, and to see him so thoughtful, such a good listener, so appreciative of other people's input and so wise and restrained in his own. When a heckler tried to take over a meeting we were holding in the Town Hall, I realized the extraordinary shrewdness and determination of the man: he simply stood a little nearer to the microphone and went on with what he was saying. By the end of the evening, the interjector had entrusted his life to Christ. I recall also Billy's interest in the plans we had made for ecumenical Nurture Groups to follow up his mission. He took that idea on board for his next crusade – and he would have taken away our church's drama and dance group if they had been available! Here was a leader who was always ready to learn.

Two other admirable American leaders come to mind. One is Dr Bill Bright, the founder of Campus Crusade, a massive international Christian organization. On one occasion, when we were lunching together, I was amazed to find him contriving apparently natural opportunities to give a copy of *The Four Spiritual Laws* to fellow diners or waiters. They all seemed so thrilled to have it. I have some reservations about that little booklet, but it has unquestionably led thousands to Christian faith, and here was its author practising what he was

urging his followers to do, and in such a natural and acceptable way. That is true leadership, exemplifying the lessons you
are seeking to inculcate.

The other American who stands out in my opinion is
Charles Colson. We first met in Germany, and he later came to
Oxford, where I arranged for him to speak in the Oxford
Union. He was a born leader who fell from a great height –
from the office next to the President in Nixon's White House
to a prison cell, because of his involvement in Watergate. He
became a Christian in the midst of the Watergate upheaval,
and incurred much sceptical mockery as a result. Yet his conversion was real and he admitted his guilt, went to prison, and
sought Christian companionship there. His time in prison was
not easy, but it was very important. It showed him the
appalling state of religious support in prison – most chaplains
were the dregs of the clergy. When he came out, he determined
to do something about it.

This was the birth of the Prison Fellowship, which has now
spread all over the world. It has brought hope to thousands,
including those kept on Death Row. It has led to the conversion
of thousands of prisoners, many of whom have, on their release,
become workers for Prison Fellowship in the very prison
system in which they were incarcerated. Godly chaplains, paid
by the Prison Fellowship, are placed in countless prisons. It is
a whole new world, and it is the brainchild of one man who
used his political disgrace as a launchpad for an entirely new
spiritual ministry. If you were to ask Chuck Colson which part
of his life he considers the most important – the part he spent
as a lawyer and political heavyweight, or the part he has spent
inaugurating and spreading Prison Fellowship – I have no
doubt what he would say. Like Bash, this man has a single
vision, and he has followed it with tremendous commitment.
He discovered that he could write, and he has used this gift
brilliantly too, not only in the substantial books he has
authored, but perhaps even more importantly in a constant
stream of magazine articles giving a Christian slant on current

events in the US. Colson is a leader from whom I have learnt much and for whom I have a great admiration.

If I were asked to pick a theologian, I should be spoilt for choice. I had the privilege of being taught as a postgraduate by two of the best theologians in Britain, Professor Charlie Moule and Professor Sir Henry Chadwick, but both were primarily distinguished academics rather than leaders. The same could be said of Dr James Packer, who, through his writings, has probably affected Christians in the US more than anyone except Billy Graham. Yet he too is known more as a theologian than a leader and, although personally warm, he does not have a following, apart from the thousands who are influenced by his books and grateful for their clarity and relevance.

Two members of the same faculty as James Packer, Dr Jim Houston and Dr Gordon Fee, show remarkable gifts of leadership. Both are deeply involved with people. Both speak widely and strategically in the world. Houston went from Oxford to be the first Principal of Regent College, Vancouver, and it was his initial leadership, warmth, vision, persistence, relational skills and academic integrity that led to Regent's acceptance on the campus of the University of British Columbia and laid the foundation for it to become the most distinguished tertiary Christian teaching institution in Canada. Houston also took the most unusual step of living in community: his house was full of students who counted it a great privilege to be there. In addition, he possesses a remarkable teaching and pastoral gift. People flock to his lectures. They do not all understand them, for this geographer-turned-theologian has a strong mystical strain about him and is not always easy to follow. Yet he is more than a lecturer: he is a friend, a father confessor, a wise counsellor. More than all the other faculty members put together, this remarkable man has proved to be a superb counsellor and a most attractive Christian leader – not least in times of adversity, when a palace revolution removed him from the principalship in favour of a North American college head.

Yes, I have learnt much from Jim Houston, just as I have from Alister McGrath, Principal of Wycliffe Hall, Oxford. I admire him for his imaginative leadership and his superb lecturing, as good as any I have ever heard. I admire him for his swift grasp of an issue and often decisive action on it, and for his massive learning, lightly held. I admire him for the way he writes definitive tomes on the one hand, and utterly lucid books for young Christians on the other – a feat few theologians can emulate. I admire him for his passion for evangelism and apologetics, and for his example of full involvement in the life of the church and university. It is not surprising that the University of Oxford has accorded him the rare privilege of a personal professorship.

I honour all these theologians, but if I had to choose one to learn from as a great leader it would have to be Bishop Lesslie Newbigin. A brilliant theologian, he worked in India as a Christian missionary, making enormous attempts to hold intelligent dialogue with leading Hindus such as Radarkrishnan. In due course, Newbigin became a bishop in the Church of South India. Stephen Neill is another great leader for whom I had tremendous regard. He came to live in Oxford during his later years and, domiciled at Wycliffe Hall, shared with me the leadership of a theological seminar for undergraduates. For me, however, Lesslie Newbigin was the greater of the two. He has left behind something of a record of his discussions with Radarkrishnan and other leading Hindu scholars in his superb book *The Finality of Christ*, in which, with infinite understanding and sympathy towards Hinduism, he shows the uniqueness and supremacy of Jesus Christ.

Half his life's work was done in India, and that is the part I know least about. When he came back to England after retiring as Bishop, however, he found that half his life's work still lay before him. Both during his years of teaching at the Selly Oak Colleges in Birmingham, and during his final retirement in London, he faced up to the prevailing plight of Christianity in the West. It was in worse shape than it had been in India, for it was no longer possible to discuss Christian claims in the marketplace of ideas – people seemed to regard it as being just as indelicate to discuss their religious faith as their sexual habits. The gospel had become, as one of his influential books called it, *Foolishness to the Greeks*, and he wanted to bring open discussion of the faith back into the marketplace of politics and boardrooms. He wanted to show that, if it was true for anyone, Christianity was true for all. He wanted to debunk the pluralism, the political correctness and the relativism about truth and morals that had infected Western thought like a plague. He wanted to show that, although mathematical certitude was inappropriate to Christian convictions, a 'proper confidence' was not, and he showed brilliantly how that confidence could be gained and humbly maintained against all comers. In so doing, he revealed both the conservative convictions that he intelligently held, and the liberal background in which he had been raised. He did a great deal to bind together conservative and liberal believers in the Christian family, and he was universally recognized as the premier apologist of our age. What an achievement to match his apologetic success in the East with his later achievements in the West!

I used to see quite a lot of him at this later stage of his life. He would come to conferences I arranged for young evangelists on apologetic issues in the early days of my work with Springboard. What moved me greatly was his continued love and encouragement of me and many others when old age hit him and he had to survive without his eyesight. He did not give in, and he showed no signs of resentment. He gathered a circle of young scholars around him, who read to him and kept him up to date with the latest issues. Thus he was still able to lecture without a hesitation for an hour or more, so excellent was his memory and so well stocked his mind. I still have some of the ill-typed letters he sent me, tapped out without sight and with many mistakes on his old typewriter. He delighted to spend time at Holy Trinity Brompton, the premier charismatic Evangelical church in the UK, balancing their proper emphasis on experiencing the Spirit of God with an equally proper emphasis on using your God-given mind to understand and commend the faith. People like Lesslie Newbigin arise only about once in a century, and I count it a tremendous privilege to hail this man both as a friend and as a leader whom I enormously admired.

One of the most impressive leaders of my own generation was Canon David Watson, who died of liver cancer at the untimely age of 50 while his ministry was at its peak. He was another product of the Bash house parties, and we became friends there. Curacies with the charismatic Evangelical John Collins at Gillingham and the non-charismatic Mark Ruston at the Round Church in Cambridge led David to York, where the Archbishop put him in charge of St Cuthbert's, a small church facing closure, to look after the dozen or so members in its concluding months. David did not see its demise as necessary. He and his wife prayed constantly for the work, and in due course people came, were converted and swelled the congregation. The congregation outgrew the building, and the Archbishop gave them permission to take over a much larger church, St Michael's, near the Minster.

At St Aldate's in Oxford we profited enormously from the ministry which David, and the small teams of parishioners he brought with him, gave us as we were fumbling our way towards renewal. It was invaluable. His church had come alive with every-member ministry, charismatic gifts, dynamic music ministry, superb youth work, drama and dance teams, and a marvellous shop where goods were cheap, love flowed and much ministry was carried out. Most impressive of all, they found that so many of the congregation wanted to give up their jobs and engage in pastoral and evangelistic ministry combined with social care, that they began to organize the church in households. Not all of these succeeded, but some did. The idea was that half a dozen or so would live in a house, sharing their possessions, and while some of them worked to finance their common life, others in the household could work within the church. So David would often have a team of 30 or more church workers, financed by this most demanding expedient of shared households, which was a tremendous challenge to patience and love.

David was a superb leader. He was warm and encouraging. He believed in team work. He was biblical through and through. He adopted the true radicalness of Scripture, daring to do what was simply not done in his day. He saw from Scripture that leadership should be shared, and he was careful that it was shared among his team. He saw that charismatic gifts were meant to equip the Church for powerful ministry, and he welcomed them without falling into the mistakes of the extremists. He was the best UK evangelist of his day, combining charm, humour, biblical teaching, illustrative stories and challenge in a way that brought hundreds to Christ in university and town missions, both in the UK and overseas in Africa, Ireland, the US and Canada. He was an excellent writer both for non-Christians and Christians, and his books continue to be reprinted. He developed training weeks at York to which he issued widespread invitations, and in addition to the English who crowded in there, you would find many from Wales, Ireland and Scandinavia. The Christian Church in all those countries was significantly affected by the teaching of the Renewal Weeks, during which guests lived in the congregation's homes and were initiated into the principles which had made St Michael's strong.

All this was accomplished at the cost of tremendous sacrifice for David himself and his congregation. They were glad to do it, however, and increasingly the country took note. In his last few years, David and his team were invited to cathedral after cathedral, where they found that evangelism and renewal went hand in hand as they celebrated the good news of the gospel. He was in great demand at Fuller Seminary in the States, where his influence was again enormous. I shall not readily forget the day when he rang me up and asked if I could go to Fuller instead of him, because he had just been told by his doctor that he had life-threatening cancer and had to go for an immediate operation. Despite a partial recovery, and an incredibly influential series of talks on the BBC which he gave as he faced death, David was a shadow of his former self. Before long he was dead, to the profound sorrow of the Christian world. He was a very close friend of mine. We did a lot together and planned very closely how the work of our two churches, his in York and ours in Oxford, could be co-ordinated for the good of the country. He was irreplaceable, but his leadership example lives on in many lives, not least my own.

Episcopal leaders

Bishops hold obvious positions of leadership within the Church, and I have respected many for particular qualities. Archbishop Robert Runcie was a gracious man who developed a reputation for sitting on the fence, but this was due largely to his ability to see several different sides of a question. Archbishop Stuart Blanch of York was a gifted evangelist and teacher, a humble and warm personality, and an excellent leader. His successor David Hope is a godly, no-nonsense leader for whom I have great affection and admiration. George Carey of Canterbury walks with God, and seeks to combine in his spirituality the best of the Evangelical, Catholic and liberal strands in Anglicanism. He has had the misfortune to be faced with more major problems than any of his recent predecessors at Canterbury. Inevitably he has not pleased or impressed everybody, but he has for many years been a dear friend and I believe he has done well in the most difficult of jobs. Bishop David Sheppard of Liverpool is another friend who did a remarkable job for the most deprived people in society and, in partnership with the Catholic Archbishop Derek Worlock, succeeded in building close bonds of fellowship between Catholics and Anglicans in what had been a very divided city.

Looking further afield, the Australian Bishop Alf Stanway of Tanzania presided over a period of tremendous growth there. He told me once that he usually opened a new church once a fortnight. He was very practically minded, but had a tremendous belief in the power of prayer. In his retirement he launched the Trinity Episcopal Seminary in the US, the only conservative seminary in the largely liberal Episcopal Church. He opened it with a tiny handful of students, none of whom could be sure that any bishop would ordain them, and he did so in the teeth of fierce opposition from the rest of the Episcopal authorities, who were busy closing down seminaries and were furious to think of an Evangelical one emerging to rock the boat!

Archbishop Trevor Huddleston proved himself an outstanding leader in three utterly diverse parts of the world, and combined the deep spirituality of a godly monk with fearlessness, vision and great personal warmth. He greatly blessed me and my family.

I could write at length about all these men: they are all distinguished leaders. Nonetheless, the bishops who have influenced and impressed me most are those in the very new Anglican Province of Southeast Asia. I have worked with at least three of them in recent years, and have written more fully about them and the remarkable situation of growth they are leading in my book *Asian Tigers for Christ*, published by SPCK. I salute them as outstanding leaders. They seem to me to combine so many of the transformational gifts we see in Jesus himself.

The first is Bishop Chiu Ban It. He was made Bishop of Singapore in 1966 and was the first indigenous bishop, although there had been an Anglican presence there since 1826. It was under his leadership that the Church in Singapore made enormous strides, despite the desperate social and economic situation when he took over. In his inaugural sermon he stressed four ideals which he hoped would characterize the Church: prayer, evangelism, witness and service. By the grace of God, he was able to see all four begin to materialize during his years of leadership. He was by nature a mild, gentle man, and he suffered considerable insubordination from his clergy. Yet in 1972 a remarkable thing happened to him. He had been handed a copy of the charismatic priest Dennis Bennett's book *Nine O'Clock in the Morning*, and was impressed by what he read. 'Lord,' he prayed, 'if you can fill Dennis with your Spirit, can you please do the same for me?' In the middle of the night he received a deep infilling of the Holy Spirit, together with the gift of tongues, and before long he found himself caught up in the healing ministry. Gone was his old fear and uncertainty. He developed a deep confidence in the power of God, and successfully piloted the diocese through the turbulent early years of the charismatic movement. Enormous advances took place, with the cathedral at the heart of the renewal.

Discerning friends could only marvel. Bishop Chiu was not a natural leader. Before his infilling with the Holy Spirit, he had actually been a very weak and uncertain one. Thereafter, however, he proved to be a marvellous example of God's strength made perfect in weakness. He himself tells us the secret of his effectiveness: 'The Lord made it very clear to me that he wanted his Church back. The Diocese of Singapore was not mine with him helping, but his with me helping! When I humbly submitted to him he began to do great things in the Diocese and Church of Singapore.' The humility and new effectiveness of Bishop Chiu, once he allowed the Holy Spirit to possess him, have been a powerful example to me of the nature of true Christian leadership. Unlike many bishops, he was small enough to allow God to fill him.

Chiu Ban It's successor was Dr Moses Tay, one of the most impressive Christian leaders I have ever known. He, too, had been profoundly filled by the Holy Spirit. He, too, was very much a man of prayer and of the Scriptures. He went through deep waters of sorrow, for, between his election and his consecration, his wife sickened and died. Yet he threw his enormous gifts into the task of building on the foundation Chiu Ban It had laid. He was deeply spiritual, clear-headed, mentally tough and highly competent organizationally. He was keen to see the four dioceses of his area combined into the new Province of Southeast Asia and that was achieved in 1996, when he was appointed the first Archbishop.

Long before that, however, he had shown his colours in no uncertain manner. He laid enormous stress on good leadership. Indeed, there was some tension between him and Trinity Theological College in Singapore, because he was more concerned that clergy should be converted, committed to Scripture, full of the Holy Spirit and inflamed with a deep love for people than that they should have gone through all the regular hoops of theological education. He was prepared to ordain good candidates if they had been to Singapore's Bible College rather than the seminary, and this led to an effective 'hands-on' type of leadership rather than one that was deeply versed in theology. This produced short-term strengths, but may lead to long-term weaknesses.

Not only was he a strong leader himself, but he took great pains to train and equip lay leadership. He developed a superb diocesan lay training programme, with basic and more advanced modules demanding biblical knowledge, practical pastoral and evangelistic ministry, and spiritual depth. There is nothing comparable in any other part of the Anglican Communion, with the exception of Sydney, Australia.

Mission and evangelism were other passions of Moses Tay. Under his leadership the Singapore diocese became a hotbed for evangelism and he saw the gospel spread widely in the island. In 1990 he held an Anglican Congress for World Evangelization, and those who came were overwhelmed both by the passion and the vision of the Christian leadership in Singapore. I recall speaking at it, and the Congress certainly gave more to me than I gave to it! Moses' passion for outreach also spread to the 400 million people of the surrounding lands. He appointed one of his senior clergy to be Dean of

Indonesia, another to be Dean of Thailand, another Dean of
Cambodia and Laos, and another Dean of Nepal. These men
were given the responsibility of evangelizing, gathering
Christians together and forming them into Anglican Churches
in their respective countries – while at the same time holding
down responsible positions in the Church of Singapore. This
is proving to be an astonishing achievement, as the
Singaporean leaders can only enter these countries for a few
weeks at a time on visitors' visas. How they are managing it all
is a story yet to be written, but I can testify that a good start
has been made, thanks to Moses' initiative.

Moses Tay is known to most people for his strong convictions, his deeply held biblical theology, and his fearless
defence of orthodoxy. This made him very unpopular in
liberal circles or when he was one of a small minority defending a position. He was regarded as hard and unyielding, but
nothing could be further from the truth. He was warm and
loving, although undoubtedly strong on conviction. His contribution to the 1998 Lambeth Conference will long be
remembered. He was one of the main leaders of the African,
Latin American and Southeast Asian bishops in rejecting
homosexual practice as an acceptable Christian lifestyle and,
despite the immense pressure from the American homosexual
lobby, Moses and his colleagues won the day by a massive
majority.

Many of the American bishops who had been defeated over
their inclusive attitude towards homosexuality paid no attention to the Lambeth decision, but went on accepting and
ordaining practising homosexual priests. One ardent advocate
of this position was Bishop Holloway of Edinburgh, and
when a meeting of the Anglican Consultative Council was
held in Scotland in 1999, Moses Tay refused to attend and
published his reasons on the Internet. He was roundly
attacked for this, but it was a principled decision.

Early in 2000, he and the Archbishop of Rwanda consecrated two theologically orthodox American priests as bishops,

owing allegiance respectively to Rwanda and Singapore, but released for missionary work in the Episcopal Church of the USA. This interference at the highest level in the affairs of another Province produced a howl of protest from worldwide Anglicanism. The Episcopal Church in the USA was both tearing itself apart through internal dissension and bleeding to death through defections. Biblically-based Christians were frankly persecuted in some dioceses. Several whole congregations were ejected by revisionist bishops. They appealed to Moses Tay to help them by providing alternative oversight. He knew that the US House of Bishops was far too divided to do anything about the ever-increasing laxity in morals and belief, and would never respond to talk, only to action. So he took this controversial step, which may yet prove to have been visionary. At all events, nobody can accuse him of lack of leadership. I honour Moses Tay, and I love him and his wife Cynthia as good friends of many years' standing. I believe they will have golden retirement years working with Love Singapore, a brilliant interchurch mission initiative in Singapore and beyond.

Moses' position as Archbishop has been taken by another dear friend of mine, Datuk Yong Ping Chung, the Bishop of Sabah. He is an inspirational leader, full of the Lord and his Spirit, full of love and vision. He has also been profoundly affected by the charismatic movement, is deeply grounded in the Scriptures and is not afraid to take a stand on their teaching, has passionate convictions about evangelism and lay training and possesses great personal warmth. Yet the quality I most associate with him in leadership is tact, possibly because that is not one of my own strong points! Perhaps it is natural to him; perhaps it has been acquired through years of chairing the Anglican Consultative Council. Be that as it may, he combines the strength of conviction which Moses displayed with a tact, political shrewdness and balanced judgement which Moses, I think, lacked. Thus, although he is strongly opposed to homosexuality, his wisdom and grace were so appreciated by his fellow primates when they met in Portugal in 2000 to discuss this contentious issue that they made him part of the small drafting committee to prepare the final statement – even though this was his first appearance among them as Archbishop. Loving tact, combined with strong convictions, a listening ear and the power of persuasion – these are invaluable gifts in a leader.

Personal convictions on leadership

When I discussed this chapter with my wife Rosemary, she said, 'Aren't you going to say anything about your own leadership?' I had no intention of doing so. After all, although I have more than once been invited to become a bishop, I know I would not have been a good one. I am too impetuous, and I loathe the endless meetings and committees with which bishops are inevitably involved. Furthermore, a bishop has constantly to resolve hard questions which have proved too difficult for others, and judgement is not my strongest suit. I make a better advocate than a judge, as Professor Henry Chadwick once told me. For all these reasons, I am thankful that I have not been called by God to that office. Nonetheless, I have been called to various positions of leadership: in the Oxford University Christian Union, in the barrack room during my National Service, in the theological college which we moved from London to Nottingham, in a marvellous church in the heart of Oxford. I think I realized how important a part of my make-up leadership was when I went to Regent College, Vancouver, an excellent teaching institution over-dominated by committees. I suddenly found that, although I was a full professor, I had nothing to lead. Instead, I launched out in evangelistic missions, taking students with me through much of Western Canada and beyond. So yes, I do know that leadership is one of my gifts.

To analyse one's own gift is a different matter, however. I suppose the first requirement in any leader is total loyalty and commitment to Jesus Christ. Any Christian leader is only an under-shepherd to the one whom St Peter calls the Chief Shepherd. That requires personal surrender to Christ. It requires a devotional life that keeps us close to him. It prompts the question, 'What would Jesus do?' in all difficult or doubtful situations. Any Christian ministry that does not reflect something of Jesus and is not modelled on the leadership of Jesus is bound to be a travesty.

It is also obvious that, if Christian leadership is based on Jesus Christ, we must be loyal to the Scriptures which Jesus studied and obeyed for his own life and inspired for his followers. Although he was the Lord, Jesus based his ministry and teaching on the Old Testament revelation. Indeed, that is one of the reasons why I regard the Bible as normative for Christian belief and behaviour: Jesus clearly did. My second reason is empirical: it works. A Christianity which detracts from Scripture, denies its authority, or adds significantly to it, is headed for the decline that the liberal churches of the world are almost without exception experiencing, while the Bible-based churches are generally growing. I have therefore tried in my leadership to follow the teaching of the Bible – not proof texts here and there, not a favourite chapter or doctrine, but the overall teaching of the book. I do not see how, in loyalty to Jesus, a Christian can adopt any other position. If Jesus was wrong about the respect he accorded to Scripture, he could have been wrong about everything else.

Example is a vital part of leadership. Time and again, on missions as well as in regular church work, I have said to my colleagues, 'I shall not ask you to do anything I am not prepared to do myself.' I have often cleared up the church after a service, or washed the dishes after a communal meal, even though that was not my normal role in the church. Example speaks loud and clear.

So does love for those whom one is leading. A warmth and lightness of touch in relationships, little gifts of appreciation now and then, letters and words of thanks after a job has been well done: these things are often forgotten in an age when the old courtesies are dying out, but they are an important part of Christian leadership and they oil the wheels of any institution you are trying to lead.

Consultation is important for any leader, and I have certainly found it so. The leader still has to make the final decision, but mistakes are less likely if he or she takes seriously and weighs carefully what other members think.

There is also the question of a fellowship of leadership. It is the answer to an authoritarian autocracy on the one hand and an unthinking democracy on the other. The opening verse of almost all Paul's Epistles shows how he constantly worked with a small leadership team. I found this crucial. It means allowing the life of the Christian body to flourish. It means recognizing and fostering gifts in other people. In the early days I had a lot to learn about leading a team. It was my colleague David Prior who taught me two crucial lessons. One was encapsulated in that phrase 'a fellowship of leadership'. He showed me how it could come about during the five years in which we jointly led St Aldate's, and I owe him a debt of gratitude for that crucial insight. The other thing he taught me is that 'nobody should minister without being ministered to'. Of course! That is why so many people burn out in church work. They are put into a job and nobody ministers to them there. They run a Sunday school class and nobody loves them, encourages them or listens to their problems. They become churchwarden and it goes on for ever. No. Everyone, most definitely including the pastor, should have somebody who ministers to them, somebody to support them. It is the universal remedy against burnout. Another helpful expedient which we developed at St Aldate's during my later years there was this: we asked people to undertake a ministry for just one year, with no obligation to continue after that. We found, not surprisingly, that people became much more ready to serve. They knew it was not a life sentence. Each September we would have a major time of commissioning scores of people in the church for a variety of ministries during the coming year.

The good leader must also be self-critical. At St Aldate's, I would sometimes get people to sit through a sermon listening to it critically, to help me improve my skills. The whole team would gather regularly to assess how we were doing as a church, where the weak points were, where we lacked vision or cohesion. The only way to stay in the game, let alone to improve, is to be rigorously self-critical, and that includes welcoming and weighing criticism from others.

I found that my skills in leadership greatly increased after I had consciously allowed the Holy Spirit to govern my life and impart to me something of his wisdom. The charismatic movement as such is often crazy, but the wisdom imparted by the Holy Spirit is a profound and welcome reality, and one which every leader needs.

Perhaps one of the most uncommon and yet essential aspects of leadership is boldness: boldness in seizing initiatives, boldness in doing the unconventional thing, boldness in making changes, boldness in standing up for biblical truth. I am tired of leaders who are timid and seem terrified of doing anything lest they do the wrong thing. We need people who can and will take a lead. The spirit of fear needs to be exorcised from many a leader. Of course, this fearlessness can easily lead to lack of tact, and I know it has often done so in my own case. Yet I still prize boldness as a Christlike gift imparted by the Holy Spirit. If the trumpet gives an uncertain voice, who will prepare for battle? If the leader gives an uncertain lead, who will follow? Nobody will, and nobody should. The fundamental requirement of leaders is that they should lead – and curiously enough, many leaders do not.

PART 4

FAITH AND THE GOSPEL

CHAPTER 11

The Evangelicals

I am a Christian first and foremost. I am happy to have been reared and to minister within the Anglican Church, of which I am an ordained priest. I am, however, unashamedly Evangelical in my churchmanship. Is this from prejudice or obscurantism? I think not. My father was a central churchman, a village clergyman whom I enormously admired. There was no Evangelical teaching or ethos in the schools I attended. How, then, did I come to these convictions?

The answer takes us back to the first chapter of this book, and the clear conversion which I experienced in my mid-teens. I was already something of a rebel, and it was only after the accident of being introduced to the almost subterranean Sunday meeting in the cricket pavilion at Clifton College, and the challenge it brought to my way of life, that I began thinking seriously about the Christian faith. I had always vaguely accepted that faith, but kept it on the back burner and did little practical about it. Now I saw it as an intellectual and practical voyage of enquiry. I was challenged by the confident claim of Rendle Short, Professor of Surgery at Bristol University and editor of the *British Medical Journal*, who spoke at the first meeting I attended. He maintained that Jesus Christ was no past figure of history but was vibrantly alive. Torn between disbelief of his claim and respect for his credentials, I determined to find out the truth.

I explained in that first chapter something of the course and the resolution of my search. I became convinced of the central claim of the Christian faith that death had not been the final act in the story of Jesus: he was risen from the dead, alive for ever more. Years later I twice returned to write about this central claim, in the popular paperback *Man Alive* and the more substantial *The Empty Cross of Jesus*. To me it is the linchpin of the veracity of Christianity. I was impressed by the attitude of Lord Darling, at one time Lord Chief Justice of England, who expressed it thus at a private dinner party: 'We as Christians are asked to take a very great deal on trust: the teachings, for example, and the ministry of Jesus. If we had to take it all on trust, I for one would be sceptical. The crux of the problem whether Jesus was or was not what he claimed to be must surely depend on the truth or otherwise of the resurrection. On that greatest point we are not merely asked to have faith. In its favour as a living truth there exists such overwhelming evidence, positive and negative, factual and circumstantial, that no intelligent jury in the world could fail to bring in the verdict that the resurrection story is true.'

I have, of course, studied the subject since then in great depth, as a New Testament scholar, an ancient historian and a Christian apologist. I remain convinced that there is no credible explanation of the empty tomb, the resurrection appearances, the start of the early Church and the transformation of the disciples *other* than the solid truth of the almost unthinkable happening, the resurrection of Jesus Christ from the dead. That is where my conscious pilgrimage began. I entrusted my life to this living Jesus and found the reality of his presence and power was such that for 50 years and more I have been unable to doubt it.

My new faith was nourished and deepened more than I can say by the leaders of the Iwerne Minster house parties. They were all Evangelicals, and I found it natural to move in that direction myself. But what exactly is an Evangelical? My answer has always been the same. Evangelicalism is nothing other than a wholehearted commitment to the unadorned Christianity of the New Testament. It is not about churchmanship or moral stances. It is not about simplicity in worship or fundamentalism. Rather, it consists in a carefully thought-out commitment to the faith of the New Testament, with perhaps six particular emphases.

Tenets of Evangelicalism

Evangelicals take the Scriptures to be normative for their belief and behaviour. This is not an easy position to maintain in the face of a hundred years of intelligent liberal scholarship, much of it attacking the central elements in the gospel. Yet thoughtful Evangelicals have faced these problems and seen a way through them. They are not fundamentalists, regarding all elements of Scripture as of equal value or literally true. There is room to differ on the edibility of Jonah or the carat-rating of the streets in the heavenly Jerusalem. Nonetheless, all Evangelicals regard Scripture as being decisive for their understanding of Jesus and of the life disciples are called to lead. If an action is shown to be unbiblical, they will seek to avoid it. If a doctrine is shown to be biblical, they will seek to proclaim it. There is room for different interpretation of the Scriptures, but once an Evangelical is persuaded of the teaching of the book for belief and behaviour, that is decisive.

This is no unthinking pietism. There are only three views you can logically take on what is the final authority, under God, in the Christian religion. One is the Christian Scriptures, and that is what Evangelicals set before themselves. One is the Christian reason, and that is where the liberals lay their chief emphasis. One is the Christian tradition down the centuries, and that is determinative for most in the Catholic tradition. It is very clear from a study of the Gospels that Jesus embraced the first of these positions. He regarded the Old Testament as decisive for his understanding of his mission, and he regarded its teachings as the inspired revelation of God. It has long seemed to me that, if that was the attitude of the Master, it should also be the attitude of the disciple. Of course proper weight has to be given to the Christian tradition, but that is far from monochrome. What are we to do when traditions clash? And of course we must give proper weight to our God-given reason, but what are we to do when our reason and the Scriptures are in conflict? Homosexual practice is a current example, where political correctness and biblical teaching are at odds. For myself, the two most decisive reasons for accepting the final authority under God of the Scriptures are these. First, such was undoubtedly the attitude of Jesus himself, and he should know. Second, this book has power to teach and transform me; it has power to change the lives of those to whom it is preached; and churches throughout the world which are loyal to the Scriptures are growing, while liberal churches are everywhere in decline.

Although belief in Scripture has never been part of the credal confession of the Church, it has been the substratum out of which those creeds have been fashioned. If, then, we grant the supremacy of Scripture as a guide for Evangelical Christians, what particular emphases within it are they at pains to underline?

One is the universal need of human beings for the rescuing grace of God. The Bible is very clear that all have sinned and come short of the glory of God. There is none righteous, not one. There is nobody who can look God in the eye and say, 'Move over, God. Here I come.' Yet I do not believe the sinfulness of humankind simply because it is a recurring theme of Scripture. It is equally obvious from the newspapers. The bottom line about human beings is that we constantly go our own way, neglect God and reject his call on our lives. This doctrine of human self-centredness and frailty is very unpopular. People like to blame their stars, their upbringing, their lack of education, their psychology or sheer bad luck for the failures in their lives. They are most reluctant to take responsibility for it themselves. Scripture, however, quietly maintains that we are all accountable to God for our deeds, our thoughts, our actions and our resultant character. 'Each of us will give an account of himself to God' (Romans 14:12). Unpopular as it is, this is realistic, and Evangelicals will not bow to political correctness, wave farewell to human accountability, and maintain that we are all OK. We are not OK, and that is where the gospel begins.

So we move to the next great tenet of the Evangelical faith. It is that God himself has intervened to put us to rights and do all that is necessary to make amends on our behalf. The deity of Jesus, his humanity and his atoning death on the cross all figure large in Evangelical theology. If Jesus were not divine, he would not be able to rescue anyone. Since he shares both God's nature and ours, he can be the appropriate – and unique – mediator between God the Father and ourselves. Accordingly, Evangelicals will have nothing to do with those reductionist Christologies which see Jesus as a magician, a witty rabbi, a Zealot leader and so forth. Whatever else he may be, he shares the nature of God Almighty *and* that of human beings. He is the bridge man. As such he offered his perfect life on the cross on behalf of sinners, and thus fulfilled the blood sacrifices of the Old Covenant.

These animal sacrifices were unwilling victims and their deaths could not make amends for human self-centredness and wickedness, but the willing self-oblation of the Son of God for a human race that had gone astray was astounding, undreamed-of love and generosity on God's part. Moreover, nobody could claim that it was unfair. Personal self-sacrifice for those in need is never unfair, although it often goes beyond the call of duty. God in Christ had done all that was necessary to burden himself with our offences, so that we could with perfect justice stand tall before God, 'ransomed, healed, restored, forgiven'. Ronnie Knox, in his book *The Creed in Slow Motion*, puts it in a slightly different way, derived from the thinking of Anselm long ago, 'The gravity of an offence is measured by the dignity of the person against whom the offence is committed, while the greatness of the reparation is measured by the dignity of the person making it.' How wise, then, of our Reformers to keep the word 'satisfaction' in the Prayer of Consecration in the Book of Common Prayer. Christ's death was indeed satisfaction for the sins of the world: it was enough. The atoning work of Christ on the cross, and the utter sufficiency of that death for our salvation, has always been one of the New Testament truths on which Evangelicals have insisted most strongly.

A further major emphasis is the physical resurrection of Jesus Christ from the dead. Evangelicals are not prepared to settle for the interpretation of the resurrection as some vague spiritual conviction among Jesus' followers. They will not swallow the suggestion made by some German scholars that the resurrection is merely an enthusiastic affirmation that the cause of Jesus continues. Evangelicals have not claimed to be able to understand the resurrection completely, but they have been strong in affirming the New Testament accounts, and seeing in the bodily resurrection of the Saviour the hope for redeemed human beings and the foretaste of a new heaven and a new earth. They see it as the assurance that the sacrifice of Calvary was accepted. They see it as the demonstration that Jesus really was the Son of God. They see it as the source of spiritual power in the Christian life. They concentrate on it because the resurrection shows that Jesus is alive and can be met – and we need to meet with him in order to become his followers.

That leads to the issue of conversion, a controversial tenet for which Evangelicals are often derided. They believe that the Christian life begins with a personal, though not visible, encounter with the risen Christ. In surrendering to him, our sins are put away, covered for ever by what he did upon the cross. In surrendering to him, we begin the new life, the new birth, the new allegiance – call it what you will. Thoughtful

Evangelicals assert the need for 'conversion'. That is our side of beginning the new life: we turn to Christ in repentance and faith. They equally assert the glorious truth of 'regeneration'. That is God's side, as he gives us new life in Christ. It is not the case that Evangelicals are committed to the notion of sudden conversion: they merely insist that there has to be this surrender, be it conscious or unconscious, gradual or sudden, to the Christ who died and rose for us. It takes two to make a friendship. His arms were held out to us on the cross. We need to run into those arms if we are to become Christians. It is not important to know the day or hour when this happened – merely that it has happened. After all, I would not know the day of my natural birth unless my mother had told me. Many believers are quite unsure when their spiritual birth took place. What matters is not when they were born, but that they are spiritually alive.

If conversion is a basic building block in anybody's relation with God, the next distinctive characteristic of Evangelical belief follows as naturally as night follows day. We must proclaim by deed and word, by testimony and gracious actions, by preaching and conversation, the story of what God has done for us and the need for human beings to respond to him. Evangelism is the lifeblood of Evangelicals. Others concentrate on it from time to time: mercifully it is not restricted to Evangelicals, but it is something to which they give themselves, impelled by the Scriptures, driven by their recognition of the plight of human beings and by the surpassing grace of God in Christ incarnate, crucified and risen. Mission in the UK and overseas has always been a central tenet of the Evangelicals.

Those seem to me to be the main emphases of Evangelicals. Like other Christians, they value holiness of life, the sacraments, human reason, the tradition of the Church, the authority of their leaders. Like others, they have generally (though by no means always) maintained a strong social concern and competent scholarship. Different strains within the Evangelical camp place varying emphases on particular New Testament truths. Yet they all seek to follow 'the faith which was once for all entrusted to the saints' (Jude 3) and are not persuaded to abandon it in favour of modern imitations and alterations.

It will be apparent that none of the six elements which I have described as central to Evangelicals is a peculiarity of theirs. All these elements are prominently displayed in the New Testament. Evangelicals can therefore claim with justice that they have no distinctives. All they want to do is to understand and apply, without addition or subtraction, the Christianity they find in the New Testament. I find that a secure position to adopt, but I have to confess that there is also justice in some of the objections that are brought against Evangelicals.

Objections to Evangelicalism

The first criticism is that Evangelicals are often less than totally loyal to their denomination. That is true. If you are a Christian, an Anglican and an Evangelical, you obviously have to range these three allegiances in order. To be a Christian must clearly be the most important. Some will want to put their Anglicanism next and their Evangelicalism third; others will wish to reverse the order. I do not wish to fault either choice, although I know where my own preference lies. Manifestly, if a particular person values his Anglican heritage more than his Evangelical heritage, he will be bound at times to offend or disappoint fellow Evangelicals. If he values his Evangelicalism more, he will be bound at times to affront or disappoint his fellow Anglicans.

I recall a bishop who came to St Aldate's to conduct adult baptisms and confirmations. He noticed that a good many more baptisms took place than confirmations, and gently reproved me for not having urged every candidate to be confirmed. I had to say to him that many of them had not come from an Anglican background, and were by no means certain of worshipping in one in future, but they had been converted through the ministry of our church and wanted to be baptized there. Baptism is initiation into Christ, not into a denomination. Confirmation is a domestic rite of Anglicans and some other churches. These young men and women valued their Evangelical heritage above the Anglican one in which they were temporarily located. I cannot find it in me to blame them.

A second accusation against Evangelicals is rather more serious, and this is the charge that they are notoriously unco-operative with other Christians. Thus they usually decline to join in mission with those who cannot sign their 'basis of faith'. The basis of faith may be a blunt instrument. It may cause offence, and it does – but it is understandable, if not always justifiable. In the past, Evangelicals have often co-operated with Christians of other stripes and found that before long the distinctive biblical teachings which they hold dear have been eroded. Evangelical students have co-operated with others on evangelistic missions in their university and have then found, to their dismay, that a gospel is preached which bears little resemblance to that of the New Testament. No wonder they react by saying, 'We will do it ourselves next time.' I can understand the decision of the International Fellowship of Evangelical Students not to co-operate with those who do not take a firm stand on Scripture. It is, however, very trying for a speaker who does seek to take Scripture as the norm to be blackballed by a narrow-minded Christian Union Executive who know no theology and whose zeal outruns their understanding. I have suffered that way myself on one occasion!

Evangelicals are often justly accused of being narrow-minded. There remains a pietistic streak in some Evangelical behaviour – a suspicion of 'worldliness' in all its forms which blinds them to the real needs of the world. Evangelicals are much better at personal than social ethics. In the days of apartheid in South Africa, I was struck by how Afrikaans

Christians were totally blind to the evils of apartheid while being very careful to avoid swearing, working on Sundays, or anything suggestive in films and on television. Indeed, for a long time they did not even have television because of the possible dangers of eroticism and violence. That is typical. Evangelical spirituality has often been anxious to keep itself 'unspotted by the world', but weak on seeing the needs of the world and taking political action to try to remedy them. As a result, many Evangelical charities have offered 'band-aid' rather than attempting to deal radically with the underlying problems. Few Evangelical Christians have, until recently, gone into parliament or the media – two places where there are many battles to be fought and much influence to be exerted.

In my student days, Christian undergraduates faced a choice of either joining the Christian Union, with its strong emphasis on personal conversion and discipleship, or the Student Christian Movement, which was strong on 'Christianity and...' Clearly both are part of authentic Christianity, but life is short and you cannot do everything. As a result, most students were driven to choose – and were impoverished whichever decision they made. In due course the SCM withered away from lack of personal commitment to Christ, while the Christian Unions persisted in a narrow-minded discipleship which often failed to connect with the real world. The big change came, for the Anglican Evangelicals at least, with the first National Evangelical Anglican Congress in 1967, which recalled Evangelicals to their social and political heritage, neglected for more than 50 years. Then the advent of organizations like Tear Fund enabled Evangelical Christians of all denominations to give to very active charities which combined biblical faith with practical action.

Obscurantism is another charge often levelled against Evangelicals: they hold a view of Scripture which is uncritical and wilfully blind to the discoveries of modern theology. Once again, there is some justice in this claim. There is no doubt that many Evangelicals are obscurantist. They hide their heads in the sand and do not want to know about evolution or the non-Mosaic authorship of the Pentateuch. When I was undertaking postgraduate New Testament studies, the dearth of competent Evangelical literature often drove me to seek out intelligent Roman Catholic books, which seemed to be able to commend an orthodox position without being deemed obscurantist. For nearly 50 years, conservative scholarship (what there was of it) was of an inferior quality and failed to challenge the tenets of the liberal establishment. Fortunately, that is no longer the case today and the temptation to defensiveness arising from ignorance is much less compelling. Evangelicals need, like others, to recognize that God and truth are never opposed. All genuine truth is God's truth and needs to be welcomed as such, even if it causes us to reconsider some dearly-held position or other. Obscurantism has no place in the mental attitude of any Christian, Evangelical or otherwise.

There is also a constant tendency among their opponents to identify Evangelicals with fundamentalists. While the controversy of the 1920s concerned 'fundamental' or basic doctrines of the faith – such as the miracles of Jesus or the resurrection – which were being assailed by modernism, the word is nowadays applied to an extreme view which magnifies the divine authorship of Scripture and minimizes the human contribution. God is seen as communicating with us through 66 secretaries! Fundamentalism tends to see everything in Scripture as flat, literal truth. Clearly this will not do. The Bible is a most complex book, embracing a whole variety of literary modes – history, fable, poetry, letter, gospel, and so forth. It is not honouring God to assess each passage of the Bible without taking any account of the literary mode employed. Literalism has no part in the Evangelical's creed. It is not piety but folly to interpret poetry as if it were sober prose. When Scripture tells us that 'the mountains skipped like rams and the little hills like young sheep', we would be fools to apply a seismograph. To do so would be to show that we were incapable of appreciating poetry.

It is therefore important to nail the charge of fundamentalism once and for all. There are, of course, Evangelicals who are fundamentalists, particularly in America, but it is no integral part of the Evangelical creed. The very loose way in which New Testament writers quote the Old should preserve us from any infallibilist literalism. Indeed, the word 'infallible' which is used in many Evangelical bases of faith has been taken in two very different ways by reputable Evangelical scholars. A narrower interpretation sees the word as meaning that there is no possibility of the least error in any statement of Scripture. This view runs into enormous problems when you compare the same story in Chronicles and Kings, for example, or in the Gospel accounts. Moreover, the Bible never makes such a claim. The broader interpretation takes the word in the sense of its Latin root, as meaning, 'If you follow it, it will not lead you astray.' That is the sense in which I regard the Bible as infallible, but, because of the ambiguity and the associations of the word, I prefer not to use it, but to speak of the Scriptures as the uniquely authoritative guide for the Christian in all matters of faith and conduct. If I am persuaded that a doctrine is taught by Scripture, I will teach it whether I like it or not. If I find that a way of life is advocated, I will seek to follow it whether or not it is my preference. That is what it means to allow the Bible to be your guide. That is a conservative approach to Scripture. To confuse it with a literalist fundamentalism is a major category confusion, but many people continue to make that mistake.

I remember preaching one night (without any concessions to literalism!) on Christ's ascension in Oriel College, Oxford. At dinner afterwards I found myself sitting next to Professor James Barr. He told me that he had just written a big book against people like me, called *Fundamentalism*. He had indeed. It was so big that it indicated an unhealthy obsession with the topic. I told him that I was not in the least worried because I was not a fundamentalist, but a conservative theologian. He told me that they were one and the same thing. I challenged him to come and debate the subject at St Aldate's, which he did – but by then he had changed his tune! A conservative attitude to Scripture is the position officially adopted by almost all churches, but fundamentalism is to be found in the formularies of very few of them.

There is one other area where Evangelicals run into a lot of criticism: their understanding of the cross of Christ. The cross is a great mystery, and none of us can plumb its depths. It shows the immensity of God's love. It shows the victory of Christ over death and evil. It is a many-splendoured thing. Yet the aspect which Evangelicals love to stress most of all is the substitutionary purpose of Christ's death. He died in place of guilty sinners. 'He himself bore our sins in his body on the tree' (1 Peter 2:24); 'Christ died for sins, once for all, the righteous for the unrighteous, to bring you to God' (1 Peter 3:18). That is music to Evangelical ears, for it is the key to our freedom, the cost of our rescue. Evangelicals love the ransom saying of Mark 10:45, where 'the Son of Man came to give his life as a ransom for many'. They recognize that attempting to win God's favour is hopeless: 'All who rely on observing the law are under a curse, for it is written, "Cursed is everyone who does not continue to do everything written in the Book of the Law"' (Galatians 3:10). Three verses later, a blazing light shines into our darkness: 'Christ redeemed us from the curse of the law by becoming a curse for us – for it is written, "Cursed be everyone who is hung upon a tree"'(3:13). Christ himself bore on the cross the curse of God's judgement which should have rested upon us.

There are many such references in Scripture, and Evangelicals are right to stress them. There is nothing that brings such peace to the troubled conscience as to recognize that Christ himself has handled our hopeless situation. He took personal responsibility for all the evil we have done. This doctrine of his substitution for us sticks in the gullet of many a self-confident person. It is very offensive. Once you become aware of your sinfulness, however, there is nothing in the world so glorious as to see that God Almighty has stepped in for you at the point of your greatest need, and has done for you what you could never do for yourself. I cannot fault Evangelicals for majoring on this aspect of Calvary, but they can and should be blamed if this is the one and only aspect of the cross they teach. St Paul is very strong on the interiorization by the believer of what Christ did on Calvary. The individual is called to die to sin and to rise to the life of righteousness. Evangelicals are not always strong in asserting this truth.

Moreover, Evangelicals often give very crude and inadequate illustrations of the cross. Sometimes it is suggested that a judge finds a person guilty and condemns that person to death, then lays aside his judicial robes and gives his own life instead. This is grossly misleading. Christ did not give his life for one person, but for the world. More importantly, in that illustration you have a clear injustice: the wrong person suffers. The gospel, however, does not suggest that the wrong person suffers. It tells us that Jesus was perfect man, heading up our rescue as Adam headed up our fall. He is representative man, taking the place of all individual men and women. In him God was reconciling the world to himself. Evangelicals also tend to speak of Christ bearing the punishment of human sin, but the New Testament never uses the word 'punishment', *kolasis*, of the cross. To suggest that an irate Father punishes a blameless Jesus for guilty you and me is a travesty of the New Testament doctrine of the atonement. It is important to keep strictly to what Scripture teaches about this most profound mystery.

Evangelicalism and the whole Church

Despite the weaknesses which many of us Evangelicals display, I am proud to be an Evangelical. It is an essentially biblical stance. The very word suggests the good news with which we are entrusted. All over the world this Evangelical Christianity changes lives. Yes, it is good to be an Evangelical – but it is not enough. None of the adjectives which Christians use to define their stance are adequate to stand on their own. The gospel is so great that we cannot take it all in, and the different catchphrases that Christians love to use must never be seen as party labels, but rather as limited pointers to what the whole Church of God should aim to be.

We should all be Catholic, in the sense of being universal. The Church of God is meant to be a worldwide fellowship, recognizably one, with interchangeabilty of members and leaders. We have a long way to go before we achieve that, but it is part of God's design for us.

The whole Church of God is meant to be Evangelical, in the sense of being committed to the good news brought us in the New Testament. Alas, many churches either take away from that gospel, or make illegitimate additions to it. We have a long way to go before the churches of the world are consumed with passion for the good news which Jesus brought.

All churches are meant to be liberal, in the sense of being open-minded, full of grace and generosity, using our God-given minds to get to grips with God's revelation. Sadly, there is much illiberal obscurantism and prejudice in all parts of the Church, including among those who call themselves liberal. We have a long way to go in this respect as well.

All parts of the Church should also be charismatic, in the sense of rejoicing in the 'gracious gifts', *charismata*, which the Holy Spirit lavishes on the Body of Christ, the Church. We fall short of that, too.

These labels can be positively sinful if they are used to exclude others and to denote our various sectarianisms. They can be most valuable if we see them as pointers to what the Church in its fullness is intended to be.

I have been enormously helped in my understanding of what true Evangelicalism is by the life and teaching of John

Stott, whose work I described in Chapters 9 and 10. His concern for maintaining and interpreting biblical truth has been a banner for me. So has his gracious way of doing it – firm yet full of love for those who disagree with him. His building up of All Souls, Langham Place, with its many gospel initiatives, has likewise been an inspiration, and his church was a beacon in the 1950s and '60s when Evangelicals were struggling to emerge from the ghetto and find their feet. I greatly value his writings, which nurture the Church, contend for the truth and face difficult social and intellectual issues. The Langham Trust, and the ministry it has exercised in providing literature for leaders in the Two-Thirds World, and the development of the Evangelical Fellowship of the Anglican Communion, with its Bursary Scheme, are outstanding and visionary achievements. All this and more has been an inspiration to Evangelicals. We thank God for John Stott, and follow in his footsteps – a long way behind.

My own awareness of the Evangelical movement began in the immediate postwar period. Between then and now, the number of Evangelicals has grown enormously in the national Church, while the influence of the Church as a whole has substantially diminished. There has been a sustained growth of Evangelical ordinands since that period, to the extent that they now outnumber those of all other persuasions. Nobody could have dreamed of this earlier in the century, but by the 1960s it was beginning to become apparent. I recall Archbishop Michael Ramsey once saying humorously, 'In 50 years the Church of England will be dominated by Evangelicals – and I am glad I shall not be here to see it!'

During subsequent decades, the major influence moved away from the liberal Evangelicals, who produced distinguished names such as Max Warren and Douglas Harrison, but did not appear to do much in terms of actual evangelization. This was attempted through a number of enthusiastic agencies and individuals, all of whom sought unashamedly to win people for Christ. Evangelicals owe an enormous amount to the Church Pastoral Aid Society, led successively by two good friends of mine, T.G. Mohan and Tim Dudley Smith. The Crusaders and the Scripture Union, the Covenanters and the C.S.S.M. beach missions all played a part too. Yet future historians will be in little doubt that the most significant influence was wielded by two institutions: the Bash camps, under the leadership of E.J.H. Nash, and the Inter Varsity Fellowship, led by Douglas Johnson and then Oliver Barclay. It would be hard to exaggerate the quiet influence of these two organizations, and it was a great privilege for me to have been intimately associated with both.

Immediately after the war a significant report was commissioned, entitled *Towards the Conversion of England*, in which Evangelicals played an important part – not least the Chairman, Bishop Christopher Chavasse, whom I got to know and admire in his old age. It was designed to 'survey the whole problem of modern evangelism with special reference to the spiritual needs and prevailing intellectual outlook of the non-worshipping members of the community, and to report on the organization and methods by which such needs can most effectively be met'. The report revealed 'a wholesale drift from organized religion', and came up with some well-tried and some innovative strategies for meeting the situation. Despite the brilliance of the report and its numerous reprints, however, nothing came of it. Archbishop Fisher declined to act on it, and instead concentrated the energies of the postwar Church on the fruitless exercise of revising canon law. A great opportunity was lost. Nonetheless, the report did a great deal to awaken the Church of England to the need for evangelism, and some developments such as the Village Evangelists, the College of Preachers and the Mission to London in 1949 may well have been inspired by it. That said, the first real Evangelical advance in Britain of which I was aware sprang from the Billy Graham Mission in 1954.

I well recall a visit by General Wilson Haffenden to Oxford in 1953, when I was president of the Christian Union for which he was preaching. He told me that he had been profoundly impressed by a young American evangelist called Billy Graham, and was going to combine with others to bring him to London. This was a bold step. At that stage Billy was little known, and his background as a farm boy in the States seemed less than propitious! Nonetheless, he came, and the Harringay Crusade of 1954 brought London to the brink of revival. Everyone was talking about this man. It became the accepted thing to go to the crusade. In fashionable society, debutantes even asked their escorts, 'Darling, have you been converted yet?' Thousands of people, from *Daily Mirror* journalists to pop singers like Cliff Richard, responded to the gospel Billy Graham preached. Initially, his simple biblical message was denounced by many in the Church hierarchy as naïve, but by the end of the crusade they were only too glad to be invited to sit on the platform from which he spoke. Archbishop Michael Ramsey was at first critical, but subsequently became a supporter of Billy Graham. 'Every time Graham came to England on a mission,' he declared, 'more young men had vocations to be priests.' At the London College of Divinity in the 1960s, we found that in some years nearly half our ordinands had been converted through a Billy Graham crusade.

During the Harringay Crusade, Billy Graham ran daily in Hyde Park for exercise, and the news-hounds tried in vain to keep up with him! His integrity of life, his freshness, his emphasis on Scripture and his refusal to preach anything that ran counter to its teaching were arresting. So was his use of story and illustration, and most of all the directness of his challenge to 'get up out of your seat' and come to the front to 'confess your sins and receive Christ'. To begin with, he had a 1,000-voice choir as backing to his preaching, and they sang 'Just as I Am' while people streamed forward. Needless to say, this was attacked as emotionalism. Billy began to preach with no choir, simply a soloist, his friend and colleague George Beverley Shea, and the critics were confounded to find that the same massive response followed. Vast numbers came forward to entrust their lives to Christ.

When people came forward, they were met and given brief advice and encouragement by counsellors, who in 1954 were rather hurriedly recruited and trained, but in later years this process was greatly refined. Advisers were on hand to help when a counsellor ran into difficulties. Follow-up literature was given, and every person was referred to one of the supporting churches, of whatever denomination. There was a lot of fallout from this procedure, but much of it was not Billy Graham's fault. God had given him an astonishing gift of precipitating decisions for Christ, but it was the task of the local pastors to nourish the new spiritual lives that fell into their laps. Many of them did not. Some of them tried to persuade those referred to them that nothing had happened, which was inexcusable. Others had no idea how to build up a new Christian, because they had never seen an adult convert before. The Evangelicals had, though. They knew how to help a new believer at least begin the path of discipleship.

The Billy Graham crusades of 1954 and 1955, followed in due course by 1966 and 1984, had an incalculable effect on the spiritual life of Britain. Hundreds went into full-time church ministry. Thousands became active Christian disciples. Others undertook missionary work in Britain and overseas. Confidence in the gospel grew, and the Evangelicals were now out of the wilderness: they had become a voice to be listened to in the councils of the Church.

Probably the most widespread and carefully prepared of all Graham's efforts in Britain was the Mission England Campaign of 1984. Recognizing the need for process in effective outreach, rather than relying exclusively on crisis, his organization designed the campaign as a three-year plan of action, involving preparation, evangelism and nurture. Its professed aim was 'to glorify God, to alert the nation to the importance of spiritual issues, to motivate local churches to do their own evangelism, and to bring large numbers of people to

a personal faith in Christ'. The outreach was fully interdenominational, as all Billy's previous work had been. Prayer
Triplets were inaugurated, where three people got together on
a regular basis to pray for three friends each to become
Christians. This year-long emphasis on intentional intercession based on personal friendships led thousands to Christ
before Billy Graham even arrived. Other aspects of training
were also important. Christian Life and Witness courses
involved some 6,000 churches. Operation Andrew strengthened the concept of friendship with people who were not yet
Christians. There was careful networking with ministers of all
denominations. There were 40 stadium events and nearly 200
video missions. It was an enormous effort, chaired by Gavin
Reid of the Church Pastoral Aid Society, who subsequently
became Bishop of Maidstone. Anglican involvement was great
– half the enquirers at Mission England were Anglican.
Overall, one in 50 of the population of England attended a
mission event. My friend the Rev. Mark Brown, of Emmanuel
Church, Northwood, has written a distinguished Master's
thesis entitled 'Anglican Evangelical Approaches to Evangelism,
1800 – the present day'. In it he records the postwar initiatives
in evangelism with great insight, and I have drawn on some of
his material here – with his cheerful agreement!

There can be no doubt that these crusades had a vast impact
on the country, and the position of the Evangelicals was enormously enhanced by it all. Before Billy Graham came, evangelism was rather looked down on by mainline Anglicans.
Tom Rees, a most gifted layman, had held large rallies in the
Albert Hall and elsewhere, including a very successful ministry in the States, while his brother Dick Rees majored on
parish missions. Yet it was very much a minority interest in
Church circles. After Billy, evangelism came increasingly into
the centre of the frame. Even in the run-up to Mission
England, however, there was a substantial number of dissent-
ing voices among leading Evangelicals. They were less than
happy about mass evangelism: was it not a crude instrument,

and could not the time, effort and money be better spent in other forms of outreach? Some of them were rather sceptical about American influence. They looked for something more home-cooked – but none of the home cooks was in the same league as Billy Graham for giftedness in drawing people to Christ. So Mission England went ahead, and was very successful, but it may well have marked the end of an era.

By then, many had become suspicious of the big meeting. They did not want their minds and feelings manipulated by an evangelist whom they had never met. Society was increasingly secularized, and people required something much more solid than a single night at a crusade if their whole lives were to be changed around. That is one of the many reasons why the 10-week Alpha course has become so effective. Moreover, by then the crusade had become a blunt tool in two particular ways. First, it affected only the fringe of the churchgoing population. Few rank outsiders found their way into its meetings. The people who professed faith were, on the whole, those who had some contact with the church and its members, but had not hitherto been personally committed. Second, the follow-up procedure had real weaknesses. It is always the most delicate part of evangelism, and a short talk with an unknown counsellor, a mass-produced response system and a referral to an unfamiliar church left a lot to be desired. The possibilities of slipping through the net were substantial, and many did fall by the wayside. They did not go to the church to which they had been referred. The pastor of that church did not follow them up. The nurture courses to which they were invited were badly run. Allowances were not made for differences of race, background and education. One could go on: the nurturing which followed these crusades was clearly indifferent.

In fact, from the late 1960s onwards, there was a growing tendency to question an overdependence on crusade evangelism, particularly by those who worked in inner-city areas, where it was least effective. There were, in any case, few preachers of the stature of Billy Graham who could draw thousands to the largest stadia in the land and could be relied upon to preach the gospel in a way that would have broad appeal. Where were his successors? And was the crusade the best way of engaging with the unchurched world? These were the questions that circulated among Evangelicals in the late 1960s, as the charismatic movement began to take off. Many Christians began to wonder whether, instead of having exaggerated expectations of a visiting evangelist, we might dare to hope for a move of God's Spirit in our country, bringing together the different denominations and drawing thousands of uncommitted people to faith. Might this be the doorway to bring about sustained outreach? Many cherished hopes that in the charismatic movement these high expectations might be met. It has been described as perhaps the most important postwar movement to cut across every denominational boundary, and the Evangelicals were profoundly involved in it from the start. It has become an ineluctable strand in the spirituality of most Evangelicals, and this is the subject I wish to examine in the next chapter.

CHAPTER 12

The Renewal Movement

At the beginning of the twentieth century a remarkable movement of the Holy Spirit took place. It was the rise of Pentecostalism. Now, a century later, the Pentecostal Churches and their charismatic cousins represent probably a third of all Christians. It is certainly one of the great renewals in history, and one we dare not neglect.

The link between the Pentecostals and the charismatics is an interesting one. The Pentecostal movement began in 1900 with Evangelical men and women who dug deep into the subject of holiness, crying out to God for a more profound experience of his love and power. The result was an overwhelming experience of God, accompanied by the gift of tongues. They saw this as baptism with the Holy Spirit, as at Pentecost, and they saw the gift of tongues as evidence of that baptism. Very quickly, therefore, Pentecostal orthodoxy required you to be baptized with the Holy Spirit as a second-stage initiation in your Christian life, and the demonstration of its reality was that you would speak in tongues. Other gifts emerged and were highly prized, such as interpretation of tongues, prophetic utterance, some remarkable healings, and the gift of knowledge – insight into a situation of which one had no cognitive knowledge.

The whole thing was hotly debated, but it seemed unassailable to those in the Pentecostal tradition who had experienced it. Opposition was only to be expected from those who had not received 'the baptism'. Imagine their surprise in the middle of the century, when God began to pour out precisely the same gifts of tongues, prophecy, healing and words of knowledge on those who were not Pentecostals and had no intention of becoming such – rather, they wanted to stay in their own denominations. Gradually these gifts spread through almost all denominations, even those which, like the Baptists and the Brethren, had been quite certain that such phenomena had died out at the end of the apostolic age, or at all events by the time the canon was formulated in the fourth century. This is a totally gratuitous claim, by the way, and one that is denied by the writings of the early Church fathers, many of whom recognized the gifts as operating in their own day. Nowadays the reality and impact of the charismatic movement, embracing both Pentecostals and those within the historic denominations who revel in the same gifts, is indisputable. So, alas, are the excesses of the movement.

Early experiences

As a matter of fact, the excesses are far less now than they were in the 1960s and '70s, at least in the West. I well remember the days in the 1960s when this phenomenon was beginning to catch on. I had recently taken up my post as New Testament teacher in the London College of Divinity. I was very affronted to hear that late one night an enthusiastic charismatic had come surreptitiously to the college, got a dozen or so ordinands into a small room, and taught them that they needed to be baptized with the Holy Spirit if they were going to be effective in their ministries, and that the evidence of that baptism was speaking in tongues. The gift was, apparently, slow to manifest itself that evening. Seeking to heat up the spiritual temperature, the visitor told them to 'yield their tongues to the Lord' and speak out whatever came.

They told me all about it the next day, and it was not a very propitious beginning to a study of the charismatic movement. I found myself in frank opposition to it. For one thing, it looked manipulative and fleshly, trying to get people to 'yield their tongues' and speak out any nonsense that emerged. For another, the person who had come was not an impressive Christian and certainly not a learned one. I studied the literature that was available, compared it with the teaching of the New Testament, and found it wanting. Their exegesis of the various Acts passages and 1 Corinthians 12–14 was poor, and in places demonstrably wrong. So I taught against it – and, because I knew a good deal more about the New Testament than any of the students did, they could not defeat me in debate. I had no difficulty, for example, in showing them that all seven of the New Testament references to baptism in or with the Holy Spirit refer to an initial encounter with the Holy Spirit, not to some rarified experience, some second blessing for superior Christians. While they could not defeat me in debate, however, they often defeated me in sheer love and thoughtfulness, generosity and prayerfulness. Despite my scepticism, therefore, I began to take them seriously. Just possibly, they might have got something I was lacking.

Shortly before we moved to Nottingham, I became Principal of the college. I noticed with some irritation that, when an applicant came who professed to have been helped by the charismatic movement, he seemed to have an immediate, unspoken affinity with those I considered to be the ringleaders of the movement among our students. How could they know that someone was charismatic without being told? It puzzled (and rather annoyed) me. Sometimes they would give me a testimony to the remarkable change in the level of their Christianity since they had been baptized with the Holy Spirit, and urge me to follow their example. Unfortunately, the change was far from apparent in some cases, and I can think of one where the claim seemed absolutely bizarre. A young ordinand went round the staff and the local hospital, claiming to have had a powerful experience of the Spirit. He maintained that he had terminal cancer of the stomach and would be dead in a month unless a certain charismatic guru came and laid hands on him. This was sheer moonshine, and gave rise to the suspicion that he was mentally unbalanced. It nearly caused him to be debarred from ordination, but I sent him to a Christian psychiatrist, who examined him and came to the conclusion that all would be well. The Holy Spirit had indeed been at work in him, and some of the mud that had lain at the bottom of his life was being churned up. The psychiatrist was of the opinion that when he settled down he would do good work in the ministry, and so it has proved. Nonetheless, it did not encourage me to take the charismatic movement more seriously if it could do such strange things to its advocates.

That summer, however, I was forced to change my mind. I was due to give a course of lectures at Regent College, Vancouver, a pleasant summer assignment. I liked to preach on the Sundays so as to experience the flavour of some of the churches from which the students came. I accepted an invitation to preach at St Margaret's Church, which looked as though it was Anglican but was in fact independent. I was amazed by what I found. When I had finished my address, they shouted out for me to go on. I was not used to this! A woman sang beautifully in a language I did not understand, but later learned was tongues, and then she sang an interpretation to precisely the same complex tune. It fitted perfectly, and left me open-mouthed. Its content was as surprising as its form. It referred, I remember, to a large Jehovah's Witness gathering in the vicinity and urged the congregation to get involved with them and, in the spirit of gentleness, display the love of Christ to them. Later, after a time of beautiful praise, there was an astonishing outburst of worship in tongues from the congregation. The harmony was so superb that I looked to

258

see who was conducting them. Nobody was – except the Spirit of God.

I had several more surprises that morning. The minister was scarcely in evidence: he sat in an inconspicuous place and others did most of the leading. Then I saw a number of people going to meet the pastor after the service. They were clearly wanting prayer for healing, and in several cases the healing was immediate and obvious to the onlooker. Finally, as I stood by the door while the congregation left, I noticed that many of them were in their twenties and thirties, dressed very casually, many without shoes or sandals. I asked several of them how long they had been Christians. In almost every case it was only a few months, or a year or two at most. These were representatives of the Jesus Movement, part of the counterculture in the 1960s who had turned to Jesus Christ. They amazed me by their intelligence and spiritual passion.

After lunch I asked the pastor, Bob Birch, to pray for me. I told him that I was the Principal of a theological college and I had seen things that morning that I had never believed possible. I expected that he would pray for the gift of tongues, but he did not. As he prayed over me with deep compassion, he was led to predict that I would have from God the gift of wisdom in running the college. That seemed eminently appropriate. The move to Nottingham was causing a new set of problems to arise daily, which taxed us greatly. I went away knowing that something had happened that afternoon, something that was profoundly enriching to my spiritual life. I had gone deeper with God's Holy Spirit. What is more, the charismatics back at the college knew it too, which was mildly embarrassing. They realized that now I was one of them, even if I did not as yet pray in tongues.

That was my first personal experience of this renewal or charismatic movement. I had been forced to recognize that, although there was a lot of rubbish in the movement, although there was much emotionalism and bad exegesis of Scripture, there was also something very important. It was essentially a matter of letting God be God, and letting him have his way with us.

My next positive recollection is of a trip to Singapore at the invitation of Bishop Chiu Ban It, where I joined him for a Friday evening prayer service in the cathedral. The last time I had been in that cathedral, they had struggled manfully but inappropriately with a Merbecke setting of the Holy Communion. I had no idea of the changes that had taken place, of the Bishop's profound experience of the Spirit, or of the regular renewal meetings that now happened in the cathedral, and I was amazed to find the place packed on a Friday evening. I was asked to preach evangelistically, which I did, and various people responded and were taken to a side room. I never saw them again! Then the Bishop preached briefly but movingly on God's power to heal, and he invited people to come up to the altar rail for prayer. To my astonishment, I saw crutches jettisoned and deaf people recovering their hearing. I do not think, at that stage in my life, that I would have believed it if I had not seen it with my own eyes.

Later that night the Bishop and I were sitting in his house rejoicing, and he invited me to praise God in tongues. I told him I was unable to do this – and anyhow, I was uptight because I was an intellectual! I allowed him to pray that I might receive this gift and, although nothing ensued at the time and I continued to praise God in ordinary language, by the middle of the night it had begun, and has been with me ever since. That night I also began to get a foretaste of the prophetic 'seeing' which has occasionally been part of my subsequent experience, although I do not get the 'words of knowledge' that some Christians do, nor do I have the gift of interpreting tongues. Mercifully, we are meant to depend on one another in the Body of Christ. Nobody has all the gifts. Such a person would be insufferable, and the Body would be robbed of its harmonious interdependence.

Spiritual gifts

In due course I discovered two gifts that were emerging in me. One was prayer for healing. Earlier, when I had written *The Meaning of Salvation*, I had investigated the question of healing without medical means rather carefully, and had come to the conclusion that this did not happen in the West, but it might do in some areas of the Third World where normal medicine was not available. I did not want to exclude God's healing power by my unbelief, but I saw no evidence of its reality in the part of the world I knew. As the years went by, however, I had to revise my opinion, and have done so subsequently in print. I know now that I was wrong in my original assumption. God does heal today.

I recall being amazed by an Air Canada pilot who told me of his remarkable healing from cancer. At the hospital in Vancouver he had been told by the consultant, a friend of his from church, that he was riddled with cancer and had only a short time to live. He told me that he turned over in bed, faced the wall and told the Lord that, if he was to die, that was OK by him, but if the Lord had a further use for him on earth, would he please heal him? That man instantaneously experienced a complete healing, so complete that he went back to Air Canada for a fresh medical and is, as far as I know, the only man ever to have been taken back as a pilot by the airline after having been discharged with cancer. I cherish a baseball cap he gave me as a memento of our conversation and his testimony of healing.

I met more and more examples of healing by God in answer to prayer alone, and gradually I dared to reach out and pray for others myself. I saw headaches and other small afflictions disappear suddenly in answer to prayer, and my faith grew. Of course, many times nothing appeared to happen, and I realized that there was a deep mystery here. There was no way anybody could manipulate God. Yet I had seen enough to know that sometimes he chose to heal without medical means, and that I had better be ready for him to do that when I prayed for people, although I needed to make it clear to them that the matter lay entirely in God's hands.

I have, to my surprise, been involved in some remarkable healings. At the end of a clergy conference in Malawi, a clergyman who could not walk asked me to pray for his leg. I could see that the leg was in a serious state, and quickly looked around for someone else to pray for it. I could not find anyone I knew to whom I could refer his request, so, rather reluctantly, I asked a few people standing nearby to join me in laying hands on the man's leg and praying for him. When we did this, he got up and started walking around, and then running! We were keen to restrain him, lest he injure himself, but he was too full of joy and gratitude to God to be still.

On another occasion I was visiting someone in hospital. The patient was a lady in our Oxford congregation who always seemed to stay on the sidelines, to criticize and grumble, and to avoid anything spiritually challenging. When I visited fairly early in the morning, the nurses told me she would be dead by the afternoon. I laid hands on her unconscious form, prayed for her, and left for a day's conference at our church which, ironically enough, was on the subject of healing. I went back that evening and, to my amazement and that of the nursing staff, the lady was far from dead. She was, in fact, very much alive and on excellent form! Moreover, her whole personality had undergone a profound change, and she was full of grace and joy for the four years before she died.

Over the years I have experienced many such answers to prayer in the realm of healing, and have long since abandoned my scepticism that such a thing is possible. I do not regard myself as possessing a special gift of healing, such as is vouchsafed to some Christians, but I have known many occasions when God has healed in answer to my prayers. The important thing, it seems to me, is to thank God when this occurs, and not attempt to systematize what is a sovereign act of God. It adds insult to injury, when people are not healed, to say that this is because sin in their life has blocked God's healing power, or that they did not have the faith to receive the healing. It is worse still, perhaps, if people are enthusiastically informed that they are healed when they manifestly are not. The charismatic movement has much to answer for in some bad teaching and practice in this area. Charlatans abound. Some 'healers' think they can tell God what to do, and command the illness to depart. This is neither sane nor biblical. In the New Testament we read that Paul, who possessed the gift of healing, had to leave Trophimus at Miletus sick and was powerless to remove the thorn in his own flesh, whatever ailment that may have been.

There is a mystery in suffering, and we must never think we have pierced its depths. Neither must we limit God by assuming that he is unable to heal without medical means. He has that power. It is also right to pray for friends who are suffering, that God will meet them in their need, whether by removing the affliction or by giving them the grace to endure it and even profit by it. The charismatic movement has taught me to pray with a fresh expectancy that God will act, but it would be impertinence for me to tell God what to do. We are totally dependent on his mercy and wisdom, and those charismatic healers who have forgotten that and played God have brought the whole movement into disrepute.

If healing was one manifestation of the charismatic movement into which I was given some initiation, the other was the ministry of deliverance. This is a highly controversial area, even more so than healing. It has two basic assumptions. One is that the Bible is not to be discounted when it tells us of dark spiritual forces which may oppress human lives. These spiritual forces are real, and it is only in the sophisticated, sceptical West that their existence is doubted. Travel to Asia or Africa, and you will find that everybody believes in the divine and everybody believes in the demonic. Scripture, at all events, is clear on the matter: there are evil spirits, emissaries of Satan, and they bring bondage and harm to human beings.

The other basic assumption is that Jesus Christ alone has the power to defeat these forces. Colossians 2:15 celebrates their defeat as part of the victory of the cross. Not only did Jesus 'cancel the bond which stood against us with its legal demands, setting it aside and nailing it to his cross', but he 'disarmed the principalities and powers and made a public display of them, triumphing over them in it [i.e. the cross]'. We see the power of these evil forces being broken in the Acts of the Apostles, and in the ministry of the early Christians. Justin, for example, writing in the second century, says,

> And now you may learn this from what goes on under your own eyes. Many of our Christian men have exorcised (in the name of Jesus Christ, who was crucified under Pontius Pilate) numberless demoniacs throughout the whole world, and in your city. When all other exorcists and specialists in incantations and drugs have failed, they have healed them and still do heal, rendering the demons impotent and driving them out.
>
> 2 Apology 6

This is not the place to examine exorcism at length. That I have attempted to do in *I Believe in Satan's Downfall*, and my friend and ex-colleague John Woolmer has recently written a magisterial book entitled *Healing and Deliverance*. Like healing, this is a gift long disused whose value is being recognized afresh in the Church. Scripture bids us not only to cry out to the Lord for his intervention, but to 'resist the devil and he will flee from you'. This is a particularly dramatic spiritual gift, and a dangerous one too. In most denominations it is hedged around with various safeguards by the ecclesiastical authorities, and with good reason. Generally those who are affected by evil spirits have a variety of other problems as well, and a simplistic approach by an inexperienced would-be exorcist is a recipe for disaster.

Abuse does not take away proper use, however, and the ministry of setting people free from evil powers (to which they have usually subjected themselves by active involvement in some aspect of the occult) is an important spiritual gift to find in a church. Personally, I would find it difficult to operate effectively in a modern parochial situation without the use of this gift by some member of the pastoral team. In an age which has largely rejected God, people have explored other spiritual forces, some of them very destructive, and this has left its mark in a trail of broken lives. These spiritual forces need to be challenged in the name of Christ, and then the power of his Spirit is displayed, driving them out. I confess that I used to be very dubious about all this – but I have seen, and have often been instrumental in, the immediate transformation of a life when a person suffering from infestation by evil forces has been set free.

One night John Woolmer, then my curate, called me to his house because he had a couple with him whom he (rightly) regarded as being heavily under the influence of evil spirits. When I entered the room, the profoundly disturbed woman who was standing opposite me by the mantelpiece shrieked out loud. Perhaps it was her awareness of another person who belonged to Christ entering the room. John clearly expected me to know what to do: I had been the Principal of his theological seminary, and we had both left the same summer to start this new ministry at St Aldate's in Oxford. Needless to say, I had no idea what to do! But I recalled the action of Jesus with the Gadarene demoniac – and this woman's wild behaviour reminded me of that story. Jesus addressed the disturbing spirit and asked it to reveal its name. It proved to be a case of multiple possession, for the name was Legion, and a full Roman legion had 5,000 men. Well, it was a case of multiple possession in this woman as well.

When I challenged the evil spirit in her to reveal its name, it responded, greatly to my surprise. I addressed it by its name and told it to leave at once, and go wherever Christ should send it. The woman then crashed most spectacularly to the floor. Our exultation was short-lived, for soon afterwards she began to speak with three different voices. The saga was a long one with this particular person, and we were greatly helped by the ministry of David Watson's church in York, which had considerable experience in this area, unlike ourselves. In due course the woman was set free from the many evil spirits which had settled in her life. It emerged that she had been cursed before birth while her mother was pregnant, and that she had been deeply involved in the occult and had deliberately handed herself over to Satan.

It was a memorable initiation for me, and it taught me the palpable reality of evil – of evil forces which could be cast out through the power of Jesus. And all of this took place in Oxford, arguably one of the most sophisticated cities in the world! It greatly affected my ministry. From then on, I realized that I might be dealing with unseen spiritual forces when handling an apparently intractable pastoral case. I recall a young woman in the church whose sleep was constantly broken by some unseen presence near the head of her bed. She asked me to go to her room and pray, which I did. I told the spiritual force that it must leave on the authority of Jesus Christ, the ultimate conqueror of all evil. We sang praises to God, thanked him for his victory, claimed it for this particular room and its inhabitant, and there was never any recurrence of the trouble.

A more recent example of this happened within the walls of Wycliffe Hall, where I am currently working. Several people felt disturbance in the small, dark and partly subterranean corridor where my room and those of two students are situated. We decided to have an informal Communion service in my room to claim God's peace and deliverance from whatever was causing the unrest. I imagined this would be effective, but it was clearly not specific enough. The occupant of the room next door to mine found himself physically unable to enter his room, and kept out of the college almost all the time. For some days he slept on the floor of a friend's room. When we became aware of this, a small group of us met to pray with him, then we entered the room – not without a strong sense of spiritual (and almost physical) resistance. We sprinkled holy water around, claimed the power of Christ to liberate, and had a great sense that the dark stuff had gone. Then we turned to praise, and there has never been any further trouble in that room. That student has had a memorable experience of the reality of dark forces and of Christ's power to set people and places free. It will do him no harm in his future ministry.

I do not like writing about this aspect of ministry. It is one where I have a gift that I do not relish. To many it seems lunacy. To those who are set free it seems glorious. I soon found that, when the word got out, people from other parts of the country would come to me in Oxford and ask me to get involved in their case with a view to deliverance. I did not feel it was right, however, to operate outside my own parish. I had the strong feeling that if I got too caught up in this area of ministry, it would eat me up. It was a wise decision. I only mention the ministry of deliverance here because it is an aspect of the charismatic movement which became important in my ministry, and is something which I would never even have imagined to be real had it not been forced upon me by encounters like these.

So it was that, in the early years of my parish ministry at St Aldate's, I found myself gifted to a greater or lesser extent in tongues, healing and deliverance. I began to wrestle with the question of how such gifts could be introduced into church life without dividing the congregation. I had heard enough of churches being torn to pieces on issues like this, and I did not want ours to be one of them. We did a good deal of teaching on the subject in public preaching and seminars. We had visits from David Watson and some of his church members from York, where the renewal was much further developed. We made a point of regarding spiritual gifts as a normal part of the Christian life, and stressed that it was natural to find tongues and prophecy sometimes occurring in services, and healing and deliverance sometimes taking place among the congregation. So many of us operate for most of the time at a sub-Christian level that it is healthy to teach about and experience a fully-orbed Christian life involving biblical, sacramental and charismatic elements.

Our worship managed for some time to combine anthems from a robed choir with modern choruses sung by a music group – until at length the choirmaster came and asked for the choir to be disbanded! It was important that this was their decision, not the decision of the Rector or PCC. Likewise, I strongly believe in evolution rather than revolution when it comes to the introduction of spiritual gifts into the life of a congregation. We also made a point of having an occasional congregational meeting after a shortened service. This was a no holds barred affair, where people could raise their disagreements in public and evaluate the level of support. In this way factious complaints were largely silenced, and we found that hardly anybody left the church over the charismatic issue, while a great many joined it.

It really is not difficult to find a place for the exercise of these gifts. To be sure, the best place to start is the fellowship group. Then a move to the midweek prayer meeting is a natural development, and from there to the services themselves. If someone gave voice to a tongue in a service I would simply say, 'If that is from the Lord, he will give us an interpretation. Let us wait on God and see if he does.' Generally an interpretation emerged. If not, the service simply proceeded. If someone felt they had received a prophetic message for the congregation, it was not difficult to incorporate it after the final hymn and before the blessing. The Corinthians are told by the apostle Paul to 'let the others judge' when a putative prophecy is offered. In our experience, when a prophetic message really did come from God, everyone realized it and there was no debate. When it did not, there was a lot of doubt and hesitation in the minds of the congregation.

I have just turned up a prophetic utterance which accompanied my induction into St Aldate's Church. I had forgotten about it until it surfaced the other day. It came by letter after the induction service, from a member of staff at St John's College, Nottingham. The writer is now a household name in Christian circles. It is a good example of the pictures in which God's prophetic utterances are sometimes given. The letter read:

I feel I should pass on to you a 'seeing' I had during Thursday's service. It was when the phrase 'the cure of souls' came in the charge to Michael. I saw a small flame above St Aldate's, which grew in brightness and beauty and became a divine beacon. Beneath the blaze was a gap, then the church – a wooden building in which, as I looked harder, there were some parts affected by worm. But other parts weren't affected. It seemed to me as though the different parts were seen to be people rather than fabric. Amongst some of the 'good wood' there was the desire to hack away the bad and throw it into the flames to be burnt (which seemed reasonable lest the disease spread – in any case, what use was 'wormy fabric'?). But there was an insistent voice, 'Attend to the cure of souls.' As I asked the meaning, I felt it to be that amongst you there must emerge (and be encouraged and trained) those who will, with practice, love and skill, attend to the needs of the 'wormy fabric', and bring cure as an alternative to destruction. In time perhaps this will mean a team of pastorally trained lay folk with gifts of faith and prayer who will exercise such a healing ministry. So I saw dedicated folk going round with great love and patience to minister the 'cure of souls' to the 'wormy', and although some others were tempted to lose patience in their desire for progress, the lovely thing was that the building grew in beauty, radiance and purity; and as it grew, so the flames of the beacon surrounded it.

And it was not consumed, but shone out in great glory
to God and attracted many.

Suffice it to say that anyone who knows the history of the
church during the next decade will have no doubts that this
prophetic picture was fulfilled.

If, as sometimes happened, there was a demonic manifestation which caused a disturbance, the person concerned was
escorted out and competent people came to minister to him
or her. There was often prayer for healing, particularly at
Eucharistic services. We also found that there was sufficient
confidence in the guidance of the Holy Spirit to make it
unnecessary for us to vote on issues that arose in the PCC. We
went for the unanimity principle, believing that it was as easy
for God to guide 15 people as it was to guide one – provided
(and this is the vital point) that everybody was genuinely
seeking God's will and was ready to follow that will once it
became apparent. When we could not agree, we deferred a
decision until the next monthly meeting, covenanting to pray
daily about it in the meantime. I cannot recall any occasion
when we failed to reach unanimity as a result. In these simple
ways, the congregation became used to charismatic gifts and
were glad to see them in operation.

Negative aspects

The charismatic movement has had such a widespread impact
on the Churches of Christ from the middle of the twentieth
century onwards, that it might be helpful to try to evaluate it.
There are, first, many negative points to bear in mind.

In the first place, many charismatics have been arrogant:
arrogant in parading their gifts; arrogant in regarding churchpeople without these gifts as less spiritual, less important. As
a result, the early days of the charismatic movement saw a
great deal of division in congregations, between those who
approved and those who did not. Division almost became

inevitable when one party urged the indispensable nature of the gifts and the other party failed to accept anything of the kind. Division became a terrible curse during the third quarter of the twentieth century, but notably improved during the last quarter, as churchpeople learned to live in fellowship with one another despite their disagreement about spiritual gifts.

Another disaster was the emphasis on the gift of tongues as a mark of having 'arrived' spiritually. St Paul, whose Corinthian correspondence figured large in this debate, is at pains to assert that he has not 'arrived' (see Philippians 3:12–16) and that tongues is the least rather than the most important of the gifts (this is the whole thrust of 1 Corinthians 14). This undue emphasis on tongues, derived in part from denominational Pentecostal literature, led to a palpable distinction between the 'haves' and the 'have-nots' which has no biblical basis whatsoever and is highly destructive in any congregation. It leads to people seeking the gifts rather than the Giver.

A further weakness has been a disregard of scholarship and an anti-intellectualism. To be sure, much intellectual discussion of Christianity, much preaching, much writing, was unbearably dull, dusty and dreary, and it was no bad thing to revolt against that. Yet many charismatics and Pentecostals despised the mind and went for the feelings instead. The songs that the movement has spawned are by no means exempt from the charge of mindless emotionalism and shortage of content, when compared with the great hymns of Wesley's day, for example. Many charismatics have been very weak on Scripture and very strong on the claim for the preacher's personal inspiration. Many have discouraged serious theological study. Many, in short, have bypassed the mind and glorified the emotions. Any movement which despises the God-given gift of reason is going to collapse before long. I have noticed that only when the charismatic movement is married to a strong biblical theology and evangelistic orientation does it have the power that the New Testament leads us to expect.

There are other weaknesses. The music embraced by the renewal lacks depth and permanence. It is not going to last. Nevertheless, it expresses the current feelings of many contemporary Christians and there is no reason why they should not use it in worship. The constant repetition of so many of these choruses can be a turn-off for thoughtful people, however. Indeed, in some circles the endless repetition seems to act like a mantra and carry people into a different level of consciousness, which may not always be helpful in public worship.

Many charismatics are always out for *more*. Yet the apostle Paul insisted that Christ and Christ alone was the blessing for Christians. 'God has blessed us with every spiritual blessing in Christ' (Ephesians 1:3). Any doctrine that adds something to Christ – as some charismatics do in their cry, 'Christ, yes, but beyond Christ you need the Spirit and his gifts' – stands self-condemned.

Particularly in the early days of the movement, charismatics were always out for power, too. They were elated by spiritual power and were always seeking short cuts to it. This, however, is to neglect the strong New Testament emphasis on sharing in the sufferings of Christ. Paul knew all about the marks of an apostle: the signs, the wonders and the mighty deeds (see 2 Corinthians 12:12). He also knew that spiritual power came from patient endurance of suffering, such as he had with his thorn in the flesh, or the patient endurance of reviling and hardship such as he submitted to in the course of his missionary work. The charismatics at Corinth (and later) had a theology of the resurrection and its power. They needed to learn afresh the secret of the cross and its weakness – which yet produced the power of God.

A further weakness of the renewal movement is its lust for certainty. That is one reason why tongues and healings and miracles have been so highly regarded among them. Paul, however, knows that we walk by faith while we are in this life, not by sight. There are many times when God calls us to trust him in the dark, without supporting evidence.

This leads on to an additional problem. There is a dangerous individualism in the charismatic movement. Such is the emphasis on immediate access to God that people gain individualistic and deeply entrenched understandings of God's guidance. They get straight through to the operator without bothering with any of the telephone exchanges, and as a result are almost impossible to move by any rational argument. They absolutize their hunches and assert that they come from God. That is very irritating for anyone who is trying to give leadership! Indeed, many charismatics have little use for their leaders, especially if the leaders do not have the same gifts as they do. The same indiscipline and insubordination was present in the early days of Christianity, among the charismatics of 2 Peter and Jude.

It has been not unfairly pointed out that the charismatic movement has offered a stage where hysteric personalities can disport themselves. That would not be true of the movement as a whole, but it is undeniably true of some churches, where spiritually unreliable people are given undue attention and opportunity simply because they claim to be speaking and acting under the power of the Holy Spirit. They need to be restrained, or disbarred, if life does not back up lip.

A final cause for concern is the continuing talk about 'baptism with the Holy Spirit'. I had hoped that this would have been put right during the past 50 years, a time when many of the movement's weaknesses have been rectified, but it shows no sign of going away. The truth of the matter is, however, that all seven references to baptism in or with the Holy Spirit in the New Testament refer to an initial encounter with the life-giving Spirit of God, not to some subsequent high-octane experience for special Christians. Many Christians do have a powerful second, third or fourth blessing in their spiritual lives, but it simply muddies the waters to call it 'baptism'. Baptism speaks of beginning, of initiation. If you talk about 'baptism in the Holy Spirit', the impression you give is that the persons concerned have not hitherto been initiated into the realm of the Holy Spirit, have not begun with him until that experience. To talk like that effectively unchurches vast numbers of godly Christians, and that is simply not good enough. I believe that this expresssion, though clear enough to those who are in the club, is a major obstacle and, indeed, an insult to those who are not card-carrying charismatics. We really should avoid this non-biblical and offensive use of the phrase and substitute some theologically correct one – such as 'filling with the Holy Spirit' or, as is common in many Catholic circles, 'release of the Holy Spirit'.

Positive benefits

If I have seemed to dwell at length upon the negative aspects of this movement (and they are serious weaknesses), it is only because I believe that the positive benefits outweigh them. The renewal movement has brought with it a new spiritual vitality. The formality and predictability of worship has been replaced by an expectancy to meet the living God. The sense of duty which propelled many reluctant feet towards church has been replaced by an eagerness to worship God. The sheer joy in worshipping God which you find among charismatic Christians is eloquent, and makes other people want to join in. That is solid gain. It is not surprising that the fastest-growing part of world Christianity is the charismatic element. It is, quite frankly, attractive – not to itself, but to the living God it celebrates.

Also positive is the new praise and worship which has emerged from the charismatic movement and spread very widely. There can be few churches nowadays who do not sing some of the short hymns or songs of the renewal. Throughout Christian history, a new intimacy with God, a new experience of his reality and power has led to a new hymnody, and today's renewal is no different. Most of the songs current today will be forgotten in five years' time, but that does not bother the congregations. They will have new songs by then! Why should one sing the same hymn for centuries – unless it has the quality of a Watts or a Wesley? Wise churches combine old hymns and new songs and do not allow a musical polarity to emerge which could split the congregation.

Another marvellous benefit of the renewal is that it has taken Christian ministry out of the hands of the professionals and allowed ordinary Christians to discover and then exercise their ministries. It has shown people that God has given them gifts to use in his service. It has thrilled them to find out that they, and not just the clergy, are called to serve the Lord. Here again, the influence of the renewal has flowed far beyond its own borders. Almost every church is now talking about, and to some extent implementing, lay ministry. You did not hear much of this before the renewal. The charismatic movement has allowed the laity to discover and use their gifts, and to do so in conscious recognition that they are members of Christ's Body, with different but complementary abilities. This has led to an enormous increase in the effectiveness of the Church, compared with the one-man-band mentality which used to prevail, and in some cases still does.

The renewal has brought a new freedom in prayer and praise to the Christian community. Informal, extempore prayer used to be rare except in explicitly Evangelical circles when I was young. Now it is natural in all types of church-manship. That is the result of the renewal. So is the idea of praying down the phone, singing God's praises in a car, or a group of friends reading Scripture by a lake. The growth of prayer and praise is unquestionable since the renewal took hold. In the West it is still weak, partly because the renewal does not burn very brightly, but in countries like Nigeria, Singapore, Tanzania, Korea and China, prayer is the stuff of life and a top priority for one and all. Many churches in these countries have prayer going on all night as thousands gather to worship God and to intercede. I am sure that the gift of tongues is not irrelevant here. Many charismatic Christians find that tongues enables them to start praying when they feel cold, and to continue long after they run out of intelligible words. So long as tongues is seen as a tool for prayer and praise, rather than as a badge of achievement, it is a beautiful gift of God.

The charismatic movement has seen a wonderful growth of fellowship across all man-made barriers. I remember an illuminating story told by one of the early founders of the movement. He spoke of a number of ducks being boxed in cages on an expanse of water. They could hear and see each other, but were separated in their own compartments. Then a flood came and the water level rose – and so did the ducks. They were no longer confined to their boxes, but enjoyed unrestricted companionship as they splashed all over the lake. God has raised the water level by the outpouring of his Holy Spirit, and this has liberated people from their denominational cages. They began by discovering that their counterparts were Christians – and that had not always been taken for granted. There was much mutual suspicion between, say, Roman Catholics and Baptists. How could a member of the other Church possibly be a Christian? Yet when you actually met members of the other Communion, and saw them lost in wonder, love and praise of Christ, heard them pray with joy and sometimes in tongues, acknowledging their love for the Saviour – how could you still unchurch them?

A fascinating fact is that this grass-roots ecumenism took place in the last quarter of the twentieth century, when the World Council of Churches had lost its vitality. My impression is that the denominational walls are now falling very fast, and the only people who seem to want to keep them intact are very conservative churchpeople on the one hand and the clergy and ministers of the various denominations on the other. Most believers these days do not much care what the label of their church is: they want life. If there is not much spiritual life in a particular church, they will go to one where there is – irrespective of denomination. I am not sure that I can

fault that. Can you? One can, of course, murmur about indif-
ferentism, tradition, disloyalty and the like, but the issue is
really one of spiritual vitality. Those who are spiritually alive
will congregate where there is life. It is as simple as that. The
form of worship, church leadership and so forth seem much
less important to today's younger generation than whether or
not there is life.

The charismatic movement has had a great deal to do with
this tendency towards transdenominational fellowship. I write
this having recently returned from a fascinating, 1,600-strong
Alpha conference in Vancouver. Guess who put it on? The
Catholic Archbishop. Maybe 60 per cent of the delegates were
Roman Catholics and the remainder were various types of
Protestant. The fellowship was marvellous, as people entered
into the spiritual gifts, joined in informal prayer and praise,
and manifested love for one another across the yawning historical gaps that once would have divided them. Surely this
is part of the renewing work of God the Holy Spirit, who is
given such a prominent place in the Alpha programme?

Whenever the renewal movement has been at its best, it has
led to widespread witness for Jesus Christ. At its worst, it has
become a 'happy-clappy' club for the cosy insiders. That is
not what God intended. The Holy Spirit is primarily given for
witness-bearing, as the Acts of the Apostles makes plain. He
is not intended to make us comfortable and complacent, but
to make us missionaries to our own circle and beyond. All
Christians have a story to tell and are intended to tell it
without embarrassment and with a joyful sense of discovery.
Not all Christians are meant to preach – thank goodness! But
whether through personal testimony or through proclamation, the Holy Spirit is given to fuel Christians for outreach.
It was so on the day of Pentecost. It still is. Throughout
the world, the majority of enthusiastic witness-bearers and
preachers are the people who have drunk deep of the renewing waters of the Holy Spirit. When you consider that the
Pentecostals did not emerge until the start of the twentieth

century and the charismatics not until its halfway stage, it is simply staggering that a majority of all new conversions should be due to them. Indeed, without the charismatics many churches would have ceased to have any discernible outreach at all. All who care about evangelism, whether or not they would claim to be charismatic, must surely thank God for raising up this renewal.

It is often (but not always) the case that this fresh experience of the Holy Spirit drives people towards the Scriptures with a new zest. This was very much the case with someone like Bishop Bill Burnett, who was brought to a powerful experience of the Holy Spirit when he was praying in his chapel in Grahamstown, South Africa. He had been trained in the liberal tradition, which tended not to go very deeply into the Bible, but now he found himself voraciously devouring Holy Scripture. It was food for his soul, food which he had neglected for so long, and it stood him in excellent stead as he faced all the problems of becoming Archbishop of Cape Town in a country that would soon emerge from the horror of apartheid. This fresh immersion in Scripture is often the case with people who have been lit up with the Spirit, and so it should be. The Word of the Lord and the Spirit of the Lord belong together. This just makes it all the more sad when some charismatic pastors give the impression to their congregations that they do not need to read the Bible, just to listen to their pastor.

There are two further areas of strength which deserve a mention. The first is the generosity of most charismatics. This springs from their awareness of the enormity of God's generosity to them, and they want to reciprocate. I am amused that several bishops I know, who really have little time for the charismatic churches in their dioceses, cannot afford to do without them because they contribute so generously and willingly, often above their quota, to diocesan funds. Freely they have received – freely they give.

Finally, charismatics are well aware of the spiritual battle which rages all around us. Many other Christians are not.

Once you have had a fresh taste of the Holy Spirit, you become uncomfortably aware of the unholy Spirit and his determination to wreck God's work at every turn. Consequently, you realize there is a battle on. The New Testament leaves us in no doubt of this. Look at Revelation 13 and Ephesians 6, for example. The Church, however, has long been silent about spiritual battle and its members have no idea that there is a war on and that they are combatants, not civilians. Until the Church in the West as a whole comes to see this, and until we are driven to prevailing prayer and fasting (a weapon of whose power the Third-World Christians are well aware), we shall not grow. I, for one, thank God for the awareness of the spiritual battle to which the charismatic movement has alerted us.

Challenges to the Church

The factors mentioned above are some of the more obvious blessings which have come through the renewal. We are not in the midst of a revival, as some Christians optimistically maintain. The level of churchgoing in Western lands continues to decrease. Nominal attachment to the Church as a mark of respectability has disappeared. Yet the vitality of Christians has been increasing, it seems to me, and it is hard to deny that this is mainly due to the renewal movement.

It is clear that much in the renewal movement is sheer froth. Many of the songs, the prevalence of guitar and drums, the raised hands, the overemphasis on tongues, the clapping – these things are totally unimportant. They may well already be in decline today. As they recede, you will find many people saying that the renewal movement has had its day. I beg to disagree. The majority of our churches have yet to discover the renewing power of the Holy Spirit. I hope the charismatic movement will long remain as a pointer to our desperate need of the Spirit's power. All Christians need to be charismatic (in the sense of depending upon the gracious gifts, *charismata*, of the Holy Spirit), but not all Christians are required to be caught up in the charismatic culture.

In every generation God tends to raise up some counter-poise to the current weaknesss and abuses of his Church. In our own day he has raised up this remarkable movement which we call charismatic renewal. It would be tragic if the Church did not learn from it. I believe that the charismatic movement presents a number of challenges to the Church at large, challenges which have a lasting relevance. I first drew attention to them in *I Believe in the Holy Spirit*, and I am per-suaded that they remain valid and important.

First of all, it is a challenge to the *institutionalism* of the Church. Too often the Church is seen as a building, a ghetto of those who like churchy things: but the Church is people, people alive with the Holy Spirit. It is immaterial where they meet or who leads them. The movement of the Spirit always poses a challenge to the conservatism of the institution. Somehow the Church of the future must manage to combine both charism and order, and the renewal movement will remain a lasting challenge to those who exalt institution over life.

Second, it provides a challenge to *intellectualism* in the Church. The movement is often weak on the importance of the intellect (a serious error which is currently, I believe, being addressed), but the traditional Churches are guilty of an even more serious error. They have so intellectualized the Christian faith that it seems beyond the reach of ordinary people. Theologians are often out of touch with the people in the pews. Ordinands are taught by academics who have little or no pastoral experience. Christianity seems all too often to be a matter of intellectual debate, assent or doubt, of churchgoing, and of middle-class mores. It makes little difference to ordi-nary life, and those who go are not readily distinguishable by their lifestyle from those who do not. Nobody could say that of the charismatics. You could call them overenthusiastic, mad, religious nutcases – but they undoubtedly embody something different. The Spirit of the Lord is that 'something different'. He is not to be intellectualized or tamed. The charismatics know that. They have found something life-changing, and this is a quality which authentic Christianity always needs to demonstrate.

Third, the renewal is a challenge to *one-person leadership* in the Church. For centuries, and in whatever denomination, monarchy has tended to reign. What the priest or pastor or minister wants, goes. The minister is the professional, and is supposed to know best. The charismatic movement will not allow this. One of its prime discoveries is the Lordship of Christ in his Body the Church and the gifts he offers to every member, so as to equip them for service. Not some, but *all* are called to serve. Not some, but *all* can have intimacy with God. Not some, but *all* have a ministry to perform for Christ. This recall to lay ministry, every-member ministry, shared ministry, is incomparably more revolutionary in the Church than is the gift of tongues, and it is incomparably more important, too. If the movement can impress on the institution that every member is called to serve and that leadership exists to equip the saints for their God-given work of service in the Church and the world, that alone would render it one of the most important movements the Church has ever known.

Fourth, the charismatic movement is a challenge to *unbelief* in the Church. It has come at a time when unbelief has reached epic proportions. As one who has spent much of his life teaching theology, I know the scepticism which underlies many of the books theological students have to study. Some of those who write these books do not believe in God, or the divinity of Christ. They do not believe he died for the sins of the world. They do not believe in his resurrection. They do not believe in biblical ethics, and they do not believe in the efficacy of prayer. Their God, if he is anything more than the smile that remains after the Cheshire Cat has disappeared, is impotent to intervene in our world. Yet this is precisely the period in history when the Almighty laughs. He sends this movement of his Spirit into the world on an enormous scale, in the most unlikely places and denominations, as if to say, 'I am alive and well, thank you!' The charismatic movement is a constant reminder that God is neither dead nor absent. It has rekindled faith in the living God who answers prayer, changes lives and equips his people with gracious spiritual gifts.

Finally, the charismatic movement is a challenge to the *introversion* of the Church. The Church is not for insiders, it is for the whole world. Its gospel is far too good news to keep to ourselves. Evangelism and service are imperative. To be sure, many other movements in history have stressed the outward thrust of the gospel, but this movement, so intimately concerned with the Holy Spirit, makes it abundantly clear that the Holy Spirit is given to equip us for service and mission, for love and worship. He cannot be muzzled or contained. The Spirit is the foretaste of the day 'when the earth will be full of the knowledge of the Lord as the waters cover the sea' (Isaiah 11:9). The supreme importance of this movement celebrating the presence and power of the Holy Spirit is to lift up our hearts in expectancy of God's future, of which the Spirit is the pledge and guarantee.

CHAPTER 13

Controversy

Theologians love to debate the marks of the Church. Classically, for example, Anglicans have maintained – in the face of strenuous Nonconformist rebuttals – that episcopacy is either an essential or at least a highly desirable mark of the Church. Yet it would not be too sardonic to say that the most notable mark of the Church throughout its long history has been controversy. This is sad in a community where the peace of Christ is meant to hold sway. What with fallen human nature and our very partial perception of divine truths, however, controversy is inevitable. From the lusty debates about the terms of Gentile inclusion in the Church at the apostolic council in AD 49 to the even more fiery debates about the ordination of practising homosexuals today, the life of the Church has been distinguished by passionate disagreements on many things. Sometimes the contestants have been able to live together, realizing that what unites them is more *etc!* significant than what divides. Sometimes this has not proved possible, and schism has resulted. In consequence the Christian Church throughout the world is very far from the loving unity intended by Jesus Christ. As one shrewd bishop put it, 'I believe in one holy, catholic, apostolic Church – but, sadly, I do not see it anywhere.'

Taboos

As I look back over the past 50 years, I realize that I have observed and, indeed, participated in a good many ecclesiastical controversies – not because I looked for them, but because they emerged at the time and it seemed imperative to take a principled position on them. One of the earliest I recall was while I was a young Christian being nourished in the Evangelical tradition. A whole host of activities were then regarded as somewhat – or very – taboo. In the Christian Union at Oxford, for example, the received wisdom was that we should not smoke, drink, wear make-up, dance, or go to the theatre or cinema. These things were dubbed 'worldly', and good Christians must 'keep themselves unspotted from the world'. Books with such titles as *Questionable Amusements* were written and eagerly absorbed by enthusiasts. Our 'soundness' was marked by the extent to which we observed such shibboleths. This will seem astonishing and laughable to today's Christian community, but quite a lot was made of it in those days. Of course, although the underlying principle of seeking to please God in everything was absolutely right, the attempt to define worldliness in terms of a list of prohibited activities was absolutely wrong. It was the kind of legalism denounced in the Epistle to the Galatians – part of the very Scripture which Evangelicals held so dear.

When I was being considered for the post of college representative for the Christian Union, I was summoned to meet the president for tea in his rooms. My instincts as a rebel were well to the fore that day! He said something like this: 'It's amazing how many in the Christian Union can't accept the first item in its Basis of Faith.' I replied that I had never read the Basis of Faith. This flabbergasted him, but he told me what that first item was. It concerned the infallibility and inerrancy of everything in Holy Scripture. I asked him to define what he meant by that. He did so at length, and I attended to him carefully. At the end I said, 'I can agree with all you have said, but that doesn't mean infallible or inerrant, and I fancy you know it doesn't.'

He hastily moved to another area where he wanted to see solidarity among the college representatives – the question of worldliness. He enunciated the sort of list I have mentioned above: no smoking, drinking, dancing, theatre, and so forth. Again I listened carefully and then observed, ' I don't happen to do any of these things, but wordliness can't be exorcised by observing a list of prohibitions.' Amazingly, I survived the interview, which was very broad-minded of him under the circumstances. Even at the tender age of 20, I had begun to latch on to the truth that holiness of life is indeed required of all disciples of Jesus, but that it cannot be exhaustively defined in terms of a list of taboos.

Nowadays that list looks ridiculous, and it soon began to be recognized as threadbare even then. Billy Graham's wife Ruth came to England one year, with massive support from the Evangelical community, and she made extensive and unabashed use of lipstick. Christian Union members going to Holland found that their Evangelical counterparts there were great smokers without the least twinge of conscience. Gradually sanity returned and Evangelical Christians became less obsessed with legalistic minutiae of conduct. The son of the prominently Evangelical Bishop of Norwich joined the Ballet Rambert, dances began to adorn Evangelical wedding ceremonies, alcohol flowed. Mervyn Stockwood, then Bishop of Southwark and renowned for his alcoholic parties for Anglo-Catholic clergy, began to complain, 'I used to have a cheap evening when I invited my Evangelical clergy: they went for soft drinks. Nowadays they drink as much booze as the Anglo-Catholics!' Evangelicals began to use pubs just as Wesley and his friends had done, and you could no longer discern Evangelical women from their non-Evangelical sisters by the little matter of make-up. Evangelicals began to get involved in the film and television industry, and in most (but by no means all) Evangelical circles the house of legalism crashed to the ground.

In many ways that is a good thing. Jesus was rigorous in his condemnation of external performance irrespective of the attitude of the heart. He was insistent that you could not merit God's favour by presenting him with a list you had satisfactorily completed. Yet I have a shrewd suspicion that those earlier Evangelicals had something we have lost. They had a greater willingness to sacrifice than we appear to have today. They had a willingness to stand up and be counted, even when they knew they would be laughed at. They may well have had a greater seriousness about their discipleship. So let us not mock their perceived narrowness. We may have swung too far in the other direction.

A question of unity

I had to face up to another very important area of controversy while I was still a student. When I became president of the Oxford Christian Union, its policy was not to co-operate with Christians of other stripes, lest the distinctiveness of the New Testament gospel be diluted or distorted. I explained in an earlier chapter how I handled the situation when the orthodox Anglo-Catholic Bishop Michael Ramsey came to lead a mission at the invitation of the college chaplains. Without co-operating as an organization, we encouraged members of the CU to take friends to the mission, and chat to them afterwards about the gospel. With the benefit of hindsight, this may appear a little jesuitical, but at the time it seemed the best compromise between maintaining the truth as we saw it, and showing love and solidarity with Christians who saw things rather differently. This is an issue that will not go away. Essentially it is a tension between perceived truth and contending for 'the faith that was once for all entrusted to the saints' on the one hand, and love, mission and the expression of unity on the other. Unreflective co-operation can emasculate the message to the point of ineffectiveness. Failure to co-operate can make you look foolish and narrow-minded, and can lead unbelievers to say, 'If they can't get their act together, they have no hope whatever of convincing me.'

A related controversy occurred many years later when I was leading a city-wide mission in Victoria, the capital of British Columbia. The Roman Catholic Bishop had grilled me carefully and had decided that he and all his clergy would back the mission. This infuriated the Baptists, however, and I had to fight my way into the arena night after night through angry anti-Roman protests, banners denouncing me and the mission as heretical, and so forth. It was a painful experience to be caught in the middle of such disunity.

Much more serious was the projected plan of unification between the Methodists and the Anglicans in Britain in the years leading up to 1969. The Methodist Church had for years been shrinking in numbers, and little apart from episcopacy separated it from the Church of England, which was always the senior partner in the discussions which took place over many years. After all, the Church of England was in no urgent need of joining up with the Methodists – or so we thought. There was no compelling reason to be generous in terms of union, especially over the issue of episcopacy. The traditional-ists among the Anglicans were clear that the Methodist minis-ters lacked the grace of episcopal ordination. The more open-minded Anglicans were not so fussy about this, but, in order to accommodate their more Catholic brethren, agreed to requiring a Service of Reconciliation which involved the mutual laying on of Anglican and Methodist hands. Apart from being a powerful symbol of unification, this act would have no effect upon the Anglicans – but the emerging Methodist ministers would thereafter be deemed to be priests or presbyters within the historic episcopate, while those declining to take part would not. Plainly, therefore, the studied ambiguity of the laying on of hands in fact meant covert ordination to the historic ministry. Some of the Methodist leaders would become bishops, and, of course, all future ordinations in the resultant Church would be episcopal.

The scheme aroused intense discussion and disagreement. The Methodists were insistent that they would not submit to episcopal ordination, but 77 per cent of the Methodist Conference and 69 per cent of the Anglican Convocation were in favour of the deliberate ambiguity of the Service of Reconciliation, which would mask – but also ensure – the fact that Methodists were being episcopally ordained. While there was intense pressure at official levels in both Churches to go ahead with the scheme, many in both denominations considered it hopelessly flawed and opposed it vociferously. They were accused of being ruthless wreckers of the proposed union. In fact, they were not at all opposed to unification, merely to the method being adduced. The Methodist Conference and the Anglican Convocation were not representative of opinion within their respective Churches. There was widespread dissatisfaction with the proposed scheme. Thus, in March 1969, 38,621 Methodists voted for the scheme and 31,810 voted against it. The figures for the Anglican Convocation were 263 in favour and 116 against. Approximately a third of the Anglican clergy also said they would not take part in the proposed Service of Reconciliation. In the event, amidst much recrimination and dire forebodings about the future of both Churches, the scheme was voted down by the Anglicans, although it was accepted by the Methodist Conference. It was an extremely painful and humiliating outcome.

I learned a lot from that whole experience about rigorous theological thought leading to principled action. As one who was unable to accept the deceitful ambiguity which lay at the heart of the Service of Reconciliation, I found myself discussing it in depth with the prominent Anglo-Catholic Bishop Graham Leonard at the 1968 Lambeth Conference, which I attended as a Consultant. We decided that, instead of merely opposing the scheme, we would call together a small think-tank of Evangelicals and Anglo-Catholics who for different reasons disapproved of the scheme, and see if we could come up with a plan based on theological principle which would merit a much wider acceptance. Colin Buchanan, member of the liturgical commission, and E.L. Mascall, both from their different standpoints equally opposed to the scheme, began conversing. In addition, Dr J.I. Packer, who served alongside me on the Church of England Doctrine Commission, brought his fine theological mind and biblical principles to bear on the problem, and we were also joined for a while by Dr Morna Hooker, the distinguished Methodist dissentient who later became Lady Margaret Professor of New Testament at Cambridge.

I was not able to be as involved as I had expected, because I had just been appointed Principal of the London College of Divinity and was working very hard to move the whole enterprise to its new site in Nottingham. In addition, I was already committed to speaking a good deal overseas. So, although the five of us presented a statement on Anglican–Methodist unity to the members of the Convocations of Canterbury and York in May 1969, giving our reasons for rejecting the proposed scheme and adumbrating what we felt was a better way, the quartet who did most of the work on *Growing into Union*, subtitled 'Proposals for forming a united Church in England', were Colin Buchanan and Jim Packer, the hard-line Evangelicals, and Graham Leonard and Eric Mascall, the hard-line Catholics.

It was a fascinating enterprise. The official view in the corridors of power within the Church of England was that the Anglo-Catholics and the Evangelicals had conspired to wreck the scheme by joining in unprincipled opposition while being quite unable to agree among themselves. It was deemed to be a deplorable and cynical political move. *Growing into Union* proved that this was not the case. It showed how Evangelicals and Anglo-Catholics could combine, with theological integrity, in producing a scheme for union which was neither unprincipled nor ambiguous, but owed much to the precedent set in the Church of South India. This method of coming together in unity and openly agreeing that all future ordinations would be episcopal was commended by the Lambeth Conference of 1988, but was shunned by the official Anglican–Methodist Commission which we had felt bound to oppose. The book published by SPCK in 1970 is a notable example of how theologians of different emphases can unite in seeking a practical way forward without for one moment sacrificing their convictions. Although it was not adopted by a Church dispirited by the failure of the official Conversations, it probably points the best way forward for future reconciliation of episcopal and non-episcopal Churches, and has the advantage of being biblically based, theologically rigorous, abundantly clear and capable of embracing everybody in the uniting bodies without remainder.

Bridging the Evangelical–Catholic divide

Another major cause of controversy was also surfacing in the 1960s. For most of the century the Anglo-Catholic view, that in the Eucharist the priest offered Christ to the Father, was dominant. With the incipient revival of the Evangelicals, however, instinctive opposition to this semi-official view emerged. Surely this was the Supper Jesus had instituted, not the Sacrifice of the Mass in which he was re-immolated? Allied to this was the debate over whether Christian ministers should be seen as presbyters or priests. Were they leaders of their congregations, or intermediaries between those communities and God, mystically offering Christ to the Father for the sins of the living and the dead? Nowadays one would not generate a lot of heat in such discussions of sacerdotal priesthood and Eucharistic sacrifice, but in the 1960s both topics were fiercely contested. It so happened that I had a hand in the resolution of both.

John Stott's 'Christian Foundations' series, initiated in preparation for the 1968 Lambeth Conference, was circulated among all the Anglican bishops and had a very considerable effect upon the conference. In my own contribution, *Called to*

Serve, I was able to show that there is no ground in the New Testament or in the formularies of the Church of England for seeing the priest or presbyter (both terms being used equivalently in historic documents) as having a mediatorial function.

I was also able to show that the 'apostolic succession' of ministers was a term capable of various interpretations, some of which could validly be applied to clergy. In one most important respect, however, the apostles had no successors. They had a unique and unrepeatable function in the Church as the *shelechim*, or plenipotentiary representatives, of Jesus. In this role they had no successors. The *shaliach* could not transmit his authority. Instead we find some indications that the last of the apostles did not attempt to appoint apostles after them, but rather bishops, presbyters and deacons. One could add that prophets and teachers also emerged for the good of the Church without any episcopal warrant. I examined the claim put forward by John Henry Newman (before his secession to Rome) that the historic episcopate, stretching back to the apostles, is essential to the Church. For many years this argument was given prominence through the work of G. Dix and K.E. Kirk in *The Apostolic Ministry* (1946). It was not difficult to show that this doctrine of tactile succession stretching back to the apostles through successive ordinations owed nothing to biblical teaching, sound theology, historical demonstrability or Anglican doctrine. Since then, and especially since the National Evangelical Anglican Congress of 1977 at which I gave a major paper on the subject, we have heard a lot less about mediatorial priests offering the sacrifice of Christ.

I was also able to help in clarifying the issue of Eucharistic sacrifice, so dear to the hearts of Catholics and so alien to the minds of Evangelicals. As early as 1961, I read a paper at the Oxford Conference for Evangelical Churchmen on the concept of Eucharistic sacrifice in the New Testament and the apostolic fathers. I was able to show that the Eucharist is nowhere seen as a propitiatory or reconciling sacrifice in the

New Testament, although, like its prototype the Passover, it is the memorial of reconciling sacrifice – that of Christ which takes away sin. Praise, thanksgiving, almsgiving, self-surrender, faith and evangelism are all called sacrifices in the New Testament, but the Holy Communion never is.

Although the early fathers frequently used sacrificial language about the Eucharist, based on Malachi 1:11, they were careful to see it as a 'sacrifice of praise and thanksgiving', not a 'sacrifice propitiatory', if we may anticipate Cranmer's crucial distinction. They were insistent that, in contradistinction to the Jews and pagans, *delubra et aras non habemus* ('we have no shrines, no altars'). To be sure, they called the Eucharist a sacrifice, but they applied that word very widely. Origen calls evangelism *sacrificale opus*, while Augustine calls mercy 'a true sacrifice, and acceptable to God'. Prayer is also frequently called a sacrifice. It is apparent that to attribute any exclusively sacrificial significance to the Eucharist is untenable in the light of the New Testament and the early Christian writers.

The distinctively Anglican position on this topic is succinctly set out by Thomas Cranmer in *The Lord's Supper*, Chapter 5:

> One kind of sacrifice there is which is called a propitiatory or merciful sacrifice, that is to say such a sacrifice as pacifieth God's wrath and indignation, and obtaineth mercy and forgiveness for all our sins ... And although in the Old Testament there were certain sacrifices called by that name, yet in very deed there is but one such sacrifice by which our sins be pardoned ... which is the death of God's Son, our Lord Jesus Christ; nor never was any other sacrifice propitiatory at any time, nor never shall be. This is the honour and glory of this our high priest in which he admitteth neither partner nor successor.
>
> Another kind of sacrifice there is, which doth not reconcile us to God, but is made of them which be reconciled

by Christ ... to show ourselves thankful to Him; and therefore they be called sacrifices of laud, praise and thanksgiving. The first kind of sacrifice Christ offered to God for us; the second kind we ourselves offer to God by Christ.

The distinction has never been better put, and any crude sacrificial significance in the Eucharist is rarely insisted on nowadays.

Professor Eric Mascall and I were able to publish an agreed statement on the subject in *Growing into Union*. A strong Anglo-Catholic and a strong Evangelical could agree that Scripture should be normative for our understanding of this mystery; that Christ's sacrifice for sins which we recall in the Eucharist is unique and unrepeatable; and that if we speak of *pleading* the sacrifice of Christ or *presenting* it, we mean that we rely exclusively on that sacrifice once made by Jesus. As for *offering*, we offer not only our thanksgiving but ourselves as reappropriated by Christ, and thus are made a living sacrifice to God. We concluded, 'If these are the factors involved in the desire of many churchmen to call the Eucharist a sacrifice, then, so long as there is no suggestion that the sacrifice of the Eucharist supplements or repeats the once-for-all offering on Calvary, and as long as the distinction between the Saviour and the saved is scrupulously safeguarded, Evangelicals and Catholics can say Amen.' It seems to me a very healthy fruit of controversy when entrenched positions on both sides of such a central issue can learn from the other and come out with a joint statement.

This leads perhaps naturally to the possibility of co-operation between Roman Catholics and Protestants in the work of the gospel. When I was young, such co-operation was out of the question. A good deal of persecution of Protestants by Catholics was taking place in Latin America, and was no doubt being reciprocated elsewhere. More importantly, the Catholic Church at that time regarded all outside her bosom as food for conversion rather than, as now, 'separated brethren'. The more dogmatic Protestants wondered if the Catholics, with their unbiblical practices, could possibly be Christians. The ground for co-operation appeared to be very restricted.

Since Vatican II, however, the climate has grown much warmer. The attitude of the Catholic hierarchy to other Christians has been considerably more welcoming, and many Protestants have been amazed by the spirituality of Roman Catholics they have come to know. The charismatic movement, which has affected Catholics and Protestants alike, has left both sides in no doubt that the other may and probably does contain large numbers of deeply committed Christians. In all probability, the massive decline in the numbers of Roman Catholics offering for the priesthood and the general increase of secularism all around us have encouraged Catholics and Protestants to embrace for warmth in a cold world. Moreover, the Roman–Anglican Conversations over the past few years have been very productive in diminishing mutual suspicion and giving a fresh insight into the enormous amount of common ground, particularly over issues, such as justification by grace, which had divided the two Communions since the Reformation.

Be the reasons as they may, the fact cannot be disputed: between Rome and other Christians there now exists a degree of warmth and co-operation that has been unknown for centuries, despite reactionary statements that occasionally still emerge from the Vatican. There are still, of course, major disagreements on doctrinal matters, particularly over the position of the Pope, the saints and the Virgin Mary in our redemption and of the Pope in his infallible teaching magisterium within the universal Church. That, however, does not prevent co-operation on a substantial scale. The Archbishop of Canterbury and the Catholic bishops are in close co-operation on moral and social issues, as well as on matters of public concern in religion. I have noticed it most clearly when taking missions. Almost always now, the Roman Catholic Church will come in on a town-wide mission, and sometimes will even give the lead. I have on occasion jointly led a mission with a Roman Catholic missioner, notably Father Pat Lynch, and we have stood shoulder to shoulder in the streets, in public services and in outreaches in schools and pubs. We do not agree on everything, but we realize that the things that divide us, particularly in the areas of Church government and the precise nature of the sacraments, are small indeed compared with those which unite us.

At a united mission, it is well understood that the Pentecostals, Anglicans, Baptists, Free Evangelicals and Roman Catholics will follow up in quite different ways those who begin seeking the Lord or profess conversion. That is eminently acceptable, since none of us has a perfect method for building disciples. Although we know from the outset that the follow-up will differ in different churches, for a week or so of concentrated outreach we can at least lay aside our denominational preferences and stand together for the King and the kingdom. This has enormous benefits. It wins much credibility for the churches in the community, and often leads town councils to offer to the combined churches facilities and opportunities they would never grant to any one denomination. It shows the members of the churches how much they have in common. It prevents the sort of escapism I used to encounter as Roman Catholics closed the door in my face, saying, 'The mission is nothing to do with me. I am a Catholic!' Most of all, it begins to provide a response to the prayer of Jesus that his followers should be united as he and the Father were united: different in person, but one in purpose and belonging.

The Doctrine Commission

I mentioned above the Doctrine Commission of the Church of England. This was set up by the Archbishops in 1967, precisely in order to deal with controversy. It was intended 'to consider and advise upon doctrinal questions put to it from time to time by the Archbishops'. In other words, it was there to handle hot potatoes. The first of these was the question of subscription to the Thirty-nine Articles, the sixteenth-century document which, together with the Prayer Book and the Ordinal, constitute the doctrinal norms of the Church of England. The issue had become contentious because one or two clergymen, on being promoted to senior positions, refused to subscribe to the Articles, which by law they were bound to do. They did not agree with the Articles, and they were not prepared to affirm a falsehood. Passions were raised on both sides. What was to be done? Well, the Archbishops' response was to appoint this Commission, on which I served for some 10 years.

On the whole, the Evangelicals wanted to retain the Articles, not because we affirmed every jot and tittle of them, but because they embodied strongly Reformation theology and practice. Other members of the Commission were less enthusiastic. After all, the Articles were old-fashioned and did not speak to today's issues. By conducting a survey of the Evangelical theological colleges, I discovered that not even their students were happy about subscribing to this dated though worthy document as it stood. The Commission toyed with the idea of revising them, but we soon saw this to be hopeless. You do not revise historic documents. Eventually we devised a preface and form of assent which is now used all over the Church of England whenever a minister moves to another post. The bishop declares:

> The Church of England is part of the Church of God, having faith in God the Father, who through Jesus Christ our only Lord and Saviour, calls us into the fellowship of the Holy Spirit. This faith, uniquely shown forth in the Holy Scriptures, and proclaimed in the catholic Creeds, she shares with other Christians throughout the world.

She has been led by the Holy Spirit to bear witness of her own to Christian truth in her historic formularies – the Thirty-nine Articles of Religion, the Book of Common Prayer and the Ordering of Bishops, Priests and Deacons. Now, as before, she has a responsibility to maintain this witness through her preaching and worship, the writings of her scholars and teachers, the lives of her saints and confessors, and the utterances of her councils.

In the profession you are about to make, you will affirm your loyalty to this inheritance of faith as your inspiration and direction, under God, for bringing to light the truth of Christ and making him known to this generation.

The candidate replies:

I profess my firm and sincere belief in the faith set forth in the Scriptures and in the catholic Creeds, and my allegiance to the doctrine of the Church of England.

I felt this was a rather satisfactory way of settling a difficult problem. We were able to contextualize the Thirty-nine Articles within the debates of the sixteenth century, and say, in effect, 'If I had been there then, this is where I would have taken my stand.' We were not there in the sixteenth century, however, and have to address our own situation. Yet we are bound to do so in a spirit of loyalty to a descending order of authorities. The beliefs of the Anglican Church are 'uniquely shown forth' in the Holy Scriptures. That was a point which some of us were determined to maintain. I recall Jim Packer and myself insisting on it. The Creeds summarize many of the key points in the Scriptures. Then come the historic Anglican formularies, including the Thirty-nine Articles, and the Church is reminded of her 'responsibility to maintain this witness'. We made room for subsequent writings and councils of the Church, and concluded by charging the candidate to 'affirm your loyalty to this inheritance of faith...' The candidate cannot proceed without making this affirmation, loud and clear, in the face of the congregation.

If this seemed to some to weaken subscription and assent to the Articles, I beg to differ. For years it had been a scandal that clergy subscribed to the Articles but then totally disregarded their content and, indeed, taught the very opposite. Now they had to acknowledge the supremacy of Scripture, the importance of the Creeds and the place of historic Anglican formularies as the inspiration and direction for any contemporary teaching they espoused.

In most of the Provinces of the Anglican Communion they do not bind up the Thirty-nine Articles even with the 1662 Prayer Book, and have no replacement as a norm of sound doctrine. As a result, clergy do and teach very much what they want, or rather what their bishops want. In the absence of clear doctrinal standards, the bishops have increasing power to make these up as they wish. This is good neither for the health of the Church nor for its identity between one country and another. I am thankful for the wisdom of our reformers, who did not leave doctrine to individual whim or to the statements of its contemporary bishops or synods.

As I write this on All Souls' Day, I will add one further example of the Commission's work. We were asked to report on the issue of prayer for the dead, 'in order to provide a background against which the Church could agree upon the forms of such prayers for use in its public services'. This proved more difficult than it might seem. Prayer for the dead figured considerably in Catholic theology, but at the Reformation there was a strong rejection of the notion of purgatory and the prayers and Masses for the dead which went with it. From the 1552 Prayer Book onwards, prayers for the dead were omitted.

Those in the Commission who wished to pray for the dead pointed out how natural it was to continue to pray for friends after death, just as one had during their lives. They pointed out how probable it is that we continue to develop after death, and prayer must surely be an aid to that growth in holiness. Scripture was crucial to this debate. There we are told to remember the dead, to follow their examples, and be conscious of their fellowship – but not to pray for them (see Hebrews 12:1; 13:7). When the Thessalonians are distressed about the death of their friends, Paul stresses Christ's care for living and dead alike, but never suggests praying for them.

Eventually we agreed that it was more appropriate to acknowledge the communion of saints by thanksgiving for their lives and confidence in the final resurrection, without attempting to frame petitions for them. Thus we could agree on prayers such as, 'We commend to God Almighty this our brother here departed…' rather than telling God what to do about it. We could associate ourselves with his purposes for all people, including the dead person: 'O God of infinite mercy and justice, who hast made man in thine own image and hatest nothing that thou hast made, we rejoice in thy love for all creation and commend all men to thee that in them thy will be done, in and through Jesus Christ our Lord.' How dated the language and bland nature of such a prayer seems only 30 years later! We suggested that, in remembering the Christian dead, a prayer like this might be widely acceptable: 'We thank you, O God, for your grace revealed in all the saints, and we pray for faith and courage, hope and love like theirs, through their example and in fellowship with them, through Jesus Christ our Lord.'

If you regard such prayers as thin, you are quite right. It is because the Evangelicals on the Commission wanted to accommodate the instinct to go on recalling the dead in prayer, which others strongly valued, but insisted that effective intercession is based on God's promises, and there are no promises and no examples in Scripture of prayer for those who have died. To countenance such petition would be in danger of compromising the decisiveness of this life for our eternal destiny and raising unbiblical hopes of a purgatory where those who had rejected Christ in this life might work through to a relationship with him. Prayer is far more than petition, however, and we were very happy to remember the Christian dead with thanksgiving and fellowship, while allying ourselves with God's purposes for those who died without faith. I believe that was a principled and reasonably satisfactory resolution of another sharp controversy in the Church.

Women in Christian leadership

Another much more significant area of controversy which has led, in most circles, to viable solutions is the question of women in Christian leadership. Women nowadays are well educated, have the vote, enter the Stock Exchange and the legal and medical professions, stand for parliament, can become prime minister, and in short show themselves in every way to be just as competent as men, if not more so. Why should they not be ministers in churches? There seems no compelling reason, and in a great many denominations this has not proved a major problem, although it has always engendered lively debate. In the Catholic, Orthodox and Anglican Churches, with their long-standing requirement of male leadership, the debate has been much sharper. At present the only one of these three churches to have accepted women clergy is the Anglican, although I fancy the other two will not be able to escape the continued pressure for ever.

Many of those in the Anglo-Catholic tradition tend to oppose the ordination of women on grounds of ontology or tradition. They argue either that women are incapable by their gender of representing the male Jesus, or that the tradition of the Church has always been against it. These arguments are not watertight. If Jesus really embodies the fullness of the deity in bodily form (see Colossians 2:6), then that nature must embody the female as well as the male, despite Jesus having of necessity to be one gender or the other. When God created mankind in his image, 'he created them male and female'(Genesis 1:27). The *imago dei* comprises both male and female. Moreover, the tradition is not uniform. Think of Pope Joan, for example, or contemplate the possibility, which the Greek certainly allows, of a female apostle called Junia (see Romans 16:7).

Many Evangelicals, on the other hand, are not in the least bothered about either of these arguments. Instead, their reluctance to accept women presbyters is due to their reading of Scripture. You do not find female presbyters in the New Testament and Jesus, who was very radical and would certainly have appointed some if he thought it right, did not choose any women as members of his apostolic band. In particular they are influenced by the headship argument. St Paul clearly states that the husband is the 'head' of the wife, who should 'obey' him. 'The head of every man is Christ, and the head of a woman is her husband, and the head of Christ is God' (1 Corinthians 11:3).

The fact that the same word in Greek serves both for 'man' and 'husband', and the same word for 'woman' and 'wife', does not make it any easier. Is this a domestic or a universal regulation? For me, this argument smacks a little of male chauvinism. Paul's words are perfectly capable of the interpretation that, just as Christ shares the Father's nature but has a different function, so it is in the married state. It may not be anything to do with any fancied male superiority. In any case, the headship argument has two serious weaknesses. *Kephale*, 'head', is a much disputed word and may not indicate authority so much as origin. It may take us back to Genesis 2, which shows the male as the origin of the female, taken from his side. Moreover, the kingdom of God is an upside-down kingdom, and often perplexes with its paradoxes. Did Jesus, undoubtedly the Head, Lord and Master of his disciples, not go down literally head over heels to wash their feet? Is this not, as he expressly told them, the sort of headship that should prevail in the Christian community? This incident above any other shows me what it is like to be the 'head'.

I confess to having changed my mind to some extent over this whole matter. When in 1983 I revised *Called to Serve*, enlarged it and retitled it *Freed to Serve*, I had already thought through the two Pauline passages that seemed at first sight to militate against female leadership. Ephesians 5 is not relevant because, while it urges submission, it is submission 'to one another' which is encouraged. Both husband and wife have a role to play in this. In 1 Corinthians 14:34, when St Paul enjoins silence on wives and tells them to ask questions of their husbands at home, he is speaking to a specific situation. Women, educationally neglected in both Greek and Jewish systems and excluded from the synagogue, were, to their amazed excitement, given a full welcome into the Christian assembly, for 'in Christ there is neither male nor female'. No doubt there was noise and chaos. The women, so long excluded, were beginning to assert themselves with noisy questions, thus creating disorder and delay in the worship. Paul bids them be quiet and ask their questions at home. That this is the correct interpretation of the passage is clear from the fact that Paul does not forbid women speaking in the assembly at all. In the same letter he allows women both to pray and to prophesy in church (11:5). Exercising the gift of prophecy is a lot more dangerous than preaching.

The passage deemed more seriously to debar women from teaching comes in 1 Timothy 2:12: 'I permit no woman to teach or to have authority over men.' That looks conclusive, but the word *authentein*, translated 'have authority over', occurs nowhere else in the New Testament. It is a very rare word associated with murder and fornication, and the Greek father John Chrysostom in his commentary understands it in that sense here. Paul is refusing to allow women in orgiastic Ephesus to slaughter men by leading them into cultic fornication through their teachings, like Jezebel in the church at Thyatira (see Revelation 2:20f.). That is a very different matter from a blanket prohibition of teaching by women! The Book of Proverbs had been clear that the prostitute's house was the high road to spiritual death (2:18; 5:5), and 'murder' is one of the other well-attested meanings of *authentein*. In this rare word, the murderous and the erotic combine. Such an interpretation makes sense of the whole context in 1 Timothy 2, where women are told to dress modestly in a city where there were many courtesans (2:9,10). They must learn that there is only one way to have union with the divine: through Jesus Christ, not through the cult prostitution which some of them had practised (2:6). They must practise their religion with decorum, not with the orgies fashionable in the worship of Artemis. The devil seduced Eve. Let them take care (2:13f.).

It is not possible to prove that this is the correct interpretation of the passage, but it may well be. And if that possibility is allowed, how can we base a ban on women's leadership in ministry on one unique and obscure word? Christianity was in the van of women's liberation in the first century. I was not keen to see the Church remain one of the last bodies in the twentieth century to allow women a significant place in leadership. In *Freed to Serve* I went on to show the wide range of ministries that the New Testament tells us was entrusted to women. I argued that we had got the concept of ordination wrong. We should see it not so much in terms of a threefold hierarchy as a shared and multiple local leadership involving both men and women. Of the gift of leadership I wrote, 'The Church will appropriately recognize this by ordination. Women will take their place alongside men within the local presbyterate.' I went on, however, to suggest that 'I believe that the creation pattern and the New Testament emphasis on the supportive role in ministry to be exercised by women might be best retained if the leadership of such a mixed team were normally, if not invariably, to be in the hands of a man.' Then I added, 'But perhaps I am unable to extricate myself sufficiently from my own cultural heritage and that of the New Testament!'

I have since come to believe, as I expressed in the 1996 revision of *Freed to Serve*, that I was indeed to some extent still in bondage to my male assumptions. Of course, this mild change of mind may well be due to the fact that in the meantime the Church of England had voted, by a narrow margin, to ordain women as priests, but I hope that was not the only reason. It is perfectly obvious that women can teach both men and women, and for ages they have been doing it on the mission field, where many ordained men have not had the courage to follow them. Now that we have allowed them to exercise their gifts in the West and the initial surprise and prejudice has worn off, that too is seen to be quite natural.

Two of my friends are very competent New Testament scholars. One of them is a little chary about the ordination of women, but on New Testament grounds unequivocally asserts that the Church should affirm the equality of the genders, encourage women's ministry, and reject any idea of 'unisex' but rejoice in God's creational differences between men and women. Those differences include the husband having some 'priority' over the wife, and he is inclined to believe that it should be the norm, in the light of the New Testament, for a man to have overall leadership in a ministry team.

My other scholar friend deals with Ephesians 5, 1 Timothy 2 and 1 Corinthians 11 much as I did above, and points out that the New Testament is clear that men and women are equally members of the Body of Christ, that it gives women more status than did the surrounding culture, that it sees the breaking down of the barriers between Jew and Gentile, male and female, slave and free as central to what Jesus has done, and that it speaks of women undertaking important ministry roles. He is enthusiastic about women's ordination. Matters to do with the organization of the Church and of society are not, he feels, of overriding importance to the New Testament writers, whereas issues of sound teaching, morality, good order and the propagation of the gospel most certainly are. Accordingly, while it does not teach that there are lasting limitations on women's ministry, the New Testament does at various points make restrictions on women in ministry either because they were causing disorder or because *in that culture* particular roles for women would cause public scandal and hinder the spread of the gospel. In terms of the current scene, he maintains there is no biblical reason for restricting women's roles – and for the Church to do so would be a public scandal in today's climate. He also resists 'unisex' interpretations of ministry – after all, only women bear children.

It is clear that these two scholars are not far apart. Indeed, they work happily in the same team. They and I can both live in a Church which maintains the 'two integrities', i.e. the genuine biblical and theological defence of women's ministry alongside those who, on the same grounds, cannot accept it. It is important not to marginalize or cast aside those whose reading of the New Testament and respect for tradition was until recently the mainstream view – although that is precisely what the Episcopal church in the USA has recently done. It is important to collaborate as far as possible with those from whom we differ, and when this issue becomes divisive it is crucial to ensure that both sides of the argument are patiently heard. Perhaps above all it is imperative that we are humble over such contentious issues. In the words of Oliver Cromwell, 'I beseech you, in the bowels of Jesus Christ: consider it possible that you may be mistaken!'

I did not play any significant role in women's struggle for ordination. This was in part accidental. I had the enormous privilege of being the Rector of a large church where male and female, ordained and unordained, young and old, served together in a team where tasks were determined by gifting, not by hierarchy or gender. Team members simply served the Lord in ways for which he had gifted them. Leading services was certainly not restricted to the clergy. A gifted layman led the PCC. The only thing that our female staff were not allowed to do was to make the prayer of consecration at the Eucharist. Yet neither were our laymen given that privilege: the Act of Uniformity forbade it – and still does, for the laity. We found no frustration among our women in ministry. They could lead, teach, preach, evangelize and do pastoral work to their hearts' content. And they were very content, for most Evangelicals do not have a burning passion to lead the Eucharist. Accordingly, it was a very easy step for me to see women ordained and officially recognized in the role which they had largely already been occupying in our church – and doing so on a proper salary and with a guaranteed career structure ahead of them.

Homosexuality

I rejoice at having seen so many controversies settled during my lifetime, but one is still very much with us: the issue of homosexual practice. When I was a young man, sodomy was a crime punishable by a prison sentence. Now it is being commended not just as an equal but as a superior lifestyle. I have lived to see the day when a leading homosexual climbs into the pulpit at Canterbury Cathedral and assaults the Archbishop of Canterbury in the middle of his address. I have lived through days when the gay lobby pestered the Lambeth Conference daily for recognition of their position, aided by a small minority of the bishops. I have struggled one night from the Houses of Parliament when a great crowd of impassioned lesbians and gays were howling for the reduction of the age of consent.

I discovered for myself the intensity of feeling over this matter when I shared with David Watson and David Holloway in writing a book entitled *The Church and Homosexuality* – 'a positive answer to the current debate', published by Hodder and Stoughton in 1980. The fury that erupted at the massive press conference which took place was a major surprise to me, although I guess I should have expected it. Our book was very mild, but it touched an extremely raw nerve.

We wrote it in response to a sensitive but unsatisfactory Report by the Church of England's Board of Social

Responsibility entitled *Homosexual Relationships: a contribution to discussion* (CIO, 1979). For my part, I examined changing standards in sexual morality and admitted that traditional Church attitudes to sexual morality in general and homosexuality in particular stand in striking contrast to the attitude of Jesus, who was far more devastating on the 'respectable' sins of hypocrisy, pride and jealousy. I went on to ask why Christians should be unhappy about homosexual activity. The answer, of course, lies in the Scriptures, both Old Testament and New. Their position is uniform and unequivocal: although not in the least homophobic, they are clear that this is not how the genitals are designed by God to be used. Whether we look at Romans 1:24–32, 1 Timothy 1:8–10, or 2 Peter 2:6–10, the attitude is clear: believers are called to have nothing to do with homosexual practice.

There is a marvellous passage in 1 Corinthians 6:9ff. which informs us that 'the unrighteous will not inherit the kingdom of God' – and that includes all of us. It is only by acknowledging that fact and turning to the Lord in repentance and faith that we enter the sphere of his kingly rule. 'Neither the immoral, nor idolaters, nor adulterers, nor sexual perverts, nor thieves, nor the greedy, nor drunkards, nor revilers, nor robbers will inherit the kingdom of God.' (The English is much less specific than the Greek which indicates both active and passive homosexual partners.) Once we are prepared to repent and change our ways, whether our particular sins are robbery, greed, alcohol addiction, bitter attacks on others, adultery, homosexual acts or fornication, then we can be 'washed, sanctified, justified in the name of the Lord Jesus and by the Spirit of our God'. The Corinthian church abounded in men and women who had been deep in idolatry, robbery, bitter talk, homosexual and heterosexual extramarital liaisons. Nobody said, 'You are not good enough to be Christians.' They were washed by Christ. Equally, nobody said, 'You can stay the way you are.' The Lord enters our lives in order to transform them, and we need to give him permission to get started on it.

That seemed to me then, and still does today, to be the essence of the biblical teaching. Homosexual activity is wrong, just as fornication, adultery and bestiality are wrong, because all of them defile the 'one man, one woman, for keeps' principle which is both the Creator's instruction for humankind (see Genesis 2:24) and the clearest embodiment we can get of the total and exclusive self-giving between Christ and his Church (see Ephesians 5:21ff.). It is written into creation. It is written into redemption. I cannot see how any Church can justifiably abrogate the clear teaching of the Bible on homosexual practice. The Episcopal Church in the USA is being torn apart on this matter. It is dominated by the cultural climate, not by the teaching of Scripture. Bishops there are ordaining active homosexuals and conducting gay 'marriages' in defiance of the Bible's teaching, in defiance of the Lambeth Conference and in defiance of the rules of their own Convention. Moreover, at its meeting in July 2000 that same Convention recognized a whole variety of sexual mores outside marriage as acceptable in the Christian Church. This, of course, means there is no point in restraint, no virtue in chastity. It means, as Ruth Graham succinctly put it, that on the Day of Judgement God will need to apologize to Sodom and Gomorrah.

This book of ours included a careful examination of homosexual claims in the light of the Bible by David Holloway, including the claim that homosexuality is as unexceptional and natural as left-handedness. David Watson wrote of pastoral considerations. He and I had both ministered to homosexuals of both sexes and had seen their practice and even their orientation change by the grace of God. I do not know if this is always possible, but I do know numerous cases where it has happened. There is abundant evidence, both from this country and from the USA, that the grace of Christ is transforming homosexuals who are willing to change. This is emphatically not a message the homosexual lobby wants to hear. They either vilify or seek to suppress this evidence of transformation. Enormous efforts are being made all the time to demonstrate that homosexuality is inherited. It is hard to see how this could be so, since every homosexual is the product of heterosexual union, but even if it were proved, which it certainly is not, it would merely show a predisposition.

We are not, however, in prison to our genes. We all have to struggle against some of the tendencies we have inherited. For most of us who are heterosexual, chastity is extremely difficult – yet it is eminently possible for those who have the heart for it and call on the grace of the Lord to assist them. So it can be with homosexuals if they offer their inherited tendencies to the Lord for him to work on. The hardest thing, I am sure, is that, if the tendency remains unchanged, it would render marriage either difficult or impossible. This would inevitably lead to loneliness. Yet I have known many of homosexual tendency, some of them my friends and tutors, who have not given in to the urges of their nature but have sublimated them into nonsexual relationships with a wide circle of friends. That is, after all, what many unmarried people – Christian or otherwise – do. The pan-sexuality of our culture and our advertising persuades us that sexual expression is a right that we must have. Is this really the case? Jesus, the most complete human being who ever lived, voluntarily remained unmarried – and was fulfilled. It is a possibility, though undeniably a very hard one, for his followers.

I am no expert in this subject, and I await further light on it. It is a controversy which continues to convulse many denominations. Society has decided to accept it, but should the Church always follow society? Is it, as great Christians like Desmond Tutu believe, an issue of liberation where the Church should sustain homosexuals in their right to whatever sexual activity they please? Or is it a matter of morality where, for believing Christians, the Scriptures must be decisive? Of one thing we can be sure: African and Asian Anglicans, who now form by far the majority of the Anglican Communion, will not tolerate the promotion of homosexual practice by the Americans. If US Episcopalians persist in this, they will run the risk of being expelled or sidelined by the Anglican family worldwide. They are very close to that point now, and the next meeting of Anglican primates will want to know whether or not they have given in to the homosexual lobby, and whether or not they have ceased to persecute (and in some cases expel) orthodox Anglican congregations which do not approve of homosexual practice. At the start of the third millennium, the Episcopal Church in the USA is dominated by this single issue. The growing churches in Africa and Asia are not. Nevertheless, they will not tolerate determined disregard of Scripture on the matter, and decision time is very near.

Of course, Christians should shun homophobia. They should realize that, if there are failures in their brethren, there are failures in themselves. They should remember that sexual sins were not the prime targets of Jesus' moral teaching. They should make a point of becoming friends with those who think differently. They should forgive as they hope to be forgiven, seventy times seven. Yet how can they condone a practice that is so manifestly against the teaching of the whole Bible? It is not without significance that the three great monotheistic religions, Judaism, Christianity and Islam, are all united not against homosexuals but against their genital activity. Is Christianity to be the first to change tack, in defiance of tradition, Scripture and reason (remember the scourge of AIDS)? The jury is still out on this, one of the most pressing controversies of our time. I have only been able to write honestly as I see things. I may well be wrong. My understanding is partial, but I can only record that over the 50 years covered by this book my opinion about the wrongness of the activity has not changed, although my understanding and compassion most certainly have. May the Lord guide us all.

Worship styles

I would like to close this chapter with a controversy which is minuscule compared to the preceding one, but which extends to almost every parish in the country. It is the issue of worship. People are extremely opinionated about the style and form of worship they like. Shall it be plainsong, the old hymns, or the new songs? Shall it be the robed choir, or the contemporary music group? Should it be the 1662 service, or Common Worship? Or should we scrap both and go for informal family services, retaining liturgy only for Communion? Even dress is involved, as young clergy are increasingly unwilling to wear antiquated robes. They wish to lead services in lounge suits, and many of them do not even use a clerical collar (after all, it only came in late in the nineteenth century).

As a Church, we have not yet resolved these matters. We live in a time of climactic change. It is difficult to get our bearings. It can safely be said, however, that the growth of the Anglican Church in the world and in Britain is primarily among the Evangelicals and charismatics, while the leadership, at least in the West, is still primarily in the hands of liberal Catholics. There is no doubt that the churches which are growing are the Bible-based churches, which have a strong doctrinal base, a warm pastoral concern, an awareness of spiritual gifts and battle, and a passionate commitment to evangelism. These are the churches that are least happy with traditional music, liturgy and dress. No doubt the current mix will continue for a while, but there is little doubt of the direction in which the Anglican Communion is moving.

If services are deemed to be dull or out of touch, people will not come. On the other hand, if radical change is made too soon or without adequate discussion, it will alienate the (often elderly) people who still attend church. One expedient is to have an early-morning Prayer Book Communion, a mid-morning Eucharist with hymns and songs, and a lively, non-liturgical service in the evening. Another is to have two morning services: a family service and a Communion, followed at night by a major time of informal praise and teaching. In some places a late-night youth service with drums, smoke and the full kit works well. In other places the youth run their own services – and these are very popular, but often hover on the edge of chaos. The trouble with all these expedients is that they subdivide a congregation according to their preferences and as a result people rarely get the opportunity (or even have the inclination) to express their unity in the Body of Christ, which must surely transcend all age and cultural preferences.

While we have not solved this problem, least of all by providing yet another new Prayer Book, certain things are clear. We must preserve the best of the old hymns and prayers. We must make room for informality. We must welcome the new songs: they are not great music, nor will they last, but they are the way in which many of today's generation want to express their worship of God, and this should not be denied them. We must not remain locked into accompaniment by an organ. In the past they had a minstrel's gallery in church, and today we are getting back to having a team of musicians leading the worship. That in itself is a proper expression of the Body of Christ, with its unity and diversity. We must go to great lengths to encourage the young. We must be willing to subordinate our own preferences to what will best serve the community in which we worship. Love and mutual consideration must be our hallmark.

I do not suggest that this approach will resolve the controversy between the 'trads' and the 'mods' in worship, but it will go some way towards it. Let St Paul have the last word: 'May the God who gives endurance and encouragement give you a spirit of unity among yourselves as you follow Christ Jesus, so that with one heart and mouth you may glorify the God and Father of our Lord Jesus Christ' (Romans 15:5–6). If that were our goal in all the controversies that arise in Christian circles, we would be much more attractive to non-members, and would much better express the character of the triune God, who is himself diversity in unity.

PART 5

FAITH AND THE FUTURE

CHAPTER 14

The World Church

Recently I was invited to give a lecture at Oxford on Anglicanism worldwide. At first this was a shock: I felt I knew nothing of the inner workings of our denomination with its 70 million or so members across the world. I had never attended the Anglican Consultative Council, nor even stepped into the Anglican Communion Office. On reflection, however, I realized I could contribute something, because I have visited and ministered in much of the Anglican Communion over some 30 years. In the East I have made some contribution in New Zealand, Australia, Papua New Guinea, the Solomon Islands, India, Pakistan, Hong Kong, the Philippines, Thailand, Sri Lanka, Korea, Singapore, Malaysia and Sarawak. I have also worked in many African countries – Egypt, the Sudan, Ethiopia, Ghana, Uganda, Kenya, Nigeria, Malawi, Botswana, South Africa, Zambia and Zimbabwe, as well as Jerusalem and several of the Gulf States. I have done some ministry in a number of European Anglican chaplaincies, and beyond Anglicanism in Germany, Holland, France, Spain, Switzerland, Belgium, Norway, Denmark, Sweden and Iceland. I have also been privileged to minister in six South American countries, together with Barbados, Jamaica, Canada and the USA.

I am no expert on any of these, but, by the providence of God, I have been around. I marvel at this when I think of the comparative poverty of my father, subsisting on his £400-a-year parson's salary, and our lack of capital resources. I do not think I have paid to go on many of these visits, but I have been invited by leading Christians in many countries to minister to them, and it has been an enormous privilege. It humbles me that I have had such a special chance to see the workings of the Christian faith in many parts of the world, particularly those covered by the Anglican Communion.

Africa

It all began in 1963, when I accompanied the Rev. Dick Lucas on university missions in South Africa. Our main destination was the University of Cape Town, where we were both busily extended for a week or more. Then he went to Durban and I went to Rhodes University, Grahamstown, for a similar period. Those missions were eye-openers for me. I was shocked by apartheid, which had been in place for over 15 years.

Some aspects of it were ludicrous: if you wanted stamps you had to go to a post office with separate access for whites and non-whites – but the same black African scuttled between the two access points to serve customers. Some aspects of it were exceedingly painful to behold: superb food was served to us by handsome black servants in the dining hall at Rhodes, and then I noticed from my guest room those same Africans going to their little hut at the bottom of the garden with one item only for themselves and their families to eat – a single loaf of bread. Some aspects were scandalous: education for white children was free, but impoverished non-whites had to pay. Moreover, the Bantu Education Act made them study in their own language, for which there were practically no textbooks, but they had to study in Afrikaans if they had the rare chance of going on to higher education. Some aspects were heartbreaking: all over South Africa were cantonments of blacks who had been evicted from their homes in the middle of the night, because they were in 'white' areas. They were ruthlessly transported into the middle of nowhere and left to get on with it, entirely without employment or education of any kind.

I did not see inside the prisons, but I met people who had been incarcerated in them. On a subsequent visit, I led a mission in the Fort Hare University in the town of Alice, and discovered at first hand what happened. If a (white) staff member invited a Coloured student to his home for a meal, the staff member got off scot free. The student was taken to police headquarters for a week or more, interrogated and beaten, and deprived of his opportunities to study for that period. I preached strongly against such practices and, although attendance was only moderate at the beginning of the week, by its end almost the whole university was at the meetings. I publicly challenged the vice-chancellor to stand up to the government, but it was all in vain. Alice was seen as a seething focus for discontent and trouble, and the many intelligent Coloured students there were regarded by the authorities as a greater threat than the blacks. Not without good reason: they had once had the vote and it had been taken away from them. It was lovely to find many of them professing conversion, and determining to throw themselves peacefully but with deep commitment into the struggle for freedom. It was a great honour to be among them.

But I digress. Back to those first two missions in Cape Town and Rhodes. The time was ripe: many students were very unhappy with government policies, and at least during their student days were quite liberal in their racial attitudes. This almost always evaporated within a year or two of graduating, but it made for quite an open, questing student body at these all-white universities. In Cape Town Dick Lucas and I were privileged to see many young men and women entrust their lives to Christ, including Jews, leading academics and top sportspeople. The same was true in Rhodes, where, among others, the Springbok rugby stand-off half came to faith. Rugby, of course, is almost the religion of South African universities, and it was good to see influential individuals surrendering to Jesus Christ.

My second visit to South Africa soon followed. This was based in a massive old home in Trovato, in the Cape, and was primarily intended to be a training visit. I still recall teaching on the steps of this great house at night while scores of students hung on the words of the Scriptures and gave themselves to prayer. Many of these later became major Christian leaders. It was on this visit that I first ran foul of the South African authorities. I started preaching about the microscopic and exploitative wages paid to their employees by powerful firms like Rio Tinto Zinc, and found myself followed everywhere by government agents. They collected a large file on me, which made further visits to South Africa somewhat problematic. On one return visit, we were met at the airport by an MP friend who was prepared to force the issue with Immigration if necessary. His intervention was not needed. My wife Rosemary preceded me in the passport queue, and had to argue with the official about the permitted length of our stay. She was a mathematician, and he could not count. She won, and in his embarrassment he let the next person through without a murmur. That person was me!

Even in those early days, I realized that you could not separate the social aspects of the gospel from the spiritual. They stood or fell together. One of the most striking examples of the need to hold the two together occurred in Durban, when Michael Cassidy, the leader of African Enterprise, packed a large hotel with people from all the country's racial groups – a real first. I was invited to give Bible studies at this remarkable congress. I arrived late and tired from the long flight, was shown to my room, and thought nothing of it when reception said they had mislaid the key. All I wanted to do was to sleep. I had not been asleep for long before a black African delegate came in. I heard him exclaim, 'Oh no, not again!' This was the second night he had been summarily evicted from his room to make way for a white delegate. No wonder they had no key to give me – he had it! I immediately demanded to see the flustered night manager, who said he would find another room for the African gentleman. 'No,' I said, 'he stays here. This is his room.' I told him to get a mattress for me and I slept (very soundly) on the floor, while the African slept in his bed. This seemed to me the most natural thing to do, but I found the next day that it had gone round the conference like wildfire. Actions often speak louder than words.

Later I was invited back to lead a second mission in the University of Cape Town. I was also invited to do some evening meetings at the prestigious University of Stellenbosch, situated not many miles away. These involved about 4,000 students, in a great 'church week' organized by the influential Dutch Reformed Church. They asked me to speak on the topic of the Church and I proposed, with their agreement, to give the first talk on 'The Failure of the Church'. I chose to speak from J.B. Phillips' fresh, modern translation of the Book of Amos, and it was eloquent against the system of 'selling the needy for a pair of shoes' – so similar to the prevailing apartheid. I simply let Scripture speak, with only two applications: one from the Church's failure in Britain and one from the Church's failure to oppose apartheid in South Africa.

The result was electric. I was surrounded by clergy telling me I had abused the pulpit by speaking of politics. I disagreed and told them that, as they were conservative Christians, they should listen to and obey the Scriptures. What had I said that was not in accord with Scripture? They could give no reply. Yet all sorts of people pushed through the press to give me little notes saying, 'We have needed to hear this for a long time.' I was debarred from speaking there for the rest of the week, and they had some problem explaining my absence. I gather that the stir continued, and one of the main topics in the Student Representative Council elections that year was the question, 'Was Green right or wrong?' Even the chaplains found themselves constrained to speak on the Book of Amos before long. Such were some of the excitements of ministry in South Africa in the days of apartheid.

On these early trips to South Africa I greatly enjoyed stopping off in a black African country on the way out and back. In those days, planes could not fly direct to somewhere so remote, and layovers were a necessity. It appealed to my sense of humour to minister in black African countries on a ticket provided by white South Africans! On one occasion I travelled via Ethiopia and had the privilege of speaking there. I also met Dr Elizabeth Duncan, a distinguished gynaecologist who combined her professional skills with unremitting Christian activity and an enthusiasm for trout-fishing. It was in her company that I sampled my first African trout. It was also in her company that I first saw Africans with their hands amputated. Their 'guilt' lay simply in gathering firewood without permission.

During a visit to Khartoum, I was most impressed by the work of the Rev. Brian Lea, a missionary who had a huge impact there. It was thrilling in the evenings to show slides of the gospel story to what purported to be an exclusively Christian gathering of youth, but in reality comprised a great many Muslims. They crowded round to watch. This was my first real exposure to Islam, and I was fascinated to see the appeal of Jesus to these young people who were forbidden to learn anything about him. It reinforced my determination to make Christ known wherever in the world I went and as long as I could speak.

The two most memorable of these side-visits emerging from South African invitations were in Ghana and Uganda. The Ghanaian invitation came from Culain Morris, the English Scripture Union worker in Accra, who asked if I would lead a conference for Scripture Union at Adisadel College on the coast. It was intended to be for Christian young people who had been brought to faith by the work of Scripture Union, but large numbers came who had no personal faith. After a day or

so, I was told I needed to change the agreed teaching programme and speak evangelistically. This I did, and the result
was remarkable. Young men and women stood for half an
hour or more in order to have the opportunity to make a
public response to the challenge of Christ and start a life of
discipleship. Those were difficult and dangerous days for
national Christians, as President Nkrumah behaved almost
like one of the old Roman Emperors who believed in their
own divinity. It was perilous to cross him.

It was equally perilous in Uganda, with Milton Obote in
command for his first spell as President. I remember meeting
him on my first visit to Uganda. He had eyes like a snake, glit-
tering and constantly moving from side to side in search of
danger. Why they ever invited this man to return from exile to
the presidency in the wake of President Amin, I shall never
know. He was as ruthless a killer as Amin. He killed Henry,
the young son of my friend and host the Rev. Amos
Betungura, who had earlier been a student with us at the
London College of Divinity. Amos became a bishop, but was
at that time Principal of Mukono Theological College, the
premier institution in the country. I was intrigued to see what
went on, since I too was engaged in theological education.
Several things stood out.

One was the warmth and generosity of these African
Christians. Amos was poor, but he had managed to purchase
a packet of English cornflakes especially for me. They were
horrendously expensive, and consequently almost stuck in my
throat. By contrast, I loved the local paw-paw and was amazed
at the variety of bananas and the myriad ways in which they
could be cooked and presented.

I was also touched by the shortage of books. The library,
such as it was, was always locked carefully after classes so that
books did not stray. Students had very few of their own. As
clergy they could only look forward to a life of financial
poverty, but this did not dim their enthusiasm. I had the privilege of doing some teaching there, and I found the hunger to

learn was intense: it knocked spots off our English students. Despite the lack of books and the spartan nature of the college, they had two facilities which were far ahead of anything in England. One was a television studio, which could put out programmes nationally and was invaluable in training students to see for themselves how they communicated. The other was a village adjoining the college where the married students and their families lived and cultivated food, and the women received some training too. Both these things made a deep impression on me, and when I came to lead St John's College I determined that we should have a television studio, as well as married and family quarters. I shall always be grateful to Mukono College for showing me the way. I am also delighted that it is now a distinguished university, of which the theological college forms a part.

I have the happiest memories of so many events in Africa. On the second mission in the University of Cape Town I shared the leadership with the black African evangelist Phineas Dube. Simply to see the two of us standing together and proclaiming Christ made an enormous impression in those days of apartheid. So much so, indeed, that the large Jewish Society in the university invited me to spend time with them debating the Messiahship of Jesus. I took them through the Old Testament prophecies, and it felt like a throwback to the first century when the apostles and their colleagues did this sort of thing all the time. One of the young women who moved from Judaism to Messianic Judaism through encounter with Christ at one of these missions has been for many years a missionary in Namibia. I have never been to Namibia, but it is a particular joy to know that this 'daughter in the faith' has been working there fruitfully for years.

Other happy memories crowd in. In Zimbabwe I saw the growth of the Church there despite tension between the two main tribes. Much of the advance was due to African Enterprise, that brainchild of Michael Cassidy which pioneered black and white partnership over 20 years before the end of apartheid, against sharp opposition from the South African government. A visit to Botswana was also very instructive. In its capital a dynamic bishop dominated the Church and had considerable power with heads of state in the area, while a small coterie of nuns gave themselves to the poor and shone for Christ in desolate circumstances. Our friend Sister Margaret Magdalen, herself a distinguished author, became the nuns' leader and, although most of them were old and infirm, they did not give up but continued to serve the local people selflessly. It was an object lesson in sacrifice and perseverance.

Before leaving the African scene, I want to say a little about Nigeria. On two occasions I had the privilege of visiting that great country at the invitation of Benjamin Nwankiti, the Bishop of Owerri. The first occasion was a training conference for the clergy of the diocese, especially in evangelism. This proved a rather novel idea to many, but we had a good time of training and ended with an open-air rally with thousands present. Dr James Allan, an Oxford University lecturer, and I preached evangelistically and the response was so great, as they surged forward, that I thought they had misunderstood the challenge. I told them to go back, and asked an archdeacon to issue the appeal in the native language. Once again, the crowd surged to the front. We assigned the 70 or so white-cassocked clergy whom we had been training in evangelism to counsel the large group of enquirers. They got their practical training, all right! It was a memorable sight.

The other occasion was a gathering of the Nigerian bishops. I had been carefully briefed by Lambeth Palace and was there-fore able to speak very relevantly. I was also able to get these bishops, most of whom are regarded as petty kings by their congregations, to engage in daily Bible reading and prayer together during the conference. This was not their normal way of going about things, but it proved invaluable in deepening the spiritual bond among them. I recall being fascinated by the Daimler cars and the leopardskin accoutrements which many of them sported, as I tried to inculcate the lessons of servant leadership!

In addition, two remarkable healings at the conference changed the whole spiritual outlook. First, during a morning's teaching in the humid heat of Nigeria, I could sense an infection building up in my throat. Infections develop very fast in such conditions, and I knew that by the afternoon I would be quite unable to speak at the scheduled sessions. So I whispered to the bishops, with what remained of my voice, that they should gather round me, lay hands on me and pray for my healing. Very cautiously, they did – and my voice was restored almost at once. Second, that very night our host, Bishop Nwankiti, was struck down with malaria. He was very unwell, and the bishops did not expect to see him again during the conference. I went to his room, laid hands on him, and prayed. By six o'clock the next morning he was up, completely healed, and bringing tea round to his colleagues. They were staggered: they must have thought he was a ghost!

I believe that these healings encouraged the Nigerian bishops to pray for healing, and to expect that God might give it. Instead of leaving sick church members to seek the ministrations of the highly charismatic and distinctly off-centre Church of the Cherubim and Seraphim, as normally happened, these Nigerian leaders began to see healing as one of their privileges as members of the Body of Christ. Now, years later, these spiritual gifts have blossomed astonishingly and the Nigerian Anglicans have exploded in number. Once a rather formal Church, they are now among the most liberated, passionate and effective evangelists in the world. Their membership has escalated in one decade from 8 million to 18 million, something paralleled nowhere else in the world. It is the Lord's doing, and it is marvellous to see.

My repeated visits to Africa in the 1960s and '70s were not without cost. It meant much separation from the children when they were very young, and put extra pressure on Rosemary. A memorable saying of our son Tim, aged two, was, 'Daddy gone to Afca. Me want to go to Afca too.' (His wish to travel abroad is now more than answered: he is a missionary in Pakistan.) Rosemary made him a cardboard caterpillar with 39 segments, one for each day of my absence, and he pulled them off one by one. Before long I determined, for the family's sake, not to do more than one extended overseas visit a year.

Europe

For a while, I found myself turning more to Europe. First there was Iceland, a magical country. I cannot recall how or why I was invited, but I was, and I delighted in the fellowship of these rather uptight but courageous and gutsy Christians. Their faces were pale because they saw so little sun. Their services were restrained: they were, after all, the most northern of Norsemen. They faced Erastianism in the Church, which was under the control of the government. They faced a lot of compromise, particularly with the old Norse religion. I was fascinated by their country, too. You could experience spring, summer, autumn and winter in a single day, so great and so sudden were the climatic changes. New islands were being thrown up offshore by volcanoes. Hot water from artesian wells was piped into the houses, and into greenhouses to nurture lush plants. I remember bringing back a magnificent sweater made from local wool of varied hue which I wore for a television appearance, after which I was rebuked by an old lady for speaking about God when 'dressed like that'!

In the years that followed, my writings percolated into Norway and Sweden, and I was asked to accompany them. I spent one idyllic winter week in Sweden, ministering to students and trying to learn how to ski. Unfortunately, I had started too late and never got the hang of it, although Rosemary did, and she still enjoys cross-country skiing whenever she gets the opportunity. As she is on the Board of the Christian Community at Schloss Mittersill in Austria, the opportunity happily comes her way each year.

Norway seems to me the most dynamic of the Scandinavian countries as far as Christian things are concerned. They have a marvellous organization called OASE, and it is indeed an oasis to many. It regularly puts on vast conferences for the deepening of spiritual life. Some 6,000 people are likely to attend, and often the subject of its deliberations becomes front line news on radio and television. This is probably unique among European nations. Their student work is equally vibrant, and Norway has the highest proportion of overseas missionaries of any country in the world. There have been repeated waves of revival in this rugged and spectacularly beautiful land for more than a century, and it shows.

Turning to other parts of Europe, I remember well a charismatic conference in Belgium hosted jointly by Catholics and Protestants. It was a joy to minister in such a setting, and to see two cases of evil spirits being cast out through the ministry of deliverance. We also visited many homes in the city two by two, a Catholic and a Protestant together, and asked the residents to a closing evangelistic service in the Catholic church, at which there were addresses in both French and English. Most of the good burghers had never seen anything like it, and I doubt if any of them will forget that utterly unexpected and, to them, unprecedented example of unity in the Body of Christ.

In the south of Germany I twice had the privilege of speaking to great Pentecost gatherings of pietistic Evangelical Christians. The talks, the daily Bible study circles, the theological conversations in broken English and German, all had a great impact on me. It was heartening to see many thousands of Germans, a large proportion of them young, gathering to deepen their spiritual lives, especially against the background of Stuttgart's war memorial. The memorial is an enormous hill, constructed from the ruins inflicted by Allied bombers towards the end of the Second World War. It was deeply moving to climb up it in the company of a wonderful friend, Friedrich Hänssler. In addition to running a Christian publishing house, he would disappear from time to time on trips to smuggle large numbers of Bibles into Eastern Europe. In those days that could be a capital offence.

Years later, I found myself giving a series of lectures on evangelism at Schloss Mittersill in Austria, accompanied by the gifted young apologist Michael Ramsden. This superb castle was once one of the Kaiser's shooting lodges and was used by the Gestapo as a headquarters and interrogation centre in the Second World War. In recent years it has become an outstanding centre for Christian education and renewal. It has a resident team of 40 or so young people, and caters for a variety of Christian groups from both Eastern and Western Europe. It has risen to some prominence largely through the visionary leadership of Dr Carl Armerding and his wife Betsy. He gave up his post as Principal of Regent College, Vancouver, in order to pioneer tertiary-level Christian education at Mittersill. A major aim was to assist the many Christians in Eastern Europe, particularly Evangelicals, who had been denied the privilege of theological study for many decades. Students now come there from far and wide. Some are moving towards doctorates and are already taking up academic posts in Eastern European universities, while others represent an impressive band of young ministers and lay leaders, determined to influence their countries for God.

In the course on evangelism which I taught there, we had students of no less than 14 nationalities, each with a passionate desire to learn. It was wonderful to see Serbs and Croats worshipping together and loving one another in Christ, despite their homelands being locked in a most bloodthirsty Balkan war. It was moving to see the dedication and commitment of young people who had practically nothing, except a deep love for Christ and a determination to make him known. It was fascinating to contrast the intellectual enquiry of the Hungarians, heirs of the Reformation, with the fresh, relaxed spirituality of the Romanians, who had never experienced it. It was instructive to discover the same old problems presenting themselves in these very varied countries. Formalism and ecclesiastical authoritarianism were to be found in Evangelical churches as well as among the Catholics and the Orthodox. The tiny Protestant minority in these countries was afflicted with the same failings as in the West: fragmentation, materialism, peer pressure, nationalism and apathy.

What struck me most, however, was the way this new generation of European Christian workers were taking risks for God and seeing fruit. They evangelized through friendship, parties, games, music, sport and social concern. Door-to-door questionnaires were surprisingly successful, as was open-air preaching. We heard of outreach in Amsterdam's red-light district through Christians providing the cheapest (and most pleasant) accommodation in the area – offering a non-alcoholic bar, Bible studies and help in getting off prostitution and drugs. I later had the privilege of visiting this most impressive hostel. We heard also of the big emphasis in Hungary on work in schools, of Romanian evangelistic services, and of bold outreach amidst the secularism of the Czech Republic. Every one of these countries has been affected by the postmodernism we have encountered in the UK – not just lands like Hungary which have been through both the Enlightenment and the Reformation, but those like Romania which have encountered neither.

I came away with a variety of impressions. I felt admiration for the vision and theological equipping offered by the Schloss, despite its slight resources, to such a broad spectrum of potential Church leaders in Eastern Europe. I felt a sense of shame that so many deplorable examples of Western cultural imperialism had flowed into Eastern Europe since the collapse of communism, gravely impeding the growth of the gospel in recent years. I felt sadness at the considerable persecution of Evangelicals by the Catholics and Orthodox, and also at the cultural insensitivity and bad evangelistic practice imported from the West, which is sure to make the growth of the indigenous churches much slower. I came away convinced that

Eastern Europe is of critical importance for the re-evangelization of the continent, and that financial support (without strings) and culturally appropriate equipping of nationals constitute the greatest service that the West can offer. Finally, I found myself praying that God will fan into flame the small fires of renewal to be found in parts of the Catholic and Orthodox Churches, for it is with them that the future must largely lie.

In Holland I have been honoured to work on some television programmes for a remarkable organization known as EO – Evangelische Omroep. This is an imaginative Christian company which enjoys so much popular esteem that it commands a great deal of State financial support, something unthinkable in Britain. I have worked with them on a number of occasions, and they are extremely professional. Programmes can go out in English because the Dutch are so proficient in languages, and the programmes are influential because they are watched by a great many people who would not call themselves Christians. The level of church attendance in Holland is very low, but the sense of philosophical and theological interest in the country is considerable. I did one series which was very well received, and this led to another – 12 programmes on Christian apologetics which were also turned into a book and a CD-ROM. The company subsequently received so many hits on their website that they invited me to return to speak and answer questions at large meetings in the country's main cities.

Another memorable occasion was the 1997 European Student Conference in Marburg. It operated under the aegis of the International Fellowship of Evangelical Students, and more than 2,500 students attended. Conditions were spartan – delegates slept on the floor and queued for over an hour for sparse meals – but love flowed among the representatives of 40 or more countries and the worship was dynamic. There were rather more delegates from Eastern Europe than from the West, but the Western students had paid most of the fares and accommodation costs of their impoverished Eastern brethren – a lovely gesture.

The largest contingent was from Russia. I met a Russian boxer who had led many of his fellow boxers to faith. Then there was a lively girl called Julia who told us how she went to university as a committed atheist, and scorned her two room-mates who began a Bible study group. After three months she found herself attending it without knowing why. An inveter-ate chain-smoker, she found herself praying for the first time in her life: 'God, I know you don't exist, but if you do, please rid me of smoking.' She woke up the next morning totally free of the craving to smoke, and entrusted her life to Christ. That little group grew rapidly and at the time of the conference they were praying for the president of the university, who had banned them from meeting on the campus. Meanwhile, they were busy multiplying on other premises.

Stories emerged of student work all over the world. Ethiopia has the fastest growth of any country. There are more than 300 groups in universities and 15 per cent of all under-graduates are members of the Christian Fellowship. Nigeria has 30,000 students meeting weekly in small groups. In Taiwan there was a recent missionary conference of 1,500 stu-dents, 1,000 of whom afterwards offered for a lifetime of mis-sionary service. This sort of thing is happening in many parts of the Two-Thirds World. It encouraged me to hear that well in excess of 2,000 cross-cultural missionaries have emerged from the student work in Asia over the past 20 years.

A Zambian student at university in Canada was won to Christ by three young people. He returned to Zambia and was soon leading a flourishing university work. This came to the ears of Dr Kaunda, the President of Zambia, who asked to see him and enquired what this message might be which was stir-ring the campus. The student leader passionately proclaimed the gospel to the President, who invited him to return a week later with some of his Christian friends to address the whole Cabinet. 'Tell them what you told me,' he said. All this happened because of the faithfulness of those three initial students.

A student from Nepal told us some astounding news. When the country was opened up to the gospel in a limited way in 1954, a mere 500 believers were known to exist. Now they number half a million and more, and the student work is vibrant. At a recent conference, 40 students cycled 300 miles to get there, preaching all the way. They have founded Christian groups not only in Nepal but also in neighbouring Bhutan, where there is no official Church.

There is also a massive growth in student ministry in South America. All 20 countries have student groups, which are particularly strong in Brazil, Argentina and Chile. In difficult circumstances they often come up with bold and imaginative means of outreach. In one university the Christian group asked the president if they could meet the professors and talk to them about the Christian faith. They were refused. They then asked if they could give any service to the university. They were set to cleaning the lavatories. Other students asked why, and the whole thing began to dominate university discussions. The president then ordered all the professors to join the Christian students in cleaning the lavatories, so they got the meeting with their teachers after all. In another university they publicly paraded five crosses. Effigies of Mau, Che Guevara, Lenin and Napoleon were hung on four of them, while the fifth was left empty. When they were asked why, they replied, 'These four great leaders are dead. The fifth cross is empty because Jesus Christ is alive.' I believe this student work, a taste of which was offered at that European Conference in Marburg, is one of the most significant Christian advances anywhere in the world in our generation.

The USA

Moving further afield once again, I have visited the United States many times, to speak at conferences, to universities, to local churches and to whole denominations. My talks have often been on the topic of evangelism and I find it mildly ironic that Americans, with all their know-how and technical efficiency, should want to hear from a benighted Brit about how to reach their friends with the gospel.

My first major exposure to a denomination's leaders was to some 1,800 ministers and lay leaders of the United Methodist Church. They met in Miami, and were acutely aware that the denomination had lost nearly 2 million members in the past 20 years. The prevailing theological persuasion in the Methodist Church at that time could only be described as liberal, however, and this does not normally make for effective evangelism. The Southern Baptists, robustly Evangelical, were operating in much the same area and were growing all the time. One section within the Methodists, known as the Upper Room, seemed to be ministering much more in the spirit of John Wesley – who would have had difficulty recognizing much of his denomination in the middle of the twentieth century. I took advice from the Upper Room leaders, and I think we began to break through the bureaucracy. I called for extended prayer on the second night of the conference, encouraging people to hang a sheet on their hotel room door if they were prepared to host a prayer meeting there. That evoked a considerable response. So did my teaching on evangelism in the New Testament, concentrating on what our forefathers in Christ had actually preached and how they depended on the gifts and power of the Holy Spirit. United Methodism was not strong in either area at that time.

Other denomination-wide efforts followed. One of the most interesting was with the American Baptists, who were very keen to distinguish themselves from the Southern Baptists. As so often happens with such polarized positions, each was strong where the other was weak. The Southern Baptists were impressive in remaining faithful to the New Testament proclamation and were very proactive, but their social care was not a patch on that of the American Baptists, who tended to be a little weak on the contents and proclamation of the *kerygma*. I also spoke at a leadership conference for one of the most liberal denominations in the whole of the US, which shall remain nameless. I am sure they did not much enjoy what I had to bring them – I rather think I was invited by mistake! What gave me most cause for surprise, however, was the condition of the Moravian Church in the US. They were kind enough to invite me to lead a conference on evangelism for their leadership, but I found that they had become rather stuck and no longer had that passion for the gospel which had launched Count Zinzendorf in the early eighteenth century. I gathered that their work in Africa was biblical and progressive, but it struck me how easily a denomination can drift away from its roots and founding fathers.

I had the privilege of speaking at many diocesan conferences for the Episcopal Church in the USA (ECUSA), and also at individual churches. As is well known, the Episcopal Church has been in internal turmoil for over a decade. People are leaving it in shoals, particularly from the more liberal dioceses. It was fascinating to see how a diocese can be controlled by its bishop: there are no checks and balances to moderate a bishop's power as there are in Britain, so whole dioceses can often be described as 'liberal' or 'conservative'. I have spoken in dioceses where the bishop has been dismissed for fornication or alcoholism, and where the bishop's heterodoxy has led several thousand parishioners to leave for more biblically oriented denominations. That exodus continues, and is receiving fresh direction through the recent action of the Archbishops of Rwanda and Southeast Asia in appointing two missionary bishops to work among congregations in the US that have been forced to leave by the 'revisionist' bishops. I mentioned this bold action in Chapter 10. It has naturally aroused enormous wrath among the Episcopal hierarchy, but ultimately it may well ensure the growth of an orthodox Anglican Mission in America. Churches are leaving ECUSA to join this Mission, and time will tell.

Of course, conservative Christians are torn. Should they abandon ship, or should they remain and seek to alter the Episcopal Church from within? The latter has been the policy adopted by most, but the sheer numbers of liberals militate against it. There is only one Evangelical theological seminary in the whole of the Episcopal Church in the US – Trinity Episcopal. All the others appear to be strongly affected by liberal theology and weak on Bible teaching and ethics. When one less-than-orthodox bishop retires, therefore, there is every likelihood that another of the same stripe will take his place. The recent President of Trinity, Bishop Bill Frey, previously Bishop of Colorado, was very nearly elected as Presiding Bishop. As it turned out, however, Bishop Ed Browning won the nomination and the denomination's decline continued under his liberal lead and the corruption of his treasurer, who had to face many years in prison.

I cannot help wondering how different things might have been had Bill Frey been elected. He gave several of his later years to leading Trinity, which has continued to pour out orthodox clergy. It is noteworthy, and indicative of the deep tensions in ECUSA, that many bishops will not tolerate in their dioceses anyone who comes from Trinity. In other words, they reject historic Anglicanism, which is all that Trinity is seeking to protect. One of its faculty, Terry Kelshaw, has been made a bishop in Rio Grande. He maintains a faithful witness there, but it lies far from the centres of power. Interestingly, Trinity's erstwhile President John Rogers is one of the two 'irregular' missionary bishops consecrated in Singapore.

It is noteworthy that all 12 of the largest Episcopal churches in the US are Evangelical. Clearly liberalism does not make for church-building. I have spoken in several of them, particularly in Virginia and Washington DC. There are three in greater Washington which hunt together to a considerable extent: the Falls Church, the Church of the Apostles and Truro. Here you will find a welcome for women of the streets,

Supreme Court judges, students and businesspeople. All three churches have strong lay leadership. All three have a clear idea of their mission and direction. A similar church is to be found in Pawley's Island down in Florida. The church itself is amazing, but the dedication of the members is even more so. I spoke at a conference there not long ago and was overwhelmed by the love, spirit of service and efficiency of scores of its members whose only purpose in life, it seemed, was to make visitors welcome and spread the influence of their church, so blessed by God. The Rector, Chuck Murphy, is the second 'irregular' bishop consecrated in Singapore. He is eminently qualified to lead the flock of God.

I must also mention the Olympic Games in Atlanta. A remarkable man called Eddie Waxer, an athletic young Jew who converted to Christ many years ago, has given his life to facilitating and co-ordinating a worldwide network of Christian ministries among athletes – organizations like Athletes in Action and Christians in Sport. The men and women who work in these organizations come together for a few days just after each Olympics to take stock and plan for the future. Someone is invited to give daily Bible teaching and encouragement to the 200 or so workers gathered there, and I had that privilege in both Korea and Atlanta.

It is a remarkable work across the athletic world. Some act as chaplains and have daily access to the Olympic village. Others work more on the outskirts, running basketball 'clinics' for local children and similar events. They organize 'Greater than Gold' outreaches in many countries of the world, arranging television coverage of Olympic events in a large centre in a city and incorporating the videotaped testimony of one or more local Christian athletes. The impact of all this is very considerable, and more recently Eddie has been arranging Kid's Games, especially in Muslim countries, which bring thousands of young people to events which feed their love of sport and arouse in them a hunger for Christ. We shall never know the full impact of what Eddie and his colleagues have done, but it is massive. In Atlanta some 1,700 pastors were specifically involved in helping the crowds at the Olympics. One delightful initiative jointly mounted by the Salvation Army and Youth With A Mission was to provide bottles of water free for the crowds and competitors in the unnatural heat. American secular organizations were selling water at more than a dollar a bottle. The contrast was stark. People were universally appreciative, and it spoke eloquently of the free grace which lies at the heart of the gospel.

Canada

I have enjoyed my visits to the USA, but Canada is the country of my adoption. I have family there, and Rosemary and I lived and worked in Vancouver from 1987 to 1992 and gained our Canadian citizenship. Our links go back much further than that, however. I used to go out to lecture in the Summer School at Regent College almost from its earliest days, and formed a great admiration for this dynamic college founded with such great faith from such small beginnings. I was delighted, therefore, to be appointed Professor of Evangelism at Regent in 1987, and have written in more detail about that time in Chapter 6. Our years there were increasingly fulfilling. We appreciated enormously the range and ability of our colleagues on the faculty, whose deep personal commitment to Christ worked through into their teaching; we loved the highly motivated students, who came from all over the world; we were proud to serve at a college which had already gained the reputation of being the most distinguished Christian tertiary institution in Canada. They were good years, and enabled me to write extensively and to minister in different parts of the North American continent – and even to have a sabbatical in Hawaii!

Regent has not been our only involvement in Canadian Christianity. In recent years two further developments have taken place. Canon Harold Percy (unquestionably the best

Anglican evangelist in Canada) and I have taken conferences on evangelism together in major cities throughout Canada. We tried to help the pastors in the afternoon and the public in the evening. I have also done some work with Wycliffe College, the seminary which is an integral part of the University of Toronto and which was kind enough to award me an honorary Doctorate of Divinity. It so happens, however, that both Rosemary and I have done more with Tyndale Seminary and Bible College, also situated on the outskirts of Toronto.

Tyndale appeals to me for a number of reasons. Toronto is one of the most cosmopolitan cities in the world, and provides the most varied opportunity for pastoral training of the students. The faculty are also for the most part practising pastors, and this gives an extra edge and relevance to their teaching which is often absent from university and college theological teachers who have no pastoral responsibilities. Moreover, there is a splendid spirit about the place. In the 1980s it ran into massive debt, verging on 6 million dollars, and it has addressed this problem boldly and imaginatively under the vigorous new leadership of Dr Brian Stiller, Dr Geoff Greenman and their team. The Jeremiahs who predicted Tyndale's demise were forced to eat their words. The college is doing a splendid job now, and proposes to seek university status. In addition to its regular degree studies, the college runs frequent short and intensive courses, often taught by visitors, which give good service to the Christian community of Toronto. We need Christian centres like this, ready and willing to share their riches with Christians in their neighbourhood. I see much more of it in Canada than in England.

I could wax eloquent about the fishing, swimming, skiing and camping in Canada, but I will restrain myself! One topic to which I must draw attention, however, is the imaginative use of television by some Canadian Christians. Toronto's *100 Huntley Street* is the brainchild of David Mainse and has a long track record. It is a daily live programme, which is very demanding on the team who put it together. They do a good job, however, and have a bank of phone counsellors to answer the calls that result from their presentations. I have done many programmes for them, but far more for *The Terry Winter Show* in Vancouver. Terry was a great enthusiast who bought air time and put out a weekly programme which attracted a wide range of viewers all over Canada and into the States. There was nothing gimmicky about it. He would interview a guest for 20 minutes, then he would give a 10-minute talk at the end. He always offered a gift to those who wrote in, usually one of the books written by his guest. He had no premises other than his own house and office, and no banks of phone counsellors. Yet every letter was answered, normally by a trio of dedicated workers. I must have done more than a hundred programmes for him, and we enjoyed a personal chemistry which enabled us to do them entirely without notes and with great spontaneity. We frequently heard of people who came to faith through these programmes.

What a contrast that is to the UK scene, where nobody can buy time on the main channels, and where the received wisdom is that there is no place for straight Christian teaching in a television programme. Terry proved that philosophy to be totally wrong. I mention him in the past tense because he had a brain aneurism in early middle age and died immediately. His death was a great loss to the Christian cause in Canada, and nobody could be found who had the time and the talent to continue the programme. Sadly it has ceased, without replacement. Yet Terry showed what one man with a vision could do in this area of Christian communication. I saw little of his initiative, faith and resourcefulness in some of the mainline churches in Canada, which seemed content to continue in gentle or accelerated decline, doing the things they had always done, without great passion or imagination for outreach. The best churches in Western Canada were and are the informal churches brought into being by talented individuals or dedicated groups. These often grow to a big size, but they have shallow roots and are apt to fragment or disappear when the founders have passed on.

The West Indies

In 1997 and 1998 Rosemary and I were asked to lead missions in the Caribbean. The first was in Barbados. We thought we were going to conduct clergy and lay seminars at the invitation of the bishop, but when we arrived we found to our astonishment that we were expected to lead a diocese-wide mission throughout that lovely island of 160 square miles. The whole thing had been prepared for by means of a Lent course, although we knew nothing of it. We, of course, were entirely unprepared.

The Anglican Church came in with the colonists 350 years ago. The island seems to have been uninhabited then, but was soon populated by slaves brought from Africa to work on the sugar plantations. The plantation owner and the Rector were the two most important people in the 'parishes' into which the island was divided, and it is easy to see how the Church became very compromised. It was in fact the Established Church of the island until 1961, fully financed by the State, and is still regarded as the proper Church to belong to. There is much nominalism, and, although congregations remain large, there is a notable falling-off of men and young people. The Church is strongly Anglo-Catholic in its externals. Unfortunately, many of the practices are a century old and the first generation of black clergy, under the first Barbadian bishop, were cautious about any innovations. There were few services other than the Eucharist, and nothing midweek. Many of the clergy teach in schools to enhance their meagre salaries.

The bishop took the initiative in calling the diocese to mission: first personal renewal, then Church renewal, leading to national renewal. This was a perfectly reasonable goal, since the population is not much more than quarter of a million and

Anglican influence is very considerable. The strategy of the mission committee was also very sound. We did two days of seminars for clergy and leading laity respectively. We spoke in the theological college and in several secondary schools. We had a day's seminar with youth leaders, and did a host of other events including press, radio and television appearances. Rosemary preached at a massive celebration for the Bible Reading Fellowship: one twenty-fifth of its worldwide membership is to be found in this tiny island! We spoke at four extremely well-attended Deanery mission services. These were evangelistic, and over 200 people made a response to the gospel and signed up for nurture groups – to the great surprise of the clergy. The final service, some 5,000 strong and held in the largest building on the island, was a moving affair and almost everyone filled in a response slip indicating what they personally proposed to do in the light of the mission.

The sequel was critical. Hundreds undertook to do an eight-week nurture course rather like Alpha. The diocese was filled with such groups, but they were under very inexperienced leaders, many of whom had never led a group in their lives and had attended one sketchy briefing session from me in the airport just before we left. It was therefore precarious, but God's Spirit was clearly at work. Many of the laity were infused with enthusiasm and had some skill, and a whole series of new midweek cells sprang up all over the island. The Church as an institution is strong, and this provided a good support for the new life that was everywhere apparent. The clergy, on the whole, tended towards an entrenched clericalism which stifled lay initiative. We tackled this head on, however, and left with every reason to suppose that at least in some areas change had ensued. The bishop had every intention that it should. We returned home (after 49 events in 12 working days, plus two blessed days of rest in a seaside cottage) tired but exhilarated. This cross between a mission and a Springboard Travelling School was one of the most exciting ventures we had been on for some time.

The next year saw us in Jamaica at the invitation of the Bishop of Mandeville. We had a gifted younger evangelist and teacher working with us, the Rev. Mark Brown from Emmanuel Church, Northwood. It did not take us long to see that Britain had not done well by Jamaica. When slaves were freed 150 years ago they were given nothing, and poverty remains acute. Bauxite, bananas, sugar, rum and tourism are the only significant industries, but there is plenty of spare labour in this charming and exceedingly fertile island. It is crying out for serious investment, and I wrote to our government to that effect when I returned home. Even the sugar is refined in Britain, thus depriving the country of its legitimate profit.

The Anglican Church is large and maintains the traditional Anglo-Catholic liturgy and music with which it was founded. This is worlds away from the reggae culture which is so apparent throughout the rest of the island. We spent much time encouraging the congregations to relax and be less formal and less 'British' in their worship. It is a great shame that the flamboyant colour and flexibility that makes Jamaica so varied and exciting is largely missing in the Church, which is dominated by a nineteenth-century British Anglicanism.

The prevailing formalism and clericalism of the Church invites the twin results of drawing the keenest members together for an occasional 'renewal' conference, and of leading many people, particularly the young, to abandon the Anglican Church for the lively Pentecostals, whose worship is contemporary Jamaican rather than an old-fashioned English import. The Pentecostals are growing fast. They target Anglicans who believe the Bible but do not know it nearly well enough to combat the rebaptism teaching which keeps coming over the airwaves from Pentecostal radio and television stations in the US. There are apparently some 365 denominations among the 2.5 million Jamaicans, and practically all of them come from the US. Baptism in the Spirit and rebaptism in water were the two issues we found most prevalent, and I think we were able to give some help on such topics in each of the three contexts in which we operated.

The first was a clergy conference called by the Bishop of Mandeville. The worship was traditional and formal. We spoke to the clergy on burnout, family life, lay training, personal evangelism, pastoral counselling and the Alpha course. This seemed much appreciated, not least by the bishop. The shortage of clergy is acute. A passive laity has resulted in a situation where many parishes are vacant – and nobody at all was in training for the ministry at the time we visited.

The contrast with the second conference could not have been greater. It was on the subject of the Holy Spirit, and was directed towards renewal. The bishop had been carefully nurturing it for years, and now the conference was 600 strong. The programme looked a hodge-podge because it was responding to requests from the previous year, but the enthusiastic participants seemed to value serious teaching on sexuality, baptism, salvation, the Eucharist, renewal and the Holy Spirit. Rosemary did a superb session on Bible study and managed to get massive participation. There was much personal ministry each day – people came thirsty because they were receiving little nourishing teaching in their parishes. The final Eucharist had everything: ritual, strong teaching, the laying on of hands and informal prayer for the whole congregation, a prophetic message, some prayer in tongues, and a few 'slayings in the Spirit'. This conference would not have been everyone's cup of tea, but it may well help to renew the Church in Jamaica. Messages of appreciation poured in from all sides.

Our third assignment was a five-day mission in and from one of the flagship churches of the country, St Mark's, the parish church of Mandeville. They expected us to lead the American type of crusade, heavy on emotion and altar calls but light on teaching. We declined. Instead we used teaching evangelism, with some drama, testimony and questions each night. Each session culminated in a challenge for people to respond to Christ by kneeling at the altar rail and undertaking to join a 10-week Alpha course (the videos for which arrived on the last day possible). More than a hundred signed up for the course, but I fear we may not have been excitable enough for the appetite of some!

One evening during that mission we took part in an astonishing open-air meeting in one of the outpost villages – on the main road among four friendly rum bars. The PA system made a tremendous noise and people came from all sides. Nobody wanted to leave. The preaching and testimony, the singing and sheer joy, together with the palpable response, went on for ages. There was a tremendous pull about these hilarious and chaotic circumstances, as cars tried to force their way through, and 20 names were collected on the spot for the Alpha course.

Nevertheless, the whole concept of this mission was that of a 'knees-up' for the congregation, rather than a serious and carefully planned attempt to meet the people in the vibrant market adjoining the church, or even to use the houses of the congregation for evangelistic meetings. It was a mission to the Church rather than from it, but hopefully next time lessons will have been learnt and things will be different. We went away trusting that our visit had been a turning point. We were deeply impressed by the bishop and his wife, whose dedication, warmth and hospitality were of the highest order. We returned home with joy and gratitude, but were left with several points worth pondering. An inward-looking Church cannot evangelize. Clericalism stifles lay initiative. Formalism feeds Anglicans to the Pentecostals. A pastoral bishop, however, can transform an unpromising situation.

South America

I would like to conclude with some cameos from South America. I have been twice to this fascinating, colourful part of the world. On my first visit, in the 1980s, I was much

involved in the indigenous student work burgeoning in difficult countries like Colombia. It was moving to see how the
Christian students were proving to be the real counterculture in
lands rent apart with revolution. Bullet holes were pointed out
to me in one wall of a building where Christians met. Those students were heroes. Night after night you would hear shots in
the streets of Bogota and know that someone else had been
killed, as revolutionaries came down from the mountains to
capture a car and dispose of the occupant. The deep commitment of the Christians, witnessing at risk to their lives, made
an indelible impression. So did the magnificent leadership of
Jorge and Gail Atiencia, who headed up the student work.

Yet it was the contrasts which emerged on my visit to the
dioceses of the Southern Cone on behalf of Springboard in
1995 which gave me the sharpest insight into the rich diversity of the world Church. I went first to Uruguay, appropriately called 'a paradise without God', for it was founded in 1828
as a secular buffer state between Argentina and Brazil, based
on French rationalism. That scepticism has remained and
dominates public awareness: 25 December was known as
'Family Day' and Holy Week as 'Tourist Week'. Until 1988
there was just an Anglican chaplaincy in Montevideo, but in
that year it became a diocese – albeit with the most slender
resources. They only had three priests and a few deacons
when I was there, together with one or two magnificent lay
missionaries. They were, however, undertaking a most ambitious social programme – a night shelter, day-care centre,
housing work in the slums, and so forth. It was visionary, but
had outrun its resources. The small team was so overstretched
that they were having to employ non-Christians to staff these
enterprises, at a financial and, I fancy, spiritual cost which they
could ill afford. My brief was to teach on evangelism, and it
was a joy to see a number of people becoming excited about
what was to some quite a new idea.

Paraguay was a tremendous contrast. In a steaming,
land-locked country of 4 million people, 70 per cent of all

inhabitants lived in abject poverty, and nearly half the population was under 16 years of age. To the left of the Chaco River live the Chaco Indians. There has been a flourishing Anglican work among them for over a century, and there is extensive spiritual fruit among these lovely, gentle people, long trodden underfoot by the Paraguayans. The urban life to the right of the river is in striking contrast to the native properties on the left. The main Anglican centres are in the cities of Concepcion and the capital, Asuncion, and they have been blessed for a good many years with a superb missionary bishop, John Ellison, and his wife Julie. Their home was the soul of hospitality (seven Chaco managed to squash into one room of the small house for the conference, as well as me in another), and the work was clearly flourishing.

My task was primarily to conduct seminars for clergy and lay leaders in areas which were concerning them: the nature of conversion, the work of the Holy Spirit and the problem of rebaptism. I also had the joy of joining with some Argentine members of the conference for practical evangelism on the streets. We worked in both English and Spanish, in different areas of the capital, and we saw considerable response to the gospel. People came to Christ then and there in the street, amidst thick clouds of bugs as we preached in open-air meetings at night and, one day, in the courtyard of a general's house. It was also refreshing to share in cathedral worship where overhead projection of worship songs was used, robes were discarded, prayer was extempore in small groups and a lot of personal ministry took place at the end of the service. I suspect that, unless the Anglican Church worldwide moves radically into these informal directions, it will lose touch even more with contemporary culture and decline will accelerate. Before I left I was invited to speak at a church service in the mud courtyard of a rented house in a rough area, a church plant which had grown from nothing and was flourishing. Not many Anglican situations in England could have shown such enterprise.

Chile was outstanding. This most European country of South America was experiencing both an economic and a spiritual boom. Long and narrow, it extends from the extremes of the Atacama Desert in the north to the Antarctic in the south. The Anglican work was brilliantly led by the experienced Bishop Colin Bazley and his wife. They have presided over an extensive and fruitful work among the Mapuche Indians, a tough race who withstood conquest by Incas, Aztecs and Spaniards. In recent years, however, the work has been reaching deep into the capital city of Santiago. Through imaginative events like Marriage Encounter and Youth Encounter, hundreds of people have been converted and thriving missionary-minded congregations have been planted, not least among the hitherto untouched upper classes.

How do they spread? They preach New Testament Christianity, with none of the vacillations which trouble Western Christians. They expect the Holy Spirit to work with power. They believe in and practise every-member ministry. They work with other denominations in mission. They care little about buildings but much about people, and they start new congregations with nothing other than a rented building. They were not too bothered with liturgical niceties, still less with pomp and ceremony. You would rarely find the bishop in a purple shirt – but he enjoyed the respect of all the denominations in the city. It was hands-on, fearless, natural Christianity. Little wonder it was expanding all the time.

A word must be said about the overall Christian situation there. I found that the influence of the Roman Catholic Church, heavily infected by animism and corrupted by its partnership with the ruling oligarchies, was declining fast, as Chile's orientation moved away from Spain and Italy and towards the more Protestant North America. Although theoretically Catholic, the country now probably has as many Protestants worshipping on a Sunday as Catholics. Everywhere I noticed Pentecostal churches. These care for the poorest of the poor so effectively that Catholics have withdrawn from whole sectors of the inner cities, unable to compete. I sensed that their social concern was matched only by their spiritual fervour, although the biblical content in their preaching was often alarmingly thin and their tendency to split was distressing.

On Sundays the Pentecostals would march to a 'temple' in the middle of the city from roads all around, singing as they went and sweeping people up in the procession. They would stop and preach every few blocks. By the time they reached the main centre, many who had unwittingly joined the procession had tasted the appeal of this dynamic brand of Christianity, and were eagerly looked after by the Pentecostals. In this way the movement rapidly advances. The main Pentecostal group is Methodist in background, and has both bishops and the Anglican Book of Common Prayer among its treasures! I attended a Saturday night gathering of some 3,000, where the bishop gave instruction to his lay workers for their ministry the next morning in small churches all over the city.

My job in Chile was primarily to teach on evangelism, and the seminar we ran was transdenominational. Since so much evangelism in Latin America is thin in content and emotional (and often manipulative) in style, my emphasis on Bible teaching and integrity in evangelism seemed to be a useful corrective, and the talks were taped for widespread distribution – as they had been in Paraguay. I had substantial evangelistic opportunities myself among professionals, at a large youth meeting and a fascinating student meeting in a highly politicized university where Castro, Allende and Ché Guevara had held forth. I was excited to speak in the open air under enormous portraits of these influential icons. That sort of thing warms my blood! One other remarkable occasion was a lunch hosted by the British Ambassador, who had invited numerous senators, Cabinet ministers, ambassadors and academics. I was given the most marvellous opportunity to tell the good news of Jesus at that meal, and there was a warm response. As we left, the bishop and I felt that it might well open several doors among the leaders of the country.

My last engagement was in a house church of some 70 people which had sprung from a family of four, meeting in the open air in a residential square and courageously worshipping God each Sunday until they began to grow. It was a remarkable community, with an hour of breakfast and fellowship among all ages before the service. Somehow or other, they all crammed into a hired house, with the bedrooms serving as meeting rooms for the children, teenagers and adults. It was highly impressive. Of course the spiritual climate is very different in Chile, but there are invaluable lessons for us in England to learn. Often our churches appear stuffy, wedded to the past, tentative about the gospel, highly clericalized and fearful of naturalness, freedom and lay leadership. The whole experience was like a breath of fresh air.

I am convinced that the churches of the Two-Thirds World have far more to teach us than we have to teach them. The future of Anglicanism lies with them, for they now far outnumber Western members of the Anglican Communion. The 1998 Lambeth Conference was a watershed, for it was then that the bishops from Africa, Asia and Latin America realized that the baton of leadership had been passed to them, and they set out to share the riches of their sacrificial, full-blooded Christianity with us in the North who have lost – and alas denied – so much of the apostolic faith.

CHAPTER 15

Southeast Asia

As I reflect on the contents of the previous chapter, I realize how fortunate I have been to minister in so many different parts of the world. Conscious of the constraints of space, I have said a good deal less than I would have liked to, and have had to omit many fascinating experiences. I am clear, however, that I need to write a special chapter on the Church in the Anglican Province of Southeast Asia, partly because I have been there time and again in the last decade, and partly because I believe it has so much to teach the rest of us. These passionate Christians remind me of a firm of furniture removers who advertised themselves as 'two small men with big hearts'. Numerically fairly small, the Province has a very big heart, throbbing with desire to reach the 400 million people in the nine nations among which it is set.

The Province of Southeast Asia is one of the youngest in the Anglican Communion. It was only formally instituted in 1966, after many years when its constituent dioceses had remained under the oversight of the Archbishop of Canterbury. Four dioceses make up this Province: Singapore, Sabah, West Malaysia and Kuching. They differ in nationality, churchmanship and culture, but they have an underlying unity: they seek to embody the principles of the first Christians. Their

Archbishop, Datuk Yong Ping Chung, expressed it passionately in his Foreword to my book *Asian Tigers for Christ*:

> We see clearly the underlying conditions for such an
> explosive growth in the early Church. The disciples were
> united in spirit and truth. They submitted themselves to
> the authority of the Scripture of their day and the teach-
> ing of the apostles received from the Lord Jesus. They
> were deep in prayer, active in ministry, vibrant in
> worship, and bold in declaring that Jesus died and rose
> again as the Lord and God of their life. They took the
> Great Commission seriously. Every situation was used
> as an opportunity to lift Jesus high for the glory of God.

That is the model they seek to follow, and to a large degree
they succeed.

During recent years I have had a number of opportunities
to work closely with the leadership and members of these
churches. I have been struck by the qualities of the New
Testament Church which I see in them more clearly than anywhere else I have visited in the world. So impressed have I
been by them that I felt impelled to write a book, *Asian Tigers
for Christ*, to alert mainline Western Christians to what our
brothers and sisters in the East are accomplishing. The whole
Province is growing fast, whereas figures in Britain and
America indicate that the Anglican Church, along with most
other mainline churches, is in decline.

It would be easy to dismiss this fact with ready excuses.
How can you compare advance in a developing society with a
postmodern one like our own? How can you compare growth
in the Two-Thirds world with that in the First World? Yet such
excuses will not hold water, because the conditions in at least
part of that Province are uncannily similar to those in the West.
Consider Singapore. It is one of the most densely populated
urban societies in the world. It is multicultural and multifaith.
It is on the cutting edge of information technology for the

whole of the Far East. It is highly industrialized and a major seaport. With English as its main language, Singapore (broadly!) follows British parliamentary procedures, marriage laws and customs, and her young people are infatuated with Western pop music. Singapore has much in common with Britain.

Nonetheless, Singapore started independent life in 1965 with many disadvantages. The island was at that time a densely populated and squalid slum, with no obvious resources, little industry, chronic unemployment and widespread corruption. How Singapore turned all that around is a modern miracle. Blessed with two great advantages, a hardworking people and visionary leaders, the island has been largely rebuilt and its population rehoused. There is almost full employment, excellent education, a massive balance of payments, a first-class airline, and it is now one of the most important financial and communications centres in the world. It is for this reason that Singapore invites comparison with the West, and the Anglican Church there with the Anglicans in the West. It should have been much harder for the Church to grow in Singapore than in the West, where there is an Anglican church on every street corner, thousands of clergy and a million people at worship every Sunday. Yet the growth there totally eclipses anything in the West. It seems important to ask why.

Spiritual renewal

The broad answer lies in a major time of spiritual renewal. It is, of course, impossible to organize such times of God's visitation, and yet there seem to be conditions of blessing, which Singapore began to fulfil and which we in the West often omit. The new life can perhaps be traced back to the appointment of the first Malaysian-born Bishop, Chiu Ban It. From the outset of his episcopate he laid great emphasis on the Bible, and determined to make the Anglican Church biblically literate. He recognized the importance of youth in Singapore, half of whose population was under 21, and took immediate steps to reach them with the gospel. Already the winds of charismatic renewal were beginning to blow in Singapore, and Chiu Ban It was not too keen on them. Then he became profoundly filled and changed by the Holy Spirit while he was attending a conference in Bangkok in 1972. He received the gift of tongues and became very effective in the healing ministry. This transformed his life and began to have a significant effect on his diocese. To begin with, it was divisive, with the Chinese clergy in particular being very suspicious. He handled it all with great wisdom, welcoming the new and exciting work of the Spirit in their midst, but encouraging people to ask seven questions of any claim for a particular work of the Holy Spirit:

1 Is it consistent with Scripture?
2 Is it motivated by *agape* love?
3 Is it for the common good?
4 Is it accompanied by the fruit of the Spirit?
5 Does it guide into truth?
6 Does it glorify Jesus?
7 Does the spirit behind it, when tested, affirm that Jesus is the incarnate Son of God?

These shrewd criteria and their implementation helped to steer the charismatic renewal in Singapore along positive and constructive channels. Bishop Chiu had the wisdom to give equal weight to the inherited sacramental worship of the Church and the new praise services which packed the cathedral as the renewal took hold. He refused to tread the path of charismatic triumphalism, and safeguarded against the extravagant claims of the lunatic fringe by his strong emphasis on the supremacy of Holy Scripture. The result was steady advance. A great many people became Christians, and a lot of long-standing believers became increasingly aware of their heritage in Christ and more active in expecting and using the gifts of the Spirit.

Under his successor Bishop Moses Tay, the renewal enjoyed tremendous advance. He presided over the diocese from 1982 to 2000, and his clear-headedness, mental toughness, organizational ability and spiritual depth proved of inestimable value. When the four dioceses came together to form the new Province in 1996, Moses Tay was the obvious man to become Archbishop – a role which their constitution restricts to four years. He got the Province off to a marvellous start in a variety of ways.

One area which he took very seriously was the training of clergy, being concerned to see that his ordinands gained a deep experience of God rather than concentrating merely on book-learning. He also put in place an outstanding lay training course. There is little comparable anywhere else in the Anglican Communion. Church members were urged to attend it, and to gain the diploma it offered. Consequently, there is a high level of Christian understanding among the lay people of Singapore.

Moses has for many years had a great passion for evangelism. He pursued this enthusiastically by putting good men into leadership, by engaging in fearless evangelism himself, and by founding new churches in secular buildings and encouraging the growth of outward-looking Christian cells, which led many to Christ. As I described in Chapter 10, he had a great sense of destiny about this: God had set this little Province in a populous and underevangelized part of the world, and he determined to attempt great things for God. The senior clergy he appointed as Deans of Indonesia, Nepal, Thailand, and Laos and Cambodia are now learning the languages of those countries and making six-week visits every six months. That is all they are allowed on the visitors' permits available. Having founded small Christian communities, their return visits concentrate on strengthening the infant churches. The leaders from those countries are also invited to Singapore for training and, in due course, ordination. All this has happened in just a few years as a direct result of the evangelistic zeal and cool strategic head of Archbishop Tay. Moreover, the close links between Singapore and the other dioceses in the Province mean that the passion for mission is inflaming the whole area.

It is worth pointing out that the evangelism which is so prominent a feature of Christian life in this Province is not mere proclamation. It means deep involvement in the life of the community. I have been very impressed to see how these churches are struggling to meet some of the crying needs of the people around them. There has been a long-standing commitment to education in all four dioceses. Medical work is another important thrust, particularly of the Anglican Church in Singapore. They are branching out into centres for the mentally and emotionally disturbed, homes for the aged, counselling centres, and refuges for battered women.

These things can, of course, be paralleled in many parts of the West, but what struck me was the spirit in which this service is rendered. It is the outworking of deep commitment to Christ, and the Christians there are not in the least afraid of mentioning his name as the inspiration for their service. This stands in some contrast to the situation in the West. Our social work is generally offered without any explicit Christian flavour, almost as though we were embarrassed to mention the name of our Saviour. Some Argentine Anglicans came to Vancouver while I was working there. They spread their enthusiastic expression of the faith around wherever they went, and were duly impressed by some of the social work being done by the Anglican Church. Yet they felt impelled to ask, 'And when do you tell them about Jesus?' There was no answer to that question. In Southeast Asia the cup of cold water is regularly proffered, but the recipient is left in no doubt that it is offered by a joyful, loving disciple of Jesus Christ, and in his name.

Thus the gospel spreads in this fascinating part of the world. The Diocese of Kuching is by far the largest of the four, and is the fruit of 150 years of dedicated work by Anglo-Catholic missionaries and priests. West Malaysia faces perhaps the greatest difficulties. The government is passionately Muslim and very alert to any attempt to evangelize Malays, although Christian mission is allowed among the Chinese and Indian inhabitants. There are some marvellous, vibrant churches there. It has been a privilege to minister in a good many of them and to see the courage and commitment of the members. In the remainder of this chapter I would like to draw attention to five areas in which these Southeast Asian churches may well have lessons to teach us in the West if we are to have any hope of seeing comparable growth.

Strong leadership

First, I think, comes strong leadership. In most cases their leaders do not seem to be in place because of ecclesiastical politics but because of the evident calling and equipping of the Lord. They are men of prayer. They are willing to take risks. They make Scripture normative and turn their backs resolutely on any activity which is forbidden in Scripture. Thank God for bishops who give this firm lead in the West. The trouble is that others, notably among the revisionist bishops in America, do not apply the standards of Scripture to ethical and social issues, but are carried along by the climate of the day and motivated by political correctness. The Asian bishops have never heard of political correctness! They seek to apply the New Testament to their situation and act accordingly. This is wonderfully refreshing. I do not want to be unfair to our Western leaders: some of them are both wise and courageous. Yet on the whole I think the quality of leadership exercised by the Asian bishops compares very favourably with anything the West can offer. They are gracious but firm, and do credit to the gospel.

This attitude among the leaders is infectious and inspires most of the clergy. They seem to be in business not to maintain the current life of the Church so much as to strategize for growth. They seem to be inspired by possibility thinking.

Armed with far fewer resources than we have in the West, and involved in hostile urban settings, they expect God to act and are prepared to make great sacrifices to see their vision take shape. They have clear goals, and a wholehearted commitment to prayer, acts of kindness, penetration of the chosen area, celebration, witness, conversion and nurture.

One of my friends in Singapore is Canon James Wong. While serving as a curate at the cathedral, he trained a group of young people to engage in door-to-door evangelism. He also realized that the existing churches were not relating to the explosion of high-rise buildings in which the government was rehousing its citizens. He and his team visited two of these housing developments and found they would welcome the presence of the church, if it brought community and social service with it: youth drop-in centres, childcare and so forth. He started his first house church on the twenty-fourth floor of the Buona Vista estate, a second the year later, and a third the year after that. It took much prayer, hard work, visiting and socializing to reach these neighbours and draw them into the life of the church – but it happened. In due course these house churches outgrew their premises and became extension centres of his main church. Now they are turning into separate parishes. The Church of the Good Shepherd to which James Wong was appointed in 1972 gave birth to the Chapel of the Resurrection, and now they have 15 congregations, seven of which are extension centres meeting local needs. Are they satisfied with this advance? Not at all. They have just produced a superb and informative magazine, outlining their plans for advance in this new millennium. That is the fruit of good leadership.

There is a developing consensus among growing churches that leadership is the single most important factor in growth. When leaders are visionary, dynamic, positive and inspirational, growth generally follows. The Church of our Saviour in Singapore is a case in point. It was a church which had long since reached its plateau, until it received a new, visionary pastor in Derek Hong. Then it leaped into spectacular and sustained advance, and has recently shared its riches with an international Anglican congress which was wonderfully inspiring and educative. The principle is no less obvious in the entirely different situation in the interior of Sabah, where Archdeacon Fred David has been at work. He is a born leader and has spearheaded a remarkable work in the jungle, bringing whole villages into the faith. When I visited the area, I was amazed both by the numbers involved and by the spiritual insight and maturity they had acquired. It was learnt from their leader, Fred.

I do not want to be negative either about selection procedures in the West or about the leadership qualities of our candidates, but I cannot help regretting the way some dynamic leaders are rejected by selection panels because they are not 'priestly' enough or because they are 'just evangelists'. These people, properly trained, could provide the toughness and vision in leadership that we sorely need. By contrast, many people who have not an ounce of leadership in them are accepted for ordination training. I have been involved in training ordinands for many years, and I know we cannot make a silk purse out of a sow's ear! If the candidate has no gifts of leadership, there is little one can do about it. They are not going to make any new tracks: the best one can hope for is that they will exercise a tolerable maintenance ministry. That is not the way to win the country back to God.

Practical love

If leadership is one quality which I have seen strongly embodied in the clergy and bishops of Southeast Asia, another is a great deal of costly and practical love. It is worth explaining what they do in projects such as Love Singapore or Love Kuala Lumpur: although we cannot expect to copy their methods, their approach is very challenging.

The missionary zeal which fires this practical caring has

strong theological underpinning. They believe that 'the king-doms of this world are the kingdoms of our God and of his Christ', so they claim his kingly power and authority in their outreach: it is his country they are trying to win back. They also take very seriously the fact that God has called them to live in their particular locality, and he has charged them to serve that area and make disciples there. Believing that in a sense they share in the reign of Christ over their particular area, they make a territorial commitment to their community and seek to win that community for Jesus Christ.

They do this by demonstrating the love of God without any strings attached. They are seeking nothing less than the transformation of their society: they want the presence of Christ to be experienced in the social, political, economic and spiritual arenas. They are well aware that premature preaching will only alienate people. They believe, with good reason, that acts of love will progressively melt hearts which are frozen hard against the gospel. They have an acronym for it, SHOW, which stands for Softening Hearts and Opening Windows. Naturally this can only be possible when the whole Church in the area is committed to it, so the leaders make a focused attempt to disciple, train and equip every member for maturi-ty and to be a flavour of Christ in the area. They do not stand apart as an ordained elite. Their role is rather to act as coach to the members of the congregation and encourage their gifts to emerge.

The project is revolutionary in other ways, too, not only in the position of the clergy. They seek to reach out to their com-munity in an integrated way, with men, women and children offering their special gifts and talents. It means that relation-ships become eloquent as Christian families engage in out-reach together. It means a reassignment of the budget so that 'there is a growing expenditure on the lost rather than on the saved'. Imagine your church giving away half its income to lavish generosity on non-members in the neighbourhood! It means that prayer for the vicinity becomes a top priority, for without it there can never be effective advance. I also found among these Christians a rather new way of looking at vocation. Rather than allow their calling to determine the direction and limits of their ministry, they see the community needs as constituting their calling. The local church sets out to become a united social, racial and economic mix that tries to represent the kingdom of God in the midst of the huge variety of nationalities and individuals who live in that one area. These are the clearly thought-out convictions and priorities of these Asian churches.

How do they actually go about it? They would describe it in four words, Prayer, Profiling, Projects and Partnership. They know that nothing happens without prayer, so they make prayer the top priority among their clergy. Only then does it take root in the members of their congregations. They have discovered the power of prayer when it springs from united vision and action, such as they have in Love Singapore. There are corporate concerts of prayer for the whole city, and long periods of prayer and fasting in which most church members take part. Private prayer is also encouraged, as well as prayer triplets, cluster prayer (when a group of friends meet together to pray) and congregational prayer (when the whole congregation prays for the area during their Sunday service). They also have prayer-walking – intercessory prayer carried out on site in a particular area. Often a group will begin by acknowledging the Lord's sovereignty, moving naturally into repentance, and then claiming the power of the ascended Christ over all the principalities and powers that oppose him. As they go round they are careful to observe what is going on. They leave plenty of time for silence in which God may reveal something to them, and they return to pool insights, making a note of them for future reference. All in all, prayer is central. That is where their loving outreach for the city begins.

Profiling is their next step. It is simply a matter of getting to know as much about their area as they can. This enables them to pray more intelligently and to express practical love more appropriately. They tend to do it in a very systematic way. They make a point of delivering small gifts such as mandarin oranges at Chinese New Year. They conduct carefully planned questionnaires, in the languages of all the people who live there. They ask the residents about the perceived needs in the community. Then they react to the results of their survey in very practical ways: perhaps laying on a free class in English, maths or computing. The point is that they set out to discover the real needs of their community, and then do something about it.

V. insprecie

Profiling prepares the way for projects, which embody Christ's sacrificial caring for the community with which they are concerned. They tend to approach this in two ways – Kindness Projects and Penetration Programmes. Kindness Projects are designed to change people's impressions of the Church. Acts of kindness with no strings attached can go a long way towards altering the Church's image. Penetration Programmes, on the other hand, are carried out with the specific aim of opening people's hearts to the gospel. In Kindness Projects the contact is often momentary – it is task-oriented, a one-off event without follow-up, making use of the element of surprise. Penetration Programmes, however, are designed to build long-standing relationships. They connect repeatedly with the same people and make conscious efforts to follow up good contacts. In due course, two things begin to happen. The Christian visitors, by now well known, tend to get invited in when the residents want to open their hearts and seek advice on some problem. And the regular contact makes it easy to invite the residents to some event in the church's programme that may be appropriate for them.

One Kindness Project I came across was the offer of free Christmas gift-wrap at a shopping mall – by agreement, of course, with the management. This was an unexpected bonus to the shoppers and a way of building relationships with the mall owners. Another expedient was to offer a free taxi wash and vacuum. A few days beforehand, the Christians go to the cafés where the taxi drivers congregate and tell them what is on offer. When the cleaning day comes, they operate a 'coffee corner' for the drivers as they wait for their cars to be cleaned. Sometimes they give them a little card saying 'Showing you God's love in a practical way'. Another approach is to arrange for the removal of bulky items which people in the area no longer want. The better stuff they take to the Salvation Army and thrift shops; the rest they dispose of in the rubbish dumps. Now, naturally one cannot move from one culture to another without adaptation. It would be inappropriate for us in the West to try to take on the Asian Christians' precise methods – yet I fancy they have hit on something of universal importance for the growth of the Christian faith. They are embodying in a very tangible way the love and generosity that God pours upon human beings whether or not they respond. That has an impact all its own.

In terms of their Penetration Programmes, they use many methods familiar to us in the West, such as holiday camps, study programmes, schools work and children's church. We do not, however, know much about 'block parties'. They decide on a theme for the party and promote it to everyone on the block. The publicity is good and the event itself radiates warmth and fun, with good food and friendship – all without cost to the residents. The Christians make a careful note of all who come, entering names on their database, and write to them later to invite them to a further event. A variation on this is a kids' club, often followed by a weekly drop-in with games, study help, craftwork and so forth. A weekend sports event is a major draw, so is free school tuition in this land where academic success means everything. They are full of ideas on how to penetrate a community, but essentially it can be summarized in another of their favourite acronyms, ABC. *Ask* God to show you the needs and difficulties of the people you hope to reach. *Be* practical in responding to them: actions need to precede words. *Commit* yourself to action. Just do it!

Partnership is a key word in this part of the world, where Christians are invariably in a minority. They do not allow themselves the Western luxury of denominational rivalry. Co-operation is becoming much better in Britain nowadays, I am thankful to say, but their partnership in mission surpasses anything we currently do. It all springs from their vision to turn Singapore towards the living God. Yet a vision remains wishful thinking unless it is allied to a strategy, and that strategy is what they call 'geo-networks'. This is simply a fancy way of carving up the territory on the island (the easy part) and then getting all the churches in that area to work together (the difficult part). They have set their sights on nothing less, and it is happening. They know that churches like doing things in their own way, so they do not try to over-regulate them. They affirm the unique contribution of each church. They help each church see how its own agenda can be furthered by being part of the geo-network. They do not have many meetings, knowing how busy pastors are, but they ensure that every moment of a meeting counts. Thus they build up confidence and partnership. I believe that this is also increasingly possible in Britain these days, when many people are not much interested in denominations but are very interested in co-operation. We have a long way to go, but it can be done, especially if we are prepared to go out of our way and make sacrifices of time, money, prayer and deep commitment.

Cell churches

It would not be possible to carry out a fraction of that ministry of kindness without the small cells into which many of the Province's churches are divided. Actually, it would be more accurate to see the cell as the basic unit, and the 'church', as we know it, as an aggregate of the cells, meeting on Sunday for the purpose of celebration. For church members the cell is the basic unit, and the (lay) cell leader is the minister. Some of the Province's leaders are convinced that this may prove an important part of the future advance of the Church. This view is enhanced by the phenomenal growth experienced by a flagship church in Sabah, St Patrick's, Tawau. The vicar is Archdeacon Albert Vun, and he has seen the congregation grow from 500 a few years ago, when the church operated in the traditional mode, to over 3,000 since he moved the church over into the cell church model. He has some 340 cells, and the number is increasing all the time.

A cell church is a group of Christians in a tightly-knit fellowship. Every cell is seen as a church, set in its neighbourhood to impact it. Every cell leader is a pastor, who always has an assistant. The cell consists of a dozen or so people. When it exceeds 15, the cell splits into two, and the assistant leader assumes leadership of the second cell. From their very outset cells have the intention of expanding and multiplying, usually within six months. No cell member is in for a static life! These cells can be of various types: a group of soldiers or civil servants, children, young people or students, or the normal mix that you would find in any congregation.

There is nothing iconoclastic about this deployment into cells. It is not change for the sake of change. It is change in pursuit of vision – the vision of building a great network of flexible Christ-centred and Spirit-filled groups which seek God's way to meet human need. Indeed, in Singapore they have a wonderful vision of planting a cell in every street within the next two years, and they are well on the way to achieving this. Here is a vigorous new instrument of the gospel which needs to be taken seriously by Christians the world over. It has much in common with the 'base communities' which have proved so effective in outreach in South America, and it may well prove invaluable in Europe and North America, especially where traditional churches seem sometimes to be in terminal decline.

The ethos in a cell church is very simple, and every member understands it clearly. It can be summarized under three Ms: *ministry to God* through praise and worship; *ministry to each other* through Scripture, the exercise of spiritual gifts, practical help, counselling and prayer – all held together with enjoyable activities which increase bonding; and *ministry to those who are not yet Christians* through a godly lifestyle, inviting non-Christian friends, verbal witness to Christ, adopting and praying regularly for a missionary, and short-term evangelistic missions. It is not difficult to appreciate the value of such a way of 'doing church'. It equips and mobilizes the entire church, since everybody is a member of a cell. It enhances the whole concept of the pilgrim status of the church, since it is always in transition. It is highly flexible and does not require any property other than a home. It promotes accountability and minimizes the temptation to be dependent on a trained minister or church buildings.

There are other important advantages. The cell church is effective for fellowship: instead of dreary committee meetings, the members are released to meet and plan with the close colleagues in their cell. It is effective for pastoral care: nobody's needs are unnoticed, nobody slips through the ring of care. It is certainly effective for church growth: an evangelistic goal is set each year for the church at large and for every cell, and the policy of 'attract, grow, divide and multiply' is extraordinarily conducive to growth. What is more, they are finding that the cell is a wonderful context for spiritual ministry. They take very seriously the New Testament teaching about the variety of spiritual gifts which are meant to be exercised in any Christian assembly, but generally are not. In cells they are. Gifts of discernment, intercessory prayer (sometimes in tongues), prophetic utterance, healing and direction are invaluable in these small groups and may come through any member who is genuinely in touch with the Holy Spirit. Naturally, a very discerning leadership is needed if freedom is to be given for these spiritual gifts, but a lot of training is given in this area and it seems to work well.

The cell is also ideal for nurturing new Christians, and it is no less valuable for growing new leaders. The leaders notice those who have a burgeoning gift of leadership, and give them opportunities to develop it. In this way, a regular supply of assistant leaders is available, who become fully-fledged cell leaders once the cell splits. Finally, cell churches are very effective both at evangelism and at church-planting. Members bring their friends, who are amazed by the dynamic Christianity they encounter, and by the power of the Holy Spirit which is manifest in the cells. Before long they have been prayed for and challenged, and most of them start following Christ themselves. As for church-planting, there are many instances of a small cell, sometimes consisting of only two or three people, setting up in a city and founding a new church. I met a young man who had gone from Tawau to West Malaysia and had planted an Anglican church in Kuala Lumpur. He began with six people. Soon there were eight of them, then 15, then 30. After four years they were 50 strong, and had subdivided into four cells. Their PCC, or church governing body, is made up of people with an average age of 22.

There are some obvious dangers in the cell church model. There is a danger of sectarianism, unless a very close oversight is exercised over the cell leaders to ensure that they are moving in the agreed direction of the church as a whole. There is the danger of biblically immature and comparatively untrained leaders. Wise clergy give more attention to equipping these leaders than to anything else they do. Moreover, within an Anglican church there is the sacramental dimension, which brings its own set of problems: who is to baptize and celebrate Communion? Baptisms can be done publicly in the river, led by the vicar. The vicar can also celebrate the Eucharist at the great Sunday gathering which all the cell members attend.

Provided the bishop is supportive, therefore, there are no insuperable obstacles to cell churches taking off within the Anglican Communion. They have already replaced the normal congregational meeting in a good many Anglican churches in Britain, and are attracting increasing interest. Near where I live, the Oxford Diocesan Missioner, Canon Chris

Neal, is not only turning his own large congregation in Thame over to cells, with conspicuous success and numerical growth, but he has also been invited by the Bishop to teach the Oxford Diocesan Synod about this risky, refreshing and imaginative new way of 'doing church'.

Church-planting

All over Southeast Asia, church-planting is top of the agenda. This may be partly due to the pressures of other faiths which surround them, but it is primarily due to the missionary zeal which is such a notable feature of the church life in this Province. The methods are much the same in each of the dioceses. Start small in a home – often in a single cell. Develop, train and nurture lay leadership. Give them encouragement, practical resourcing and some seed money to get off the ground. Do not wait for a minister to be ordained or a church to be built, but commission a lay leader to found a new congregation in a home or hired building. That is the way they go about it. The remarkable thing is not the method but the passion and determination with which they prioritize this goal.

There is usually a definite cut-off period for major support, and this in fact strengthens the plant because it forces it to take responsibility. These outposts then become mission churches and in due time, if they succeed, new parishes. The church plant is lay led, and the minister comes round from time to time to conduct the sacraments. Unlike their Western cousins, in this Province they do not wait until they feel financially secure to begin. They tend not to put money into bricks and mortar, but into people. If they need a building larger than a house, they hire one. The House Churches have been doing this in Britain for 30 years, and more recently there has been a massive growth in Vineyard groups, based on the charismatic ministry of John Wimber. It can be done in the West, therefore, but do we have the passion, the commitment, the willingness to put our money and our manpower where our mouth is?

Canon Ng Moon Hing is the vicar of a large and thriving Anglican church in Ipoh, West Malaysia. I have several times had the privilege of ministering there. As I mentioned earlier, evangelism is difficult in West Malaysia because it is illegal to evangelize a Malay. It happens, of course, but converts go underground and are generally forced to leave the country. Moon Hing's church is largely Chinese, and he majors on training. To begin with, he had to train the PCC of his own church to take a share in the work of the gospel, and that was not easy after long years of leaving everything to the vicar. Then he set about training capable young Christians to spread the gospel and offer leadership. He trains them as lay assistants in his church before sending them off to seminary, and so they learn from him on the ground how to minister effectively in church growth. He takes them out on evangelistic missions, village work and practical social work, especially in education. They rent or borrow a house, and the local people are initially drawn by curiosity to the vibrant worship which goes on inside. He tells me of one such church which grew to 60 people in 18 months and is now hopeful of achieving parish status. He and his colleagues have planted no less than 38 Chinese-speaking churches in recent years. Seven of them have failed, but the net gain of 31 new congregations speaks for itself. These churches are entirely lay led. Moon Hing trains the leaders, and they teach and lead the church. He visits all of them each month to exercise oversight and celebrate Communion.

If this all seems too radical for the English traditionalists, let them learn from Bishop Moses Poniah, who describes himself as a very traditional Anglican. Assistant Bishop of West Malaysia, he is also Rector of St Christopher's, Johor Baru, a church which initially was not interested in outreach. He told me, 'About four years ago we started visiting in a town about 20 miles away, from which three people came to St Christopher's. Soon we planted a small group in the home of one of them. Then they said, "We must have a service." So we started a service in that house, and it began to grow. Within a year it grew into 30, 40, 50, and so we had to move to a larger house. St Christopher's Church made all sorts of opposition. They did not think it was necessary to plant a church because they were still doing building work at St Christopher's. But we kept on pushing, and the Lord has blessed us. Today we have bought a double shop lot for the church plant, and St Christopher's has given half the price of it.'

The missionary heart of this gentle bishop has motivated the parent church, St Christopher's. They are now prepared to take on the lion's share of the financial needs of the church plant. What is more, instead of one cell round the bishop, they now have eleven. Moses Poniah is very interesting about all this. He stresses that the minister must give the lead – must have a personal burden for mission, must teach the congregation regularly about it, and must see that the whole enterprise from first to last is soaked in prayer. 'We need to wait on the Lord to show us where to plant,' he says. He also began to train a small group of people for lay leadership – going through various relevant passages of Scripture with them, and helping them prepare to speak on certain passages. This seems to me to be admirable training, and really should not be beyond the capability of any competent parish priest in Britain, provided the motivation is there. It is encouraging that in 1994 the House of Bishops in England published a report on church-planting, called *Breaking New Ground*. Our record of actually planting new churches is less impressive, however. We need more of that restless Asian passion, commitment and imagination if we are to plant congregations in the many parts of Britain that are devoid of churches. Church-planting is not only a gospel necessity, it is a sign of life.

Spiritual gifts

I do not think I have ever ministered anywhere that takes as urgently as this Province the need for the power and gifts of the Holy Spirit if Christian ministry is to be effective. They live with a profound awareness of the Holy Spirit of God, and they seek to draw him into everything they do. They consciously seek to keep in step with the Spirit. Let me introduce a few of the leaders who walk in the Spirit's power.

The Very Rev. John Tay, Dean of St Andrew's Cathedral, Singapore, writes, 'A significant event in 1976 was my baptism in the Holy Spirit, which brought the gift of spiritual discernment and other spiritual gifts into my life. The baptism did not come easily to me because I had a long struggle with intellectual blocks.' That is not what one normally hears from a cathedral dean! Nor are most deans active in church-planting, as he is. In recent years he has planted churches in seven of the provinces of the Philippines and also in North Thailand, where new churches are accompanied by community care projects. That is the practical outcome of his moving into deeper water with God's Holy Spirit.

Another friend in these parts is the Rev. Madavan Nambiar, who grew up in Penang in a Hindu family. Addicted to heroin, he was unable to hang on to any job. First he was hospitalized, then he was locked up in a mental hospital for treatment. After coming out, he resumed his habit. His father took him to see an Indian priest-medium, hoping that through the intervention of the goddess Kali he would be able to change. He had to drink the blood of a chicken and a pigeon, mixed with ashes, and was assured that Kali had removed the desire for drugs. No such luck! He returned to his addiction, sleeping rough on the streets. In due course he was noticed and cared for by a Christian pastor who took him, filthy as he was, back to his home and spent the whole night in prayer for him. When Madavan woke up in the morning, he entrusted his life to Christ and found that the craving for heroin had gone. That man is now in the ordained ministry.

Canon Soh Chye Ann is a very interesting man. Born into a family which practised traditional Chinese religion, he became dissatisfied with it and in due course became a

Christian, thereby drawing down on himself a great deal of odium from the rest of the family. They felt he had betrayed them and angered the ancestors. Things did not get any easier as he set out on the path towards ordination. Shortly afterwards, his sister fell ill. Repeated visits to the hospitals and temples achieved nothing: she was dying. The family did the sensible thing and said to Chye Ann, 'Can your church help us?' Intense prayer was offered by the Christians and a miraculous, complete and instantaneous healing took place, while the whole family was gathered round her bed. They all became Christians. Chye Ann is currently working with the Church Mission Society in Britain.

A notable example of the power of the Holy Spirit took place in the life of Bishop John Savarimuthu, the Indian Bishop of West Malaysia. It would be fair to say that in the early part of his episcopate he was rather opinionated and difficult to get on with. I only got to know him after all this had begun to change. His heart consultant told him he needed a triple bypass. He said he was too busy. The operation was eventually rearranged, by which time his condition was very acute. The night before the operation was to take place, Bishop John placed his whole situation before God in prayer, felt a lot of heat in his chest, and fell asleep. When he woke up he was completely healed, and this was confirmed by his consultant. No operation was necessary. In his few remaining years he had a simply amazing ministry of healing. God used him in an extraordinary way. One of the most remarkable occasions was when he personally petitioned the Muslim Prime Minister of Malaysia to allow him to conduct a Christian healing mission in the stadium at the heart of Kuala Lumpur. Can you imagine this in such an aggressively Muslim state? He told me that thousands attended and the results were phenomenal.

When he prayed for people, they normally fell to the ground. I recall him coming to a church where I worshipped in Chilwell, just outside Nottingham. Some 70 people gathered one weeknight to hear the bishop tell what God had done in his life, and then he offered to pray for people. Most came forward and all but a couple fell to the carpet, myself included, as he prayed for them. Many of them testified afterwards to some area of healing in their lives as a result, and others to a fresh awareness of God's love for them personally.

This falling to the ground seems very strange to us in the West. I remember how amazed I was when I began ministering in Southeast Asia and found people sinking to the ground, semiconscious, as I prayed for them. This did not happen as a result of any particular action or technique on my part. Nobody touched them or suggested they should lie on the floor. I think that the spiritual atmosphere was so warm that God was able to act in this way. It would be a great mistake to suppose that this sort of thing is just an extravagance of the so-called 'Toronto blessing'. It happens in many parts of the world, including Britain, and not only among Evangelicals and charismatics. I have seen it in Roman Catholic circles too. It seems to be a way in which God encourages his children to relax in his love and rest in his faithfulness. I have rarely seen anyone unaffected by the experience when they got up. Some found their mouths filled with laughter, some shed tears of repentance and renewal, some experienced healing, and some were simply refreshed with a new touch of the love of God. I shall never forget the robust common sense of Archbishop David Hope of York on the topic: 'I don't mind people falling down, but I want to know if they are any good when they get up!' These people are.

A challenge to the West

Such is the quality of spiritual life in much of the Province of Southeast Asia. Of course there are terrible failures, but this is the prevailing wind, irrespective of churchmanship, nationality, background and culture. It faces us in the West with a serious challenge. Why is our Christianity so much less aware of the presence of God, so much less dynamic than theirs?

Why do we not expect to grow, as they do? The multifaith, pluralist, postmodern urban culture is reasonably similar in both areas. Why are things so different with us? Why is it that in these spheres of leadership, spiritual gifts, church-planting and cell churches we are so far behind them? To be sure, there is a God-given revival in that part of the world, and nobody can organize that, but I think there are clear reasons why our Christianity is subnormal. We are incapacitated by our materialism. We do not bring God into the affairs of daily life. We do not expect him to intervene. We are deeply trapped in the secularist presuppositions of our society. The Christian mind has almost disappeared. We do not make serious efforts to think and act biblically about the pressing issues of the day. We are drowning in a sea of materialism, relativism, pluralism and scepticism. It is hardly surprising that we do not see the Lord so powerfully at work in our midst.

It seems to me that we have a simple choice. Either we continue as we are, with our bland, inoffensive but fairly powerless Christianity, while the churchgoing statistics plummet and the Christian influence in the West diminishes – or else we start to change our attitudes and learn from these courageous Christian brothers and sisters in Southeast Asia, Africa and other parts of the Two-Thirds World. They have not got it all right, but they have got a lot more of it right than we have.

Surely they are right, even if politically incorrect, to take an unequivocal stand on the uniqueness of Jesus and the incompatibility of Christian discipleship with any form of idolatry. They are right to lay emphasis on the need for personal conversion and a genuine acceptance of the Bible as the supreme norm for faith and practice. They are right to make repentance an important part of their lives, rather than glossing over their sins or hiding them away. They are right to open themselves up to the powerful work of the Holy Spirit and to expect him to be active in and through their lives. They are right to expect not only the graces but the gifts of the Holy Spirit to figure regularly in church members and their worship. They are right to have a passionate burden to evangelize the countries around them, and not to desist because the inhabitants are Muslims, Hindus or Buddhists. They are right to expect their leaders to lead courageously. They are right to engage in outstanding acts of love for their neighbours. They are right to pray through the night and to give until it hurts for the growth of the gospel.

I have come away time and again from Southeast Asia with the conviction that they know and practise an authentic Christianity of which ours in the West is only a pale imitation. I long to see their passion translated into our culture. That is why I have written a whole chapter about the impact they have made on my life, and on the lives of the thousands they have won to the faith in recent years.

CHAPTER 16

Tomorrow

It would be a brave man who would dare to make many predictions about the future when the past 50 years have seen such amazing and undreamed-of developments in almost all areas of human existence. Nonetheless, I would like to end this book with a few reflections on three particular dimensions of the future: the 'tomorrow' of the world, the Church, and our own lives.

The tomorrow of our world

As I write, the media are alive with reports of a mentally unstable man who forced his way into the cockpit of a British Airways Boeing on the way to Kenya and wrested the controls from the pilot. Before he was overwhelmed and tied up, he sent the plane into a massive dive. The whole plane shuddered and was near to disaster. That might seem to be an apt parallel for the condition of today's world.

Some years ago, the academic and diplomat Ronald Higgins wrote an important book. Although by no means a member of the 'doomwatch' brigade, he showed from personal experience in the Diplomatic Service how frail and bumbling are the human safeguards against disaster. Then he went on to outline the reasons for believing that 'mankind is blundering towards multiple calamity'. He predicted a world of rapidly rising confusion and horror, with the starvation of hundreds of millions, the growth of local war and disorder, and the impossibility of maintaining the current injustice of the world's massive economic disparity. All over Africa democracy has collapsed, as it has in Pakistan, and the attempts to introduce it in China were smashed to pieces at Tiananmen Square. In the wake of the protracted and pathetic struggle between Al Gore and George Bush for the American presidency and the chaos in Florida upon which it all hung, we may well witness major changes in the vaunted but flawed democracy of the world's remaining superpower. It would be salutary to review the seven reasons which led to Higgins's pessimistic analysis of the future. They are even more impressive now than when he wrote *The Seventh Enemy* 30 years ago.

The first is the massive population explosion. At the time of Christ the world population was perhaps 300 million; by 1750 it was about 800 million; today it is approximately 6 billion. It took some 1,200 years from the time of Christ to double the world's population. After 1650 it took about 200 years. Now it takes about 30 years. A continuation of this growth rate would be horrifying, and China, the most populous country in the world, has taken the draconian step of allowing only one child per family as a result – an injunction which appears to be failing. What is more, nearly three-quarters of our present births occur in the poor South amidst scenes of increasing deprivation. Birth control is not an answer. When a substantial proportion of children born in the South die early, a large family is the only form of support and insurance available.

The second great threat is the food crisis. I have travelled widely in both First and Third World countries. The problem in the North is obesity. The problem in the South is starvation. America uses more fertilizer on its golf courses than India can afford to fill the hungry stomachs of its people. Britain's 10 million cats and dogs eat enough protein to satisfy half a million humans. We in the West have reduced our food production in the name of 'sound economics', while thousands starve every day in the Horn of Africa and the slums of Bolivia. We have our mountains of unsold butter, grain and meat, while famished Southerners strip trees of their leaves for sustenance. As Gandhi once said, 'The earth has enough for every man's need but not for every man's greed.' In addition, much of the planet's richest ground is being lost every year – in the North to tarmac, industry and towns; in the South to soil erosion, floods and salination. Back in 1974 a UN report showed that, of 97 developing nations, 61 had a deficit of food energy supplies, and in Asia and Africa 30 per cent of the population suffered significantly from undernutrition. The situation is far worse today. Moreover, a factor which was only dimly foreseen by Higgins in the 1970s is everywhere apparent today: the greenhouse effect that is playing havoc with the world's climate and is entirely the product of human industrial mismanagement.

The third great threat is the overconsumption of scarce resources. It stands to reason that you can only cut a limited number of slices from a finite cake. We have been taking enormous slices, in the greedy pursuit of growth and development, to the detriment of succeeding generations. We have been ravaging the earth with greed and wastefulness. Fossil fuels and minerals are irreplaceable, yet we pursue them with no thought for tomorrow. The authors of the first Club of Rome report, *The Limits to Growth*, assumed, perhaps optimistically, that five times our present known reserves of minerals would eventually be found – but reckoned that most of these reserves would be exhausted within a century, and several would be gone in half that time. Even more serious is the growing scarcity of fresh water. About 95 per cent of the world's water is saline. Of the remainder, some three-quarters is frozen in glaciers and icecaps. Only about an eighth of the rain falls over land, and most of this is inhospitable terrain where the water cannot be used or collected. When you consider that the production of a pound of wheat requires some 60 gallons of water, a pound of meat 2,500 gallons, and the production of a car 100,000 gallons, it is plain that a massive problem faces us as the dry parts of the world become drier. Water shortage may be the cause of the next war. A UN conference on water in 1977 took as its motto, 'A generation later may be too late.'

Fourth, there is the degradation of our environment. The whole biosphere is infected by our waste. Our poisons have penetrated everywhere: DDT has been found in polar bears at the North Pole and in penguins at the South. Our atmosphere is increasingly polluted by hydrocarbons, carbon monoxide, sulphur dioxide and other harmful pollutants. The ozone layer, our protection against solar radiation, has great holes in it, caused by aerosols, fridges and the effluents of cars and planes. It has been argued that half of it will disappear in the next 50 years, with incalculable results for the world. And who can tell the long-term effects of the disastrous nuclear emissions from Chernobyl? We are abusing the land, too. There is a massive increase of erosion, as topsoil is washed away as a result of widespread deforestation. North Africa, once the breadbasket of the Roman Empire, is now dominated by the irreversible deserts of the Sahara. The American Dust Bowl is another example. Our abuse of the seas and rivers is also shameful. Massive quantities of sewage and rubbish are constantly discharged into them. The River Tiber has a hundred times the safe level of pollution. Oil is a major pollutant of the seas. Hundreds of miles of dragnets litter the oceans, clogged with decomposing fish. Cod have almost been eradicated from the Grand Banks, once the best fishing ground in the world.

Attempts to rectify situations such as these usually run into intransigence from one or more countries. Russia, Norway and Japan, for example, have defied attempts to save the whale. Meanwhile, all the factors contributing to ecological pressure are still multiplying – population, urbanization, industrial growth, high-pressure agriculture, hunger for resources and the spread of harmful technologies. Things will get worse.

The fifth threat to the world is nuclear abuse. When the first atomic bomb was tested in the deserts of New Mexico in 1945, a genie was let out of the bottle which could never be replaced. Over 50 years later, familiarity has bred a dangerous indifference. If the prospect of nuclear war between superpowers has receded with the collapse of the Soviet Union, plenty of other problems remain: the proliferation of nuclear powers, radioactivity in the atmosphere, human mistakes like Chernobyl, the disposal of nuclear waste, nuclear terrorism, the existence and indestructibility of nuclear weapons sufficient to blast the world into desolation many times over. That is a whole nest of problems! The clock cannot be turned back. We shall have to live with these problems – or die because of them.

Higgins defined the sixth threat as the uncontrolled spread of science and technology, giving a quotation which struck me as widely descriptive of technological advance. In early 1945, while working towards the first atomic test, the physicist Enrico Fermi frequently told questioners, 'Don't bother me with your scruples. After all, the thing's superb physics.' What a contrast to Leonardo da Vinci, who wrote that he had suppressed his invention of the submarine 'on account of the evil nature of men'. They would employ it, he saw, 'to practise assassinations at the bottom of the seas'. Higgins drew attention to the development of chemical and biological weapons, the invention of new weapons such as high-energy laser beams and genetic engineering. What would he have said, had he known of Star Wars or thermobaric bombs? How would he have regarded our ability to create a foetus without any sexual congress, to clone human beings, and to design children to order by tinkering with their genes? How would he have regarded the starvation of persistent vegetative cases or the destruction of one twin in order to attempt to preserve the other? What would he have made of fertilizing eggs to make human spare parts? Brilliant science is involved in all these ventures, but the moral questions are sidestepped or laughed out of court.

These are six of the threats which Higgins unveiled with careful documentation in the 1970s. Since then several other massive threats have emerged. One is the emergence of 'mad cow disease' and its human counterpart, the direct result of our greed and perversity in feeding animal waste to herbivores. Another is the advent of AIDS, the most serious threat to world health since the Black Death. A third is the moral collapse in almost all the developed nations and their disregard for God, in contrast to the strong Muslim or Christian faith to be found in most of the rest of the world. The contrast between the godless materialism of London and the God-centred observance of Islamabad, which I recently visited, is striking. No less significant is the growth of postmodernism, denying any objective stance for truth or morality. The dangers inherent in such a world view cannot be exaggerated. Nor is it only Christians who see them. The Chief Rabbi, Dr Jonathan Sacks, has drawn attention to them in his Reith Lectures for 1990 and in his book *Faith in the Future*. He maintains that the future of civilization may well depend on the survival of three things: faith, family and community – and of these faith is the most fundamental.

Yet Higgins spent nearly half his book on the seventh threat, which has two roots. One is political inertia: few politicians look beyond the next election, and policies which are popular invariably eclipse those which are necessary. The other is individual blindness: the average man or woman does not like to be bothered with unpleasant thoughts which might give check to the pursuit of pleasure and a comfortable standard of living. As Barbara Ward put it in *Only One Earth*, the rich nations suffer a kind of tunnel vision: 'Like the elephants round a water hole, they not only do not notice the other thirsty animals. It hardly crosses their minds that they may be trampling the place to ruin.' Higgins concludes that 'we are becoming steadily immunized against moral perceptions'.

Who can argue with that? 'We persist in believing that we are kind and harmless, good people at heart. Despite the world's evident atrocities, greed, lies, neglect and cruelties most of us cannot accept that we are in any fundamental way party to them. Our blindness lies in our imagination that the evils always dwell in the others.' I do not know if Ronald Higgins is a Christian, but it is a very Christian understanding of human nature that he presents.

What, then, is the Christian hope for tomorrow? Is there any future for *homo sapiens*? Christianity claims humbly yet confidently that there is. We do not agree with discouraged liberals like H.G. Wells that 'there is no way out or round or through'. There is hope for the world, hovering though it may well be on the brink of destruction. What is it?

There are two ways of reading an Agatha Christie crime novel. One is to read straight through it. The other is to read the penultimate chapter first, where the perpetrator is unmasked, and then to turn back and read the whole story in the light of this knowledge, picking up the clues you would otherwise have missed, confident of the conclusion. The book of human history is rather like that. The New Testament, however, does not encourage us to begin with either the beginning or the end, but with the secret. That secret is what God has done through Jesus Christ crucified, risen and exalted. In the light of that crucial event in the middle of history, we can turn back to the beginning. It was through him that the world came into being: the universe is not to be seen as the product of blind chance, but as the creation of a personal God who made human beings in his own image and, when they had gone wrong, came in person to find and rescue them.

As those first Christians looked at the cross and resurrection of Jesus, and saw him bearing the consequences of human wickedness and then rising to a new and endless life, they saw the clue to the whole mystery. Truth, final truth, is personal. Truth loves. Truth suffers. Truth goes to the scaffold. But truth does not stay on the scaffold. It emerges from the tomb, triumphant. The whole philosophy of Christian optimism about the future, despite the evil and suffering in the world, is built upon the historical cross and resurrection. That is the sure foundation for the world's tomorrow. The crucified and risen Jesus at the centre point of history gives meaning to the start of the story and assurance about the end. The future is controlled by the one 'who holds the keys of death and Hades', or, as Revelation puts it, 'The Lamb once slain sits in the midst of the throne of God.' In the cross and resurrection we have a demonstration that 'the Lord God omnipotent is reigning'. It is the trailer of the main film of God's future for this world, a future to be worked out in history and transcending history.

The overwhelming way in which the New Testament gives expression to this confidence about the culmination of all history is in the extensive teaching it gives about the return of Jesus Christ at the end of time. This has evoked much incredulity. After all, it has not happened for 2,000 years, and it is precarious to assume it will. Date-fixers and cranks have brought discredit on the whole idea. Jesus himself spoke extensively on the subject, however, and it cannot be omitted from his teaching. For example, in Matthew 24:36–42 he makes five main points: Jesus will return in person (v. 37); nobody knows when (v. 36); it will be totally unexpected (v. 39f.); it will be final (v. 40); it will be decisive for human destiny (v. 40).

What are we to make of such teaching? All ideologies and faiths have convictions about the future. Communists used to look forward to the fulfilment state: but only one generation would enjoy it after the struggles and bloodshed of all the preceding ones. Some materialists expect the contraction of the globe, others its expansion: either of which will wipe out all life. Hinduism looks forward to constant recycling of lives until all personality is eliminated. Humanists look for a man-made society where all are kind to one another: but such hope is wrecked by human wickedness. You cannot really live without some goal, however poor – and these are poor. How does the Christian expectation of the future stand up? Does it make sense?

I believe the Christian hope makes sense of our innate hunger for justice: the day is coming when all evil will be rectified and all injustice put right.

I believe it makes sense of human freedom: we are at liberty to use our God-given freedom as we wish, but we will be held accountable for what we have done.

I believe it makes sense of human nature: at the end we will not be assessed by one who is alien to us, but by the embodiment of human nature as it was meant to be. Human nature, in the Christian view, is not destined to be scrapped. God has set the highest value on it – so much so that he came to share it. The Ideal has lived and loved as one of us. By that man we can be saved, and by him we will be judged. We are neither judged nor saved by someone who does not understand us, but by someone who has stood in our shoes. He will be there at the end of all things. That is another way of saying that self-sacrificial love is the most enduring entity in the universe.

I believe it makes sense of our quest for purpose. Many today wonder if life is going anywhere. Most Greeks saw time as a circle imprisoning the soul until death releases it into the undifferentiated Beyond. History is therefore meaningless, this world unimportant, the body insignificant. To the Hebrew and Christian mind, however, time is not a circle from which you escape at death, but a line: a line of past, present and future, the line of God's redemption. The world is moving on, not to chaos but to Christ and his return, to the final manifestation of him whose first coming for ever settled the world's destiny. That is what the doctrine of the second advent means. At the end of the road (and the road has an end – it is not a ring road), God steps in. The God who has already been along this road, and is even now in charge of its traffic, will one day rip aside the veil which hides him from our sight and show himself to be what by faith the Christian knows him to be – ever present. That is the Christian hope. It is anchored in the historic life and death of Jesus Christ. It is grounded in the fact of the resurrection, the ultimate assurance that God's will shall prevail on earth as it does in heaven. It is not demonstrable, this Christian hope, but it makes sense.

The tomorrow of God's Church

Theoretically the Christian Church embraces some 34 per cent of humankind. It stretches into every corner of the world. It is the largest religion the world has ever known. Its future should therefore be secure. It is very apparent to anyone living in the West, however, that this is far too rosy a view of the situation. Countless hordes of the baptized show no sign of Christian discipleship whatsoever. Western countries on the whole have given up the Christian faith that has been a major factor in making them what they are. The media pour scorn on Christianity. It is marginalized in this post-Christian society. Almost any view is acceptable today except full-blooded New Testament Christianity. Can it survive?

When we look beyond the West towards the Two-Thirds World, a very different picture emerges. It is a picture of financial poverty and spiritual faithfulness. It is a picture of Christian growth: never in all human history has expansion been so fast. Apparently some 90,000 people a day are becoming Christians, mostly in Africa, Asia and Latin America. Some 20,000 a day become believers in Communist China. There are now more non-white than white Christians in the world, and the whole dynamism of Christianity has passed from Europe to Africa and Asia. Who knows what the future may bring?

Several things can be said with assurance. The 'death of God' confidently expected in the 1960s has not come about. The social commentator Paul Johnson observed, 'The most extraordinary thing about the twentieth century was the failure of God to die. God survived, and flourished even.'

Even in post-Christian Britain, far more people go to church on Sunday than attend football matches on Saturdays. Moreover, the future of organized religion is not only important to those involved. Surveys have shown that regular churchgoers are three times more likely to be involved in some form of voluntary work than those who do not worship. The Charities Aid Foundation has discovered that those who consider religion very important are 10 per cent more likely to give to charitable causes than those who do not consider it important at all. The health of organized religion is therefore important for the good of society, not simply for the Church.

There is, nonetheless, a very clear and sustained trend against organized religion. In 1900 there were 9 million regular church members in the country. In 2000 there were 6 million. A Mori poll of those who were aged 18 in the year 2000 found that in answer to the question 'Do you have any religious beliefs?' a staggering 77 per cent said 'No'. This may be due partly to the collapse of Sunday schools and youth groups in many parts of the country, partly to the lack of Christian homes, partly to the smattering of comparative religions taught in school without commitment to any, and partly to the boring unattractiveness of many churches, resulting in a youth culture that feels the Church has nothing for them. It is, however, mostly due to the fact that Christianity is no longer a part of the plausibility structure of our society. You are odd if you go to church. Christians today are attempting to reach the third generation of the unchurched, and it is harder than starting from scratch.

The remarkable thing, as another poll has revealed, is that no less than 76 per cent of people claim to have had an experience of God at some time in their lives. Traditional churches seem to be unable to capitalize on this, and exercise less and less appeal. In this consumerist society people are looking for something tailor-made to their own requirements, in spirituality as in all else. In most churches, however, everyone is expected to conform to church custom – standing to sing and recite the Creed, sitting to listen to a monologue, kneeling while someone reads or says prayers. People are allergic to being treated in this standardized way: the expression of the gospel must connect with their condition. Thus I find people increasingly impatient of denominational loyalties. They will go where there is life. They are not prepared to listen to someone who is six feet above contradiction. There has to be opportunity for them to make discoveries for themselves. They want time for reflection, not to be caught up in a torrent of words. They want a church where there is proper care for the whole family, particularly the children, in a way appropriate for their age and ability. They want to be able to comment and ask questions. They want to find an expression of true fellowship. Privatized religious experience does not offer the friendship we hunger for. It does not enable us to share in the values and experience of others, which reduce the uncertainty of the human condition and promote the sense of being uplifted and taken out of yourself in worship.

It is noticeable that the mainline churches have on the whole failed to engage with the radically changing nature of society. Energy has been dissipated over internal issues like the ordination of women and the pros and cons of homosexual unions. Vast amounts of time and money have been squandered on maintaining buildings scarcely ever used during the week. Paid clergy have continued to be appointed to serve buildings that are nearly empty, rather than to minister among networks of people outside the church, or as facilitators to lay leadership teams. The effort to maintain widely scattered congregations has militated against co-operation with other clergy in planting new congregations where they are needed. Not many clergy seem to have the imagination and skills needed to guide people in their own exploration of faith. The result of all this is that the main Christian denominations have continued to shrink. Yet the 'new churches', with their greater flexibility, hired premises, lay leadership, interactive worship, modern songs, relevant preaching and relatedness to people's needs, have grown enormously. From some 50,000 in 1980, they now draw 200,000 or more people a week in the UK.

A good deal of research has been done on characteristics of growing churches throughout the world. Here are 10.

1 A passionate, energizing, scriptural faith: members who have opened their lives to the Spirit of God and whose commitment springs both from the head and the heart.

2 A loving community which is genuinely open to the needs of the community, and active in trying to meet some of them.

3 A prayerful community, corporately and individually, aware that nothing is achieved for God without prayer.

4 A positive attitude to change, and a hunger to grow even if it means taking risks and trying out new directions.

5 A clear sense of direction: the church leadership and members have clear short-term and long-term goals, which are understood and embraced by all.

6 An enabling rather than an authoritative and hierarchical leadership.

7 A participating laity, keen to share in worship, acts of generosity and witness.

8 An outward-looking focus: a church that is not obsessed with its internal problems but is attractively and imaginatively seeking to do good to other people in very practical ways, and continually trying to win them to Christ.

9 A church which is undeniably a sign of the kingdom: a small manifestation of the way God meant people to be, act and relate.

10 A church marked by the sacrificial obedience of its members.

As these characteristics take root, there is every prospect of a thorough renewal of Christianity in Britain. There will be a dropping of denominational barriers. New congregations will be formed among people who have never been to church, in homes or rented buildings. There might be, in many an ordinary town, a Saturday-morning congregation in Tesco's for the children of parents who are shopping; a Sunday-night gathering for teenagers; an early breakfast meeting on Wednesday for businesspeople; worship in the local pub on a Sunday morning; and traditional services are sure to continue in many places. There will hopefully be much more co-operation between denominations, especially in planting new churches. Clergy training will involve much more emphasis on adult learning and the gaining of skills in sensitive evangelism. In all probability, many more people will be ordained who continue in regular employment and who lead traditional services on Sundays, releasing the paid and more fully trained clergy to supervise new congregations and to relate to non-church organizations.

Of course, things may not pan out this way in the next half-century. I shall not be here to see! Yet I am certain that the quality of leadership will be critical. Robert Bellah, the American sociologist, believes that if only 2 per cent of a nation has a new vision of what they want their society to be, they can change that society. He instances Japan, where Christians are a microscopic minority but women's rights, labour conditions, public policy issues and many other aspects of life have been greatly influenced by Christianity. A Chinese philosopher observed, 'There are only three kinds of people – those who are immovable, those who are movable, and those who move them.' I believe there are enough 'movable' people in our churches. It is the task of leaders to move them, and they can only do it by example. General Eisenhower made this point once to his senior aides. He placed a piece of string on the table and said, 'If I try to push this string from behind, it simply bunches up. But look what happens when I pull it.

387

That string will follow wherever I go.' The supreme function of leaders is to lead, and the wisest of them follow the advice of Peter Drucker, the doyen of management consultants: 'At the heart of everything I have done has been the aim of enabling others to become all that they can be.' Enabling leaders like that will help the Church to regain its momentum in the West – a momentum that is very obvious in the Two-Thirds World.

Of two things I am sure. The New Testament is very clear that the gates of hell will not be able to withstand the advance of the Church. History during the past 2,000 years shows the truth of that prediction. For all its failure, corruption and sin, the Church continues to grow in numbers and worldwide influence. As I look at it, I am often appalled by the mess, and yet in a paradoxical way that only serves to increase my confidence in God's purpose for the Church. If it were not a divinely ordained (and preserved) society, it would have packed up centuries ago, so massive are its gaffes and failures. The other abiding conviction I have about the Church is that it is not only Christ's chosen instrument to express his life in this world, but it is also his bride. At the end of time he will present it 'without stain or wrinkle or any other blemish' to the Father. That is the ultimate 'tomorrow' for the Church.

The tomorrow of our lives

Death is the certainty we all have to face. Contemporary society does its best not to think about it, but it comes to us all. It is no good having a philosophy of life if it does not have anything to say about death. The more I look around the faiths of the world, the more convinced I am about the future which Jesus Christ offers to believers. What alternatives are there? The leading humanist J.H. Blackman observed, 'On humanist assumptions life leads to nothing, and every claim to the contrary is a cruel deceit.' The poet Dylan Thomas looked on death with savage anger and advised:

Do not go gentle into that dark night,
Old age should burn and rage at close of day;
Rage, rage against the dying of the light.

What good does that do? Better by far to listen to Martin Luther King: 'Only that man is free who is not hung up on his own dying, who can live as though death is dead.' The agnostic route is no more satisfying. Thomas Hobbes, the seventeenth-century rationalist wrote, 'When I die worms will devour my body and I will commit myself to the Great Perhaps.' There is no hope, either, in the Hindu postulate of reincarnation. Although it has become popular in some Western circles as an avenue for continued existence which offers the hope of even better conditions the second time round, it has no such overtones in the East, where the doctrine originated. Not hope but dread accompanies it there, for reincarnation is a manifold series of lives of purgation, until one is ready to be assimilated to the universal Monad with all shreds of personhood eradicated.

In contrast to views such as these, the Christian hope of resurrection shines out like a beacon. It is not based on any assumed immortality of the soul. That is what Socrates argued for, but it is no part of the Christian hope. Our dependence is simply on the sheer grace of God through which we live every day. Eternal life is his gift and his alone. He will not scrap those who are precious to him. That is surely the thrust of Jesus' discussion with the Sadducees about levirate marriage and the succession of brothers who took the same wife, one after the other. Their trick question, 'Whose shall she be in the resurrection?'(in which they did not believe) was answered by Jesus from the only part of Scripture which they accepted – the Pentateuch, where one might have thought there was least reference to any life after death. Jesus told them, 'Even Moses showed that the dead are raised, in the passage about the bush, where he calls the Lord the God of Abraham, and the God of Isaac and the God of Jacob. Now he is not the God of the dead but of the living: for all live to him' (Luke 20:37f.). Jesus derives his confidence about life after death explicitly from the faithfulness of God, who remains the God of Abraham, Isaac and Jacob long after they have passed from this earth. God does not jettison those on whom his love has been lavished.

Jesus also gave an even more revolutionary understanding of life after death. In John 17:3 he is represented as saying, 'This is eternal life, that they may know you the only true God and Jesus Christ whom you have sent.' In other words, eternal life is not a commodity which God dishes out to his favourites, but a relationship to be enjoyed with himself and the Jesus who has made him known. That is presumably what Jesus meant when he said, 'I have come that they may have life, and have it to the full' (John 10:10). That life begins when we entrust ourselves to Christ and start to taste his reality. It continues throughout our earthly journey, and it culminates in the fulfilment of that relationship with him for ever. A continuous quantity of life is unattractive, but an endless love relationship is the most wonderful thing one could imagine. He offers no less.

The supreme reason for Christian confidence in the face of death, however, is the resurrection of Jesus. The empty tomb, the resurrection appearances to a lot of people who had a great variety of temperaments, the transformation of the disciples from a bunch of cowards into an army of fearless witnesses, the start of the worldwide Christian Church, the change of the day of rest from Saturday to Sunday (the day of his resurrection), and the witness of multimillions down the ages that they know Christ and experience his risen power in their lives – these factors are enough to persuade me and countless others of the reality of the resurrection. The Jesus who rose from the dead on the first Easter day had uttered these immortal words to his volatile followers just three days earlier: 'Do not let your hearts be troubled. Trust in God: trust also in me. In my Father's house are many rooms; if it were not so I would have told you. I am going there to prepare a place for you' (John 14:1ff.). That has been the confidence of Christians in the face of death from that day to this. No wonder St Paul, after being harried and persecuted all over the Roman Empire, could write as he did:

> If God is for us, who can be against us? He who did not spare his only Son, but gave him up for us all, will he not also give us all things with him? Who shall separate us from the love of Christ? Shall tribulation or distress or persecution or famine or nakedness or peril or sword? No, in all these things we are more than conquerors through him who loved us. For I am persuaded that neither death nor life, nor things present nor things to come, nor powers nor heights nor depth, nor anything else in all creation shall be able to separate us from the love of God in Christ Jesus our Lord.   Romans 8:31–9

That was St Paul's conviction, and as he faced up to his impending death he was still able to rejoice:

> I am on the point of being sacrificed: the time of my departure has come. I have fought the good fight. I have finished the race. I have kept the faith. Henceforth there is laid up for me a crown of righteousness which the Lord, the righteous judge, will give me on that Day, and not only to me but to all who have loved his appearing.
> 2 Timothy 4:6f.

Shortly afterwards he walked out to his execution on the Via Appia.

We are not all St Pauls, but we have the same Saviour and Lord. We take our stand on the same resurrection of Jesus. We rely on the same promises. I can honestly say, as I face my own forthcoming death, that I am looking forward to being dead, for 'to depart and to be with Christ is far better' and 'blessed are the dead who die in the Lord'. I confess, however, that I am not looking forward to the actual process of dying! That can be messy, protracted and very painful, but I am persuaded that the Lord I have followed these past 50 years will keep his promise and never fail me nor forsake me. That gives me great confidence and joy.

One of the best insights about life after death came my way quite recently. For many years I was friends with Terry Winter, the Canadian evangelist who had a remarkable television ministry. I did three programmes with him shortly before he died suddenly and unexpectedly. His last programme was on resurrection and in it he said, 'You will hear one day that Terry Winter is dead. Don't you believe it. He will be more alive than ever.' That programme was aired, in its regular scheduling, two days after he died. I could not have expressed it as well as he did, but I share his confidence as I look to the 'tomorrow' of my own life.

APPENDIX 1

Lifeline

1930   Born in Shenington, near Banbury, Oxfordshire.

1937   To Montpelier School, Paignton, Devon.

1944   Scholarship to Clifton College, Bristol.

1945   First visit to Christian house party in Iwerne
Minster.

1949   Scholarship to Exeter College, Oxford, to study
'Greats' (i.e. Classics).
Became a leader at the Iwerne Minster camps.

1952   President of Oxford Christian Union.

1953   First Class Honours in 'Greats'.
Start of two years' National Service.

1954   Commissioned in the Royal Artillery. Became
Assistant Adjutant of 64 Regiment, RA.

1955   Fenced for the Army and Combined Services.
Went to Queens' College, Cambridge and Ridley
Hall Theological College.

1956   Fenced for Cambridge v. Oxford.

1957   First Class Honours in the Theology Tripos, pt. 3
(New Testament), and the University Carus Prize
(New Testament).
Marriage to Rosemary Storr.
Curacy at Holy Trinity, Eastbourne.

1960   New Testament tutor at the London College of
        Divinity.

        Birth of our first son, Tim. He was followed by
        Sarah in 1962, Jenny in 1964 and Jonathan in 1966.

1966   Awarded the Cambridge BD.

1967   Member of the Doctrine Commission of the Church
        of England.

1968   Consultant at the Lambeth Conference.

1969   Principal of London College of Divinity, overseeing
        the move to St John's College, Nottingham in
        1970.

1970   Became Canon Theologian of Coventry.

1975   Rector of St Aldate's, Oxford.

1978   Made Canon Theologian Emeritus of Coventry.

1987   Professor of Evangelism and New Testament at
        Regent College, Vancouver, Canada.

1992   DD (honorary) University of Toronto.

        Return to UK as Archbishops' Adviser on
        Evangelism with the Springboard project.

1996   DD (earned) Lambeth.

        Senior Research Fellow at Wycliffe Hall, Oxford.

APPENDIX 2

Book List

Called to Serve	1964
Choose Freedom	1965
The Meaning of Salvation	1965
Man Alive	1967
Runaway World	1968
Tyndale Commentary on 2 Peter and Jude	1968
Evangelism in the Early Church	1970
Growing into Union[1]	1970
Jesus Spells Freedom	1972
New Life, New Lifestyle	1973
I Believe in the Holy Spirit	1975
You Must Be Joking!	1976
The Truth of God Incarnate[2]	1977
Evangelism Now and Then	1979
Why Bother with Jesus?	1979
The Church and Homosexuality[3]	1980
I Believe in Satan's Downfall	1981
What is Christianity?	1981
The Day Death Died	1982
To Corinth with Love	1982
Freed to Serve	1983
World on the Run	1983

1 Jointly written with Colin Buchanan, Graham Leonard, Eric Mascall and Jim Packer.
2 Editor. Jointly written with Christopher Butler, Brian Hebblethwaite, John Macquarrie and Stephen Neill.
3 Jointly written with David Holloway and David Watson.
4 Jointly written with Gordon Carkner.
5 Jointly written with Alister McGrath.
6 Jointly written with Paul Stevens.
7 Contributor.

Index

Ward, Barbara 379
Warner, Canon 209
Warren, Max 143, 248
Washington DC 334
water 376-7
Watergate 215
Watson, David 64, 69
  controversy 306
  evangelism 178
  leadership 219-21
  renewal 266-7
  writing 134, 138, 143
Waxer, Eddie 335
Wells, H. G. 380
Wenham, David 143
Wenham, John 105
Wesley, Charles 271, 275
Wesley, John 87, 172, 285, 332
West Indies 339-43
West Malaysia *see* Malaysia
West Malaysia, Bishop of 370
Westminster Foundation 67
WH Smith 123
White House 215
Whitefield, George 172
Wimber, John 366
Winter, Terry 338, 392
women 95, 101-2, 300-6, 385

Wong, James 356
Wood, Maurice 45
Woolmer, John 264, 265
Woolwich, Bishop of 130
World Church 315-48
World Council of Churches 46,
  162, 276
worldwide web 155, 164
Worlock, Derek 221
worship styles 310-12
Wright, Tom 145
Wright, Walt 107
writing 118-45
Wycliffe College, Toronto 337
Wycliffe Hall, Oxford 40,
  112-14, 217, 266

York 266-7
York, Archbishop of 194, 221,
  371
youth clubs 83, 85
Youth Encounter 346
Youth With A Mission 336

Zambia 315, 330
Zimbabwe 315, 322
Zinzendorf, Count 333
Zulus 126